A FIELD GUIDE

TO THE

BIRDS OF MEXICO

Second Edition

by

ERNEST P. EDWARDS

and
principal illustrator:
Edward Murrell Butler

Parrots, parakeets, macaws by:
John P. O'Neill

Published and distributed
by
Ernest P. Edwards
Box AQ
Sweet Briar, VA 24595

Library of Congress Catalogue Card No.: 88-83374

ISBN:911882-11-1

Second Edition

Composed and Printed in the U.S.A.

To my wife
Mabel T. Edwards

PREFACE

This, the first new or revised Mexican field guide to appear in 15 years, is unique in illustrating approximately *350* Mexican bird species which are not illustrated in any other Mexican field guide to date, in addition to the approximately 500 species which the other guides do depict.

Thus, with its color plates illustrating 856 Mexican bird species as well as several distinctive subspecies, and a black-and-white plate illustrating 18 additional species, this *Field Guide* provides an abundance of aids for bird identification in Mexico. The text reinforces and supplements the informational content of the color plates, with details about colors, patterns, size, distribution, habitat, behavior (including voice) in some cases, and other important features, for each of the more than 1000 bird species which regularly occur in Mexico.

The bird-finding companion-books for this *Field Guide* have already been published (see Edwards in Bibliography), and the use of the bird-finding books together with the field guide will enable any observer to use available time to the best possible advantage in relation to his or her own interests, whether to list as many species as possible, or to study carefully a certain habitat or a few kinds of birds. The bird-finding guide also describes in greater detail the regional system (used in this *Field Guide* as well) for organizing and communicating our knowledge of the distribution of Mexican birds.

This edition has been completely rewritten, and the number of species illustrated in color has been nearly doubled. Edward Murrell Butler painted 45 of the color plates (26 of them new for this edition) and the black-and-white plate. John P. O'Neill's painting of parrots, parakeets, and macaws from the first edition has been used again. Miguel Alvarez del Toro and Allan R. Phillips provided much information for the first edition, thus helping to provide a solid foundation for this revision. Mabel T. Edwards helped in all phases of the work, and did the exacting work of preparing the layouts for all the plate captions. I sincerely appreciate the help of all these persons.

Ernest P. Edwards
January, 1989

TABLE OF CONTENTS

LIST OF MAPS

LIST OF ILLUSTRATIONS

INTRODUCTION

Mexico is rich in bird life, readily accessible, and almost unique in its mixture of some typically temperate zone species with many distinctively tropical birds. Although considerably smaller than the United States it has many more species of birds. More than 1000 species of birds occur regularly in Mexico. Almost half of Mexico's birds are not found in the United States, and many others cross the border only a short distance into our southwestern states. The Atlantic (or Gulf) Lowlands of Mexico, and the adjacent mountain slopes, are richest in variety of species and numbers of typically tropical species; and the observer need penetrate only 200 to 300 miles south of the border into the eastern lowlands of Mexico to be met by a host of exotic species, among them parrots, motmots, "new" kinds of woodpeckers, hawks, jays, and the like. Likewise, in many cases, the Mexican resident need travel only a couple of hours, or less, to find an assortment of birds quite different from those around his or her home. This book, with its detailed descriptions of all of Mexico's regular species, and color illustrations of more than 850 of them, is designed to provide assistance and greater enjoyment for the rank amateur and the seasoned professional alike, who might wish to know more about the birds which are to be found in Mexico and other parts of Middle America.

How to Use This Book.

It is important, first of all, for the observer to begin to develop a concept of the different regions of Mexico, the elevations, the habitats, the behavior of certain kinds of birds, and the distribution of various species within the country. No matter where the observer is situated, only a portion of the total number of species in this book need be taken into consideration. For example, a dull, brownish bird, slightly smaller than a robin, flying across the road in rather open, dry, highland country in northern or central Mexico may quite likely be a Brown Towhee. A similarly plain brownish bird, about the same size, in the humid lowland forests of southeastern Mexico might be a Rufous Piha, a Rufous Mourner or one of the ovenbirds or tropical creepers. It is difficult to imagine even a remote possibility that a Brown Towhee would ever be found in the lowland rain forests, or that a Rufous Piha would ever be seen flying across the road in arid, semi-desert, highland country.

In order to assist the observer in developing the regional and elevational concepts, particularly, we have divided the country into regions and sub-regions, and have described the distribution of each species in terms of these areas, and in terms of the elevations at which the species is to be expected. Within any sub-region the states in which the species occurs will be indicated in parentheses, unless the species occurs virtually throughout the sub-region, in which case only the sub-regional designation is listed. Similarly, if a species occurs only in one or some sub-regions of a region, these sub-regions are listed, whereas if it occurs in all sub-regions of a region, only the regional designation is used.

The regional system is based partly on elevation and partly on position within the country (see maps, Plate 48). The letter H (or ncH or csH, etc.) refers to the highlands of Mexico, more than 5000 feet above sea level except in the nH sub-region where some parts of the plateau close to the U.S. border are as low as about 3500 to 4000 feet above sea level. The letter P, or some combination ending in P, indicates that the species occurs in the Pacific lowlands of Mexico, or on the lower mountain slopes falling away toward the Pacific Ocean, *below* 5000 feet elevation. The letter A (or sA, ncA, etc.) indicates that the species occurs on the Atlantic (Gulf of Mexico) slope or lowlands *below* 5000 feet elevation. This is a convenient system because much of Mexico consists of a high central plateau bordered by higher mountain ranges on each side; these ranges then slope in the direction of the Atlantic and Pacific Oceans, respectively. The BC Region, however, consists of the entire peninsula of Baja California in northwestern Mexico, therefore extending from sea level to a little more than 10,000' elevation. We now divide this region into nBC and sBC, roughly corresponding to Baja California Norte and Baja California Sur, respectively. The Y Region consists of the drier northern portions of the states of Campeche and Quintana Roo, and all of the state of Yucatán. No part of this region rises more than a few hundred feet above sea level. It is not divided into sub-regions.

Some species may be found regularly in the highlands, and perhaps down to 4500 or 4000 feet elevation on the mountain slopes. In these cases it may be listed as simply a bird of the H Region (but note that the elevation of occurrence is given for resident birds). Similarly, a distinctively lowland species may go to 5500 or even 6000 feet above sea level, and yet be listed only as P or A. The 5000-foot line is significant in many cases, and helpful in most, as a boundary between upland and lowland species. Other species are widespread above *and* below this line, and this pattern is indicated by listing the regions and sub-regions in which it occurs.

Within each species account the regions of occurrence are indicated in sequence from BC, through P, H, A, and Y, as appropriate for the particular species, with the initials n, c, or s indicating whether the bird is in the northern, central, or southern portion of the region (except BC with only two sub-regions and Y with none.). If the bird is to be expected in *all* sub-regions of any region, *only* the regional designation is indicated, not the sub-regions (for example, A, not ncsA).

Species which are accidental or casual in Mexico are listed separately (p.107). That list also includes two species which have been introduced or have spread to northwestern Mexico and which may or may not have become firmly established. It also includes some species once thought to be accidental or casual, but very recently found to be regular. Neither that list nor the regular list includes species included in some Mexican books solely on the basis of occurrence in the vicinity of Clipperton Island.

Families (or subfamilies) and species are treated in the sequence used in the *AOU Check-List* except in the case of the Icteridae (orioles, blackbirds, etc.) which is raised to family rank and placed just after the Thraupidae (tanagers - also raised to family rank), and the Highland Honeycreeper (Cinnamon-bellied Flowerpiercer) which I have taken out of the Subfamily Emberizinae and placed in the Family Thraupidae.

Please refer to the maps in this book for a graphic indication of the limits of the various regions and sub-regions, and if possible have a large, up-to-date road-map of Mexico at hand. For a much more detailed account of the Edwards regional system of indicating distribution, and for details of weather, topography, types and distribution of vegetation, habitats preferred by the common birds, and other information about each region and sub-region, as well as many specific localities, please see the book *Finding Birds in Mexico*, and its *1985 Supplement*.

In addition to the customary discussion and information about each species, a condensed family discussion is provided in the case of each family with more than two species *in* Mexico. As you work at identifying a bird by means of the color plates and the species accounts, you should find it worthwhile to read the family account as well.

A sample species account (for the Blue-crowned Motmot) follows:

Blue-crowned Motmot. *Momotus momota.* X4a9.   Turco Real
M-SAm. Resident up to 4000', sP, A, Y. Rare; river-border woods, dry or humid forest, orchards, near dirt bank; switches tail side to side. V: low-pitched *hoot, hoot.*
Pl.20. 16" Green above (or with some rufous); olive green (or rufous) below; crown pale blue with black border (nA, n.cA), or crown has black center then blue circle then black border (s.cA, sA, sP, Y); short bare space on tail; black breast-spot.

An analysis and explanation of the species account follows:

"Blue-crowned Motmot." This is the English (or common, or vernacular) name of the species, and generally it is the name used in Edwards's *A Coded Workbook of Birds of the World.* In most cases in which this name differs from that used by the A.O.U., the A.O.U. name is included in parentheses. Ordinarily my English name nomenclature will differ from that of the A.O.U. only if the name I use is more convenient or appropriate. In an age of TVs and K'birds it seems preferable not to call a Geronimo Swift a Great Swallow-tailed Swift, or a Savanna Vulture a Lesser Yellow-headed Vulture, or a Leafgleaner a Foliage-gleaner. The latter name in each case sounds more alluring in a tour brochure, but field guides and checklists should use the former.

"Momotus momota." This is the scientific name of the species, in Latin form. The names used here generally follow *A Coded Workbook of Birds of the World.* In a very few cases these may differ from those used by the A.O.U., because of differing concepts of specific and generic limits.

"X4a9." This is an alphanumeric code for the species, taken from *A Coded Workbook of Birds of the World.* The "X" is the code for the Order Coraciiformes; the "4" is the code for the Family Momotidae; the "a" indicates the subfamily, or as in this case indicates that the family is not divided into subfamilies; the "9" is the code for the species, which is ninth in the family in taxonomic sequence.

"Turco Real" This is the Spanish name of the species. You will find that there is great variation in the Spanish names used for the same bird in different parts of Mexico. The ones we use here are almost entirely those suggested by Mexican ornithologists for the First Edition of this *Field Guide.*

"M-SAm." This is the New World range of the species - Mexico to South America, including all the countries of Middle America. If the species should occur from Alaska to Panama, except in El Salvador, the statement would read, "AK-Pan,x.ES." Countries in which the species occurs only accidentally or casually north of Mexico are not included; those Middle American countries south of Mexico in which this is the case are included.

"Resident" This indicates that some individuals of the species occur all year round in the areas named, and presumably nest in those areas. Other possible indications include "Summer resident" (occurs only in summer and presumably nests there); "Transient" (goes through the area, usually on migration in spring or fall); or "Winter visitor" (comes to the area and stays there during late fall, winter, and early spring, but goes elsewhere during the summer).

"up to 4000'" The species occurs mainly between sea level and 4000' above sea level. You might find it at 4300', but generally the limits mentioned are inclusive.

"sP, A, Y." The species occurs in the southern sub-region of the Pacific Lowlands Region, and in all sub-regions of the Atlantic Lowlands Region, and in the Yucatan Region. When the species occurs in only a small part of a sub-region or region the limiting states may be mentioned.

"Rare;" Judgment of the abundance of the species is subjective, and refers mainly to its abundance within the range and habitat indicated. This can vary considerably from one part of Mexico to another, but should be a good average indicator. The categories used are "very rare, rare, rare+ (=moderately common), common, and abundant". If the bird occurs in only a few scattered localities, the word "local" or "irregular" may be used.

"river-border woods, dry or humid forest, orchards, near dirt bank;" These are the types of situations in which the species is to be expected.

"switches tail side to side." Characteristic mannerisms are noted in some cases.

"V: low-pitched *hoot, hoot.*" When the song or call is distinctive it may be mentioned here, or in the next paragraph along with the description of the bird.

"Pl.20." The illustration of the bird is to be found on Plate 20.

"16" " This is an average length for the species, including bill and tail. In case the male and female are quite different in size the length of each may be given, the male first.

"Green above (or with some rufous); olive green (or rufous) below;" etc. This is the description of the bird, usually emphasizing plumage colors and patterns, but also may include eye- or bill- or leg- or soft-part colors, or bill shape. In case other species are quite similar, some distinguishing features may be indicated in a direct comparison. The standard terminology for the different parts of the bird is used in most cases, but sometimes I use the word "chest" to refer to the upper part of the breast, nearer the throat, if that part is a different color from the lower part of the breast, nearer the belly. In addition I have coined the words *uptacs* for *up*per *ta*il *c*overts, and *untacs* for *un*der *ta*il *c*overts (called crissum in the First Edition).

Bird Finding

A good guidebook for bird finding is now considered to be a part of any serious birder's library, even for birding in areas close to home. For a birder traveling far from familiar territory such a book becomes virtually indispensable. *Finding Birds in Mexico,* and its companion volume *1985 Supplement to Finding Birds in Mexico,* both by Ernest P. Edwards, author of this Field Guide, can add greatly to the interest, pleasure, and efficiency of a birding trip to Mexico. These volumes are available from the author at Sweet Briar, VA, 24595.

List of frequently used abbreviations (mostly not in bird names):

A	Atlantic	H	Highlands	ph.	phase
Ad.	Adult	H	Honduras	s or s.	south(ern)
AK	Alaska	I.	Island	SAm	South America
B	Belize	Is.	Islands	se.	southeastern
BC	Baja California	Im.	Immature	S.,Sum.	summer
Bl.ph.	Black phase	Juv.	Juvenile	sw.	southwestern
c	central	M or m.	male	US	United States
Can	Canada	M, Mex.	Mexico	w.	west(ern)
CR	Costa Rica	N	Nicaragua	W.,Win.	winter
D.ph.	Dark phase	N., n, n.	Northern, north(ern)	x.	except
e.	eastern	ne.	northeastern	Y	Yucatan
ES	El Salvador	nw.	northwestern		
ex.,exc.	except	P	Pacific		Note also that
F or f.	female	P	Panama	untacs = under tail coverts
G	Guatemala	Pan	Panama	uptacs = upper tail coverts

If an <u>alternate</u> English bird name is abbreviated (in parentheses in the heading of a species write-up), you could find the bird's full name in the *AOU Checklist* or the *ABA Checklist* .

In case a bird's scientific name or English name is abbreviated in the heading or the descriptive part of a species write-up, you should be able to match it with the name in the heading of that species or of the one just above or just below in the sequence, or with another name in that family.

In case a bird's name is abbreviated on a page of illustrations it should correspond to a full spelling of that name somewhere else on the same page, or it should be readily recognizable.

In a very few cases we use a <u>modification</u> of the four-letter standard designation used by bird-banders, for example (our modification) LeNi = (standard) LENI = Lesser Nighthawk. This is only used when the full name is also used on the same page.

If the name is still not clear in any of these cases, referring to the Index should help.

The Birds of Mexico

TINAMOUS - TINAMIDAE - PERDICES

Four regular residents, mostly sA; medium-large; plump body, medium-length legs and neck, rounded wings, very short tail; neotropical; shy walkers in dense lowland vegetation, almost never fly. Identify species by voice; or size and barring. **Plate 2.**

Great Tinamou. *Tinamus major.* F1a4.   Gallina de Monte
M-SAm,x.ES. Resident up to 2000', csA (se.Puebla to Quintana Roo). Rare+; undergrowth of humid forest or dense woodland. V: A tremulous whistle, followed by short notes, usually some of the notes in pairs, some paired notes descending in pitch.
   Pl.2. 15" Large; olive plumage lighter below; noticeable tail; bluish legs and feet.

Little Tinamou. *Crypturellus soui.* F1a11.   Ponchita
M-SAm,x.ES. Resident up to 2000', csA (n.Oaxaca to Quintana Roo). Rare+; humid forest, woodlands, borders, luxuriant hedgerows. V: a slow series (ascending in pitch) of tremulous notes; or a long, tremulous note ascending, and then descending.
   Pl.2. 9" Unbarred grayish brown or reddish brown plumage.

Rufescent (Thicket) **Tinamou.** *Crypturellus cinnamomeus.* F1a21.   Perdiz Canela
M-CR,SAm. Resident up to 5000', P (s.Sinaloa to Chiapas), A, Y. Common; undergrowth, from tall humid forest to scrubby woods to thorny thickets. V: a loud, clear, extended, whistled note, usually on one pitch, but may go down or up or both.
   Pl.2. 11" Barred back; buff-brown (nP) to olive brown (humid sA); legs orange.

Boucard's (Slaty-br.) **Tinamou.** *Crypturellus boucardi.* F1a22.   Perdiz de Boucard
M-CR. Resident up to 2000', csA (n.Oaxaca to Quintana Roo), Y. Rare; in undergrowth of dense humid forest.   V: two extended, unobtrusive, low-pitched notes.
   Pl.2. 11" Legs orange; plumage similar to dark races of Rufescent T., but mostly unbarred. M: Very dark olive brown to slaty. F: Dark reddish brown; untacs barred.

LOONS - GAVIIDAE - SOMORGUJOS

Three regular winter visitors, mostly BC, nP; large; long heavy body, short legs, medium-short neck, pointed wings, very short tail; medium-long pointed bill; north temperate and arctic; mostly coastal (in winter) swimmers, surface-divers; winter and summer plumages. Distinguish species by bill shape, back pattern, and (winter) light-and-dark contrast, and (summer) neck-stripes, color of head and throat. **Plate 1.**

Red-throated Loon. *Gavia stellata.* B1a1.   Somorgujo Garganta Roja
AK-M. Winter visitor BC, nP. Rare; mostly in coastal salt water, lakes or large rivers.
   25" Bill slender, upturned. Win: Gray above, white below; more speckled on back, less contrast on head and neck than Pacific L. Sum: Dark gray above, whitish below; head pale gray; throat reddish brown; hind-neck streaked black and white.

Pacific Loon. *Gavia pacifica.* (B1a2).   Somorgujo Pacífico
AK-M. Winter visitor BC, nP. Common; mostly coastal waters; bays, inlets, lagoons.
   Pl. 1. 25" Smaller, smaller-billed than Com. L. Win: Contrasty gray and white; no back-speckles (see Red-thr.L.). Sum: Barred black and white above; throat purplish.

Common Loon. *Gavia immer.* B1a3.   Somorgujo Común
AK-M. Winter visitor BC, nP, nH, nA. Rare+; coastal, or lakes, rivers, on migration.
   33" Larger than Red-throated or Pacific L., with larger, straight, dark bill, and few back-speckles. Win: Gray above, white below; less contrast than Pacific L., more than Red-throated L. Sum: Black above with rows of large white spots; white below; head and neck black with greenish gloss; two partial, striped collars.

GREBES - PODICIPEDIDAE - ZAMBULLIDORES

Six regular residents or winter visitors, mostly northern Mexico; plump body, short legs, medium or long neck, very short tail; world-wide; swimmers, surface-divers, mostly in ponds, lakes or coastal lagoons; winter and summer plumages. Distinguish species by neck and head patterns, colors, size, bill shape. **Plate 1.**

Least Grebe. *Tachybaptus dominicus.* C1a2.   Zambullidor Chico
US-SAm. Resident up to 8000', all sub-regions (exc.BC recently?). Common; ponds,
lakes, pools in marshes, swamps and lagoons; often in loose flocks in winter.
*Pl.1. 9" Shorter-necked than other Mexican grebes; darker than Pied-billed G.,
and has short, slender, black bill, orange-yellow iris, dark gray untacs; plumage
mostly dark gray. Win: Throat whitish. Sum: Throat and crown blackish.*

Pied-billed Grebe. *Podilymbus podiceps.* C1a8.   Zambullidor Pico Pinto
M-Pan. Resident up to 9000', all sub-regions. Rare+; pools, marshy ponds, and lakes,
rivers, and lagoons. V: a loud, staccato *ca-ca-ca-co-co , co-uh , co-uh, co-uh, co-uh.*
*12" Largely dark grayish brown, paler below, with white untacs; bill short, stout,
pale. Win: Throat white, bill plain. Sum: Black throat, black bar on bill. See Least G.*

Horned Grebe. *Podiceps auritus.* C1b2.   Zambullidor Cornudo
AK-M. Winter visitor nBC, nP (Sonora). Rare; coastal waters, or large lakes, ponds.
*13" Blackish gray above, and hind-neck and crown; bill short, slender. Win:White
below; throat and sides of head and neck contrasty white. Sum: Much of neck and
underparts chestnut; hind-neck and head black, except tawny plumes behind eye.*

Eared Grebe. *Podiceps nigricollis.* C1b5.   Zambullidor Orejudo
Can-M,G. Resident up to 7000', nBC (?), ncH (Chihuahua to Veracruz); winter visitor
BC, nP, sH, nA. Rare, local in summer, common in winter; often in colonies or loose
flocks, resident on inland lakes and ponds, winters on lakes, ponds, rivers, lagoons.
*13" Bill short, slender, slightly upturned. Win: Blackish gray above,whitish below;
neck medium to dark gray with little contrast; white throat-patch and patch behind
eye small, not contrasty. Sum: Belly, sides reddish brown; but back, most of breast,
entire neck, most of head, black; tawny plumes behind eye. See Horned Grebe.*

Western Grebe. *Aechmophorus occidentalis.* C1b10.   Achichilique Occidental
AK-M. Resident, 4000 to 8000', ncH (Chihuahua to Guerrero+Puebla); winter visitor
BC, nP. Rare, local; summer, marshy ponds, lakes; winter, lakes, bays, lagoons.
*Pl.1. 28" Blackish above, white below; crown, hind-neck, and area around eye,
black; lower sides of face, white; long neck; slender, yellowish bill. See Clark's G.*

Clark's Grebe. *Aechmophorus clarkii.* C1b11.   Achichilique de Clark
AK-M. Distribution and seasonal occurrence similar to that of Western Grebe (above),
but Clark's Grebe may be more common than Western Grebe in summer, in Mexico.
Pl.1. 28" Like Western G., but white of side of face extending broadly around eye.

ALBATROSSES - DIOMEDEIDAE - ALBATROSES
Very large; short legs, neck, and tail, very long slender wings, rather long stout
hooked-tipped bill; oceans of the world; dynamic soaring over open ocean. **Plate 1.**

Black-footed Albatross. *Diomedea nigripes.* D1a5.   Albatrós Pies Negros
AK-M. Ranges BC (w. side), cP (Revillagigedo Is.). Rare, summer; very rare, winter;
usually far offshore, occasionally near shore; soaring close to the surface, solitary.
*Pl.1. 30" Ad: Bill, feet, and plumage blackish brown, but white around base of bill,
white or pale gray untacs (rarely belly), and (in some) white uptacs. Im: Less white.*

Laysan Albatross. *Diomedea immutabilis.* D1a6.   Albatrós de Laysan
AK-M. Resident, near sea level, nBC (Guadalupe I.); ranges BC, cP. Rare; over open
ocean, usually far offshore, or on or near nest island; soars rather close to the surface.
*30" Back, upper surface of wings, and tail, black; mostly white otherwise except
black patch around eye; pink bill and feet; under-wings white, bordered with black.*

SHEARWATERS, PETRELS - PROCELLARIIDAE - FARDELAS
Eight regular visitors or residents, BC, P; medium-large; short legs, neck, and tail,
long slender wings, rather slender, hooked-tipped bill; world-wide; oceanic, flapping
and gliding; light and dark phases. Distinguish species by bill and foot colors; colors of
back, under-wings, belly, untacs, and crown; shape of tail. **Plate 47.**

Northern Fulmar. *Fulmarus glacialis.* D2a4.   Fulmaro del Norte
AK-M. Ranges BC (w.side), nP (Sonora). Rare+; offshore, flapping and long glides.
17" Stouter, broader-winged than shearwaters and large petrels; bill short, heavy, yellowish. D.ph: Uniform medium gray to dark gray. L.ph: Mantle pale gray to medium gray with darker wing-tips; white head, tail, underparts, and under-wing.

Cook's Petrel. *Pterodroma cookii.* D2a31.   Petrel de Cook
AK-SAm. Ranges BC, ncP (sBC to Rev.Is.). Rare to common; offshore ocean waters.
13" Slender wings; upperparts (including crown) dark gray, but blacker bar on spread wings and across rump, forming an "M"; underparts white; bill short, black.

Pink-footed Shearwater. *Puffinus creatopus.* D2c10.   Fardela Pies Rosados
AK-M. Ranges BC, P (Nayarit to Oaxaca). Common; over open ocean; "heavy" flight.
16" Dark grayish brown above, white to pale gray below, with mottled sides and under-wings; bill slender, pink with black tip; feet pink; tail short, slightly rounded.

Wedge-tailed Shearwater. *Puffinus pacificus.* D2c7.   Fardela Pacífica
M-SAm,x.B,H. Resident cP (Revillagigedo Is.); ranges sBC, nsP. Rare+, open ocean;
common, near nest islands; found mostly offshore, over ocean or on or near islands.
*Pl.47. 16" Tail not short and rounded; bill slender, pink with black tip; feet pink.
L.ph: White below, contrasty dark above. D.ph: Uniform medium to dark brown.*

Sooty Shearwater. *Puffinus griseus.* D2c12.   Fardela Gris
AK-SAm,x.H. Ranges BC, P. Abundant; mostly spring to fall, offshore ocean waters.
17" Blackish gray, slightly paler below, dark bill and feet. See Short-tailed Shearw.

Short-tailed Shearwater. *Puffinus tenuirostris.* D2c13.   Fardela Colicorta
AK-M. Ranges nBC (w.side), cP (Guerrero). Very rare; offshore, open ocean waters.
14" Dark bill and feet; plumage blackish gray, slightly paler below, less contrast between gray under-wing coverts and dark body and flight feathers than Sooty S.

Manx Shearwater. *Puffinus puffinus.* D2c15.   Fardela de Manx
Black-vented group. *P. puffinus opisthomelas.*   Fardela Cachiruleado
US-M. Resident nBC (w.islands); ranges BC, ncP (Sonora to Guerrero).
Common; over open ocean waters, and on and near offshore nest islands.
14" Blackish brown above; black bill, pink feet, short tail; underparts white except black untacs and blackish-brown mottling on (especially sides of) breast.
Townsend's group. *P. puffinus auricularis.*   Fardela de Clarión
M. Resident cP (Revillagigedo Is.); ranges sBC (w.side), P (Sinaloa to Chiapas).
Common; offshore ocean waters, and on and near offshore nest islands.
14" Like Black-vented group, but has black legs; little or no mottling below.

Audubon's Shearwater. *Puffinus lherminieri.* D2c18.   Fardela Chica
US-SAm,x.B,H. Ranges csP (Guerrero to Chiapas). Common; open ocean waters.
12" Wings shorter, tail longer than those of Manx S.; feet pinkish; upperparts blackish; unmottled white below, except black primaries and blackish-brown untacs.

STORM-PETRELS - HYDROBATIDAE - PETRELES
Six regular residents or visitors, BC and P; mostly black; medium-small; rather long legs and wings; world oceans; flying, fluttering near ocean surface. Identify species by patterns, type of flight, rump patch, color of legs and feet, and shape of tail. **Plate 47.**

Wilson's Storm-Petrel. *Oceanites oceanicus.* D4a1.   Petrel de las Tormentas
US,M,G,CR,Pan,SAm. Ranges csP (Oaxaca+Chiapas), cA (Veracruz). Rare; over
open ocean waters; flying with fluttery, shallow wing-beats, close to the surface.
7" Black; pale gray wing-patch; white rump-patch extends to flanks and sides of untacs; tail square to rounded; feet yellow-webbed, extend beyond tail-tip in flight.

Leach's Storm-Petrel. *Oceanodroma leucorhoa.* D4b6.   Petrel Rabadilla Blanca
AK-SAm,x.B,H. Resident nBC (w.is.); ranges BC, P. Rare+; over the open ocean.
8" Black, except pale wing-patch; and white to gray to dark brown rump-patch, not

extending to flanks or untacs; *tail forked; wings pointed; legs and feet short, black.*
Ashy Storm-Petrel. *Oceanodroma homochroa.* D4b12.   <u>Petrel Ceniciento</u>
US-M. <u>Resident nBC (Los Coronados Is.)</u>. Rare+, nest islands; very rare, open ocean.
7" Blackish brown; wing-patch duller than in Leach's P., and under-wing paler than
in Leach's P. or Black P.; *tail rather long, deeply forked; feet and legs short, black.*
Galapagos (W.-r.) **Storm-Petrel.***Oceanodroma tethys.* D4b3.   <u>Petrel de la Tempestad</u>
M,G,CR-SAm. <u>Ranges BC, ncP (Sinaloa to Revillagigedo Is.)</u>. Rare; offshore waters.
Pl.47. 6" Blackish, except dull wing-patch, <u>longer</u> white rump-patch than in
Leach's,Wilson's P.; *tail notched; feet, legs short, black. Flight "bounding", uneven.*
Black Storm-Petrel. *Oceanodroma melania.* D4b10.   <u>Petrel Negro</u>
US-SAm.,x.B,H. <u>Resident BC, nP (Sonora); ranges P</u>. Common to abundant; inshore
and offshore ocean, flapping and gliding swiftly, close to the surface, in wake of a ship.
*9" Large size. Blackish brown (appears black), except inconspicuous gray
wing-patch; tail forked; legs and feet black, extend slightly beyond notch of tail.*
Least Storm-Petrel. *Halocyptena microsoma.* D4b2.   <u>Petrel Mínimo</u>
US-SAm.,x.B,H. <u>Resident nBC, nP (is. off Sonora); ranges BC, P</u>. Abundant, north;
rare, south; offshore islands and ocean, flies rapidly, erratically, with deep wing-beats.
6" Blackish brown; wing-patch barely paler; tail very short, slightly wedge-shaped.

TROPICBIRDS - PHAETHONTIDAE - RABIJUNCOS
Large; short legs and neck, pointed wings, pointed bill; warm oceans of the world.
Red-billed Tropicbird. *Phaethon aethereus.* E1a1.   <u>Rabijunco Piquirojo</u>
US-SAm.,x.B,H. <u>Resident BC, ncP; ranges sP</u>. Rare over open ocean waters, ranging
widely; common on offshore nest islands or over ocean waters in the vicinity of islands.
*Pl.1. 35" Ad: White, with long, slender, white, central tail-feathers, fine black
barring on back; black wing-tips; red bill. Im: Tail short, bill orange-yellow.*

GANNETS, BOOBIES - SULIDAE - BUBIAS
Five regular residents or visitors, mostly BC, P; large; short legs, medium-short
neck, long pointed wings, pointed tail, straight heavy medium-long bill; world oceans;
open ocean or near-shore, fliers and aerial deep-divers. Distinguish species by patterns
of white, black, and brown; and by color of feet, legs, and bill. **Plate 47.**
Masked Booby. *Sula dactylatra.* E4a6.   <u>Bubia Cariazul</u>
US-SAm. <u>Resident sBC, cP (Revillagigedo Is.), Y; ranges sP, nA</u>. Rare; coast, ocean.
*32" Ad:White except black wing-tips, and black trailing edge of wing, <u>black</u> tail, and
black around eye and on chin ; bill yellow, feet orange-yellow. Im: Grayish brown,
breast, belly, and untacs white; whitish patch across hind-neck; feet blackish olive.*
Blue-footed Booby. *Sula nebouxii.* E4a4.   <u>Bubia Pies Azules</u>
M-SAm.,x.B,H. <u>Resident BC, nP; ranges csP</u>. Rare; islands, coasts, over open ocean.
*32" Feet bright blue; bill dark grayish blue. Ad: Mantle and tail blackish brown with
faint streaks and spots; rump and patch on upper back white; hind-neck and head
streaked brown and white. Im: Darker, with head and rump more streaked;
darker below than im. Masked B.; paler below than im. Brown B. or Red-footed B.*
Brown Booby. *Sula leucogaster.* E4a8.   <u>Bubia Vientre Blanco</u>
US-SAm. <u>Resident BC, ncP, Y (is.); ranges sP</u>. Rare+; over open ocean or coastal
waters, bays, harbors, islands; flies with strong wing-beats and long, sweeping glides.
*28" Ad: Feet, bill yellow; upperparts, entire head, neck, and <u>upper breast</u> dark brown
(but head and much of <u>neck</u> whitish in w.Mexican male); rest of underparts white,
including under-wing coverts. Im: Like brown-headed ad. but duller, less contrasty.*
Red-footed Booby. *Sula sula.* E4a7.   <u>Bubia Pies Rojos</u>
M-SAm. <u>Resident ncP (Tres Marias+Revillagigedo Is.); ranges P (Sinaloa to Chiapas),
Y (Quintana Roo)</u>. Rare+ (common at nest islands); open oceans, islands; flies rapidly.

Pl.47. 27" Ad: Feet red; bill blue with pink base. Wh.ph.: White, but tips and trailing edge of wing black. D.ph.: Dark brown; or dark brown with some white, such as white rump, uptacs, untacs, tail. Im: Dark brownish gray; feet yellowish.
Northern Gannet. *Morus bassanus.* E4a1. Bubia de Norte
US-M. Ranges cA. Very rare; over open ocean waters, flying strongly, gliding, diving.
38" Ad: White except black wing-tips and tawny wash on head and neck. Sub-ad: Feet black; younger birds mostly mottled dark brownish gray above, whitish below; older birds contrasty white below, and on rump, wings, and (slightly tawny) head.

PELICANS - PELECANIDAE - ALCATRACES
Very large; short legs, long neck, very short tail, very long bill; temperate, tropical.
White Pelican. *Pelecanus erythrorhynchos.* E3a6. Alcatraz Blanco
Can-G,B,N,CR. Resident up to 8000', nH (Durango); winter visitor BC, P, ncH, A, Y. Rare,local; coastal bays, lagoons, or inland lakes; in groups, swimming, or soaring.
60" Ad: White, except broadly black wing-tips; very long, heavy, pouched orange-yellow bill, orange-yellow feet and legs; some yellow or gray on head and nape in breeding season. Im: Similar but wings mottled, much gray on head and neck.
Brown Pelican. *Pelecanus occidentalis.* E3a7. Alcatraz Moreno
Can-SAm. Resident coastal BC, P, A, Y. Common; ocean beaches, rocky shores, and bays, often groups flying in an irregular line, perching on rocks, or diving from the air.
Pl.1. 50" Mostly gray. Ad: Head and neck white (win.), white and brown (sum.).

CORMORANTS - PHALACROCORACIDAE - SARGENTOS
Four regular residents, mostly BC, P; large; short legs, long neck, medium-length hooked-tipped bill; world-wide; fliers, and coastal or inland swimmers, surface-divers; bright face colors in breeding season. Distinguish species by patterns, white in plumage, soft-part colors, metallic sheen; eliminate some by range and habitat. **Plate 1.**
Double-crested Cormorant. *Phalacrocorax auritus.* E5a6. Cuervo Marino
AK-M,B. Resident, near sea level, BC, nP (Sonora); winter visitor ncP (Sonora to Guerrero), Y. Common; rocky islands, headlands, ocean waters, bays, inlets, lagoons.
Pl.1. 32" Ad: Black, dark green sheen; rather large, rounded, orange-yellow throat-pouch. Im: Dark brown above; very pale brownish gray throat and breast, shading to dark brown belly and untacs; throat-pouch yellow; plumage darker, except throat and breast, than Olivaceous C.; much paler below than Brandt's and Pelagic C.
Olivaceous Cormorant. *Phalacrocorax olivaceus.* E5a7. Corvejón
US-SAm. Resident up to 9000', sBC, P, csH (Michoacán to Chiapas), A, Y. Common; coastal lagoons, estuaries; inland ponds, lakes, rivers, swamps and marshes.
Pl.1. 26" Ad: Black, may have purplish sheen; except small, triangular, yellow throat-pouch (bordered by narrow white line in breeding adults). Im: Dark grayish brown above, pale gray below; throat-pouch dull yellow. See Double-crested C.
Brandt's Cormorant. *Phalacrocorax penicillatus.* E5a10. Sargento Guanero
AK-M. Resident, near sea level, BC, nP (Sonora). Rare+; coast waters, bays, inlets.
30" Ad: Black, with purplish and greenish sheen, except blue throat-pouch bordered buff; Im: Dark grayish brown above, slightly paler below; throat-pouch dull blue.
Pelagic Cormorant. *Phalacrocorax pelagicus.* E5a17. Pato Sargento
AK-M. Resident, near sea level, nBC; winter visitor sBC. Rare; headlands and rocky islands, and nearby coastal and open ocean waters.
27" Slender neck, small head, and slender bill. Ad: Black; dark red throat-pouch and white flank-patches in breeding season. Im: Very dark grayish brown all over.

ANHINGAS - ANHINGIDAE - HUIZOTES
Anhinga. *Anhinga anhinga.* E6a1. Huizote
US-SAm. Resident, near sea level, P (Sinaloa to Chiapas), A, Y. Rare+; swimming in

ponds, lagoons, rivers, fresh or salty water, or perching open-winged, or soaring.
Pl.1. 32" Very long, slender neck; slender, sharp bill; short legs; very small head; long, full tail; large silvery patch on wings and upper back. M: *Glossy black otherwise.* F: *Blackish otherwise, but head, neck, upper breast dark buffy brown.*

FRIGATEBIRDS - FREGATIDAE - FRAGATAS
Very large; short legs and neck, long, pointed wings; warm oceans. **Plate 47.**

Magnificent Frigatebird. *Fregata magnificens.* E2a1.   Fragata Magnífica
US-SAm. Resident or visitor coastal and offshore waters, BC, P, A, Y. Common; ocean, coastal lagoons, bays, estuaries; very rare inland over lakes, ponds, or rivers.
39" Long, forked tail; long wings; rather long, hooked-tipped bill. M: *All-black wings; inflatable red throat-sac.* F: *Like male, but has white breast and sides.* Im: *White head, throat, breast, and sides; progressively less white in older immatures.*

Great Frigatebird. *Fregata minor.* E2a3.   Fragata Grande
M,CR,SAm. Resident cP (Revillagigedo Is.). Rare+, at nest islands; rare, open ocean.
Pl.47. 40" Like Magnificent F., *but* M: *pale brown upper-wing-coverts and inner secondaries; and* F: *white throat; and Im: rusty wash on white head and underparts.*

HERONS, BITTERNS, EGRETS - ARDEIDAE - GARZAS, PEDRETES
Fifteen regular residents or visitors, mostly P, A, Y; medium to very large; legs and neck long or very long; wings rather short, rounded; bill medium-long, pointed; world-wide; mostly waders in inland and coastal waters; mostly nest in trees or shrubs in or near water, or in marshes; immature and adult plumages and color phases. Identify species by size, proportions, plumage colors and patterns; to identify white individuals note color of legs, feet, and bill (Great Egret, Snowy Egret, Cattle Egret, young Little Blue Heron, white phase Great Blue Heron and Reddish Egret). **Plates 2 + 3.**

Pinnated Bittern. *Botaurus pinnatus.* I1d10.   Pedrete Lineado
M-SAm,x.H,Pan. Resident up to 1000', csA (Veracruz to Quintana Roo), Y (Quintana Roo). Rare, secretive; in marshes, or marshy edges of ponds, lagoons, sluggish rivers.
Pl.2. 25" Neck and crown narrowly barred (no black patch on side of head); breast streaked, not barred. See American B., immature Tiger H. and Lineated H.

American Bittern. *Botaurus lentiginosus.* I1d11.   Torcomón
AK-Pan. Resident, 4000 to 9000', ncH; transient and winter visitor, all sub-regions.
Rare, irregular; in open fresh-water or brackish marshy areas, often among cat-tails.
Pl.3. 26" Resembles Pinnated B. *but has black patch on head; streaks on neck.*

Least Bittern. *Ixobrychus exilis.* I1d3.   Garcilla
Can-SAm. Resident, transient, or winter visitor, up to 9000', all sub-regions. Rare, local, secretive; in fresh-water or brackish marshes, and marshy ponds and lakes; flies more often, farther, and with slower wing-beats, than rails of comparable size.
Pl.3. 12" Rich buff wing-patches contrast with black wing-tips and tail. M: *Black back and crown.* F: *Dark reddish brown back and crown.*

Tiger (Bare-throated Tiger-) **Heron.** *Tigrisoma mexicanum.* I1c1.   Garza Tigre
M-SAm. Resident up to 3000', P, A, Y. Rare+; solitary, along wooded rivers, fresh-water or brackish marshes, swamps, or marshy borders of ponds, lakes, lagoons.
Pl.2. 30" Throat bare, yellow. Ad: *Sides of neck, and upperparts, narrowly barred; white streak down underside of neck; belly brown.* Im: *Boldly barred buff and black.*

Great Blue Heron. *Ardea herodias.* I1a4.   Garzón Cenizo
AK-SAm. Resident or visitor up to 10,000', all sub-regions. Dark phase common; white phase rare ("Great White Heron" - occurs only in coastal Y); on ocean beaches, coastal lagoons, bays, estuaries; also lakes, ponds, sluggish rivers, marshes or swamps.
Pl.3. 45" D.ph: Much larger than other dark Mexican herons; bluish gray above; darker flight feathers; brownish wash on neck; whitish head. Wh.ph: White, with yellowish legs and yellow bill. Larger than Great Egret, *which has* blackish *legs.*

Great Egret. *Egretta alba.* I1a13.   <u>Garzón Blanco</u>
Can-SAm. <u>Resident or visitor up to 10,000', all sub-regions</u>. Common; coastal and
inland waters, lagoons, marshes, swamps, lakes, rivers; often in mixed wader flocks.
Pl.3. 38" White; note *large size, mostly yellow bill, and blackish-gray feet and legs.*

Snowy Egret. *Egretta thula.* I1a22.   <u>Garcita Nívea</u>
Can-SAm. Resident or visitor up to 8000', all sub-regions. Rare+; mostly in lowland
waters, brackish or fresh-water lagoons, marshes, swamps, ponds, rivers, and canals.
Pl.3. 22" Like Cattle E. and im. Little Blue H., *but has black bill, black legs (or
front of legs dark and rear of legs yellowish in im.), yellow or yellow-orange feet.*

Little Blue Heron. *Egretta thula.* I1a21.   <u>Garcita Azul</u>
Can-SAm. <u>Resident or visitor up to 8000', all sub-regions</u>. Rare+; mostly in lowlands, in lagoons, tidal flats, fresh-water ponds, lakes, canals, or marshes and swamps.
*Pl.3. 25" Bill <u>yellowish</u>, black-tipped. Ad: Slaty blue, with greenish to black legs;
purplish neck and head. Im: White, or white and blue, legs and feet dull greenish.*

Tricolored Heron. *Egretta tricolor.* I1a8.   <u>Garza Flaca</u>
Can-SAm. <u>Resident or visitor up to 8000', all sub-regions</u>. Common to rare; mostly
lowland, lagoons, estuaries, mangrove swamps, or sluggish rivers, or marshes.
*Pl.3. 24" Bill long, slender. Plumage white below, narrow white stripe down front
of long, slender neck. Ad: Neck and upperparts mostly dark blue. Im: Upperparts
partly dark brown, neck mostly brown.* See Little Blue Heron and Reddish Egret.

Reddish Egret. *Egretta rufescens.* I1a14.   <u>Garza Melenuda</u>
US-SAm,x.H. <u>Resident or visitor, near sea level, BC, P, A, Y</u>. Rare, local; brackish
lagoons, quiet bays and inlets, coastal swamps; moving about erratically when feeding.
*Pl.3. 30" Bill mostly pink, with black tip; legs dark grayish blue. D.ph:Dark
grayish blue, but (shaggy) head and entire neck rich reddish brown. Wh.ph: White.*
See much more common and smaller Little Blue Heron.

Cattle Egret. *Bubulcus ibis.* I1a28.   <u>Garcita de Ganado</u>
AK-SAm. <u>Resident or visitor up to 8000', all sub-regions</u>. Common to rare; often
with livestock in moist to wet pastures, fields, large clearings, swamps, marshes.
*Pl.3. 20" Neck, and yellow bill, relatively short; yellowish to orange legs. Breeding
adults have rich tawny-buff wash on crown, upper breast, and back.*

Green (Green-backed) **Heron.** *Butorides virescens.* I1a35.   <u>Garcita Verde</u>
Can-Pan. <u>Resident up to 8000', all sub-regions</u>. Rare+; usually in swampy or marshy
areas, or shrubby or marshy borders of ponds, lakes, rivers, brackish lagoons, inlets.
*Pl.3. 16" Ad: Gray and dark green above; sides of neck reddish brown; crown
black. Im: Duller; streaked dark brown and white on sides of neck and underparts.*

Agami (Chestnut-bellied) **Heron.** *Agamia agami.* I1a38.   <u>Garza Estilete</u>
M-SAm,x.ES,N. <u>Resident up to 1500', sP (Chiapas), sA (se.Veracruz to s.Quintana
Roo)</u>. Very rare, local; swamps, or swampy forest streams, sluggish rivers, or ponds.
*Pl.2. 28" Rich reddish brown, and iridescent dark green; bill <u>very</u> long and slender.
Im: Dark and dull above, streaked brown and buffy below.*

Black-crowned Night-Heron. *Nycticorax nycticorax.* I1b2.   <u>Pedrete Gris</u>
Can-SAm. <u>Resident up to 9000', BC, P, cH (Michoacán to México), A; visitor nsH, Y
(Yucatán)</u>. Common; fresh-water or brackish swamps or marshes; ponds, lagoons.
*Pl.3. 26" Ad: Back black or dark gray; wings gray; underparts white. Im: Brown
above,with pale spots; heavily streaked brown and buff below.* See Boat-billed H.

Yellow-crowned Night-Heron. *Nyctanassa violacea.* I1b1.   <u>Pedrete Enmascarado</u>
Can-SAm. <u>Resident or visitor up to 9000', BC, P, cH (Guanajuato to Distrito
Federal+Tlaxcala)</u>, A, Y. Rare+, local; in mangrove swamps, wooded brackish
lagoons, inlets, or fresh-water swamps, wooded ponds, rivers, occasionally marshes.
*Pl.3. 26" Head large. Ad: Medium gray body and wings, black-and-white head.
Im: Streaked, mottled; grayer, has smaller spots, than* im. Black-crowned Night-H.

BOAT-BILLED HERONS - COCHLEARIIDAE - MACACOS
Medium-large; long legs, medium-long neck, rounded wings, short tail. **Plate 2.**
Boat-billed Heron. *Cochlearius cochlearius.* I2a1.   Macaco
M-SAm. Resident, near sea level, P (Sinaloa to Chiapas), A, Y. Rare+, local; active at
night, often in colonies, mangrove swamps, wooded rivers, ponds, brackish lagoons.
*Pl.2. 20" Bill very broad, inflated. Ad: Reddish-brown below, with black sides.
Im: Brownish to gray above, and buffy or whitish below.* V: a guttural *cah-cah-co.*

IBISES, SPOONBILLS - THRESKIORNITHIDAE - IBISES, ESPATULAS
Three residents; mostly lowlands; large; long legs and neck, rounded wings, short
tail; long bill, slender and decurved, or broad and spatulate; temperate and tropical;
coastal or inland waders. Distinguish species by bill shape, color, pattern. **Plate 3.**
White Ibis. *Eudocimus albus.* I5a1.   Ibis Blanco
US-SAm. Resident up to 6000', sBC, P, nH (Guanajuato), A, Y. Rare+; open
swampy or marshy areas, shallow ponds, wet meadows, mangrove lagoons, estuaries.
*Pl.3. 23" Long legs and long decurved bill pinkish. Ad: White, with black
wing-tips. Im: White below; brown above (may be mottled); head and neck streaked.*
White-faced Ibis. *Plegadis chihi.* I5a5.   Atotola
Can-SAm,x.B,N,Pan. Resident up to 8000', ncP (Sonora to Colima), ncH (Chihuahua
to Oaxaca), ncA; transient or winter visitor sA, BC. Rare+, local; large marshes, wet
meadows, mud-flats, open swamps; neck and legs outstretched in flight.
*Pl.3. 20" Sum.Ad: Bronzy reddish brown, white face-line.Win.Ad: Dark bronzy
gray; paler, streaked head, neck, no* white. *Im: Paler; heavy streaks on head, neck.*
Roseate Spoonbill. *Platalea ajaja.* I5b6.   Espátula
US-SAm. Resident or visitor up to 6000', P, nH (Guanajuato), A, Y; casual nBC(?).
Rare+; in small ponds, borrow pits, fresh-water or brackish marshes, swamps, lagoons.
*Pl.3. 30" Much shorter-necked and shorter-legged than Flamingo. Bill long, heavy
with broad, flat tip. Ad: Mostly pink and red, with white upper back and neck;
greenish bare skin on head; legs red. Im: Mostly white to pale pink; yellowish legs.*

STORKS - CICONIIDAE - CIGUENONES
Very large; long legs, neck, bill; broad wings, short tail; temperate and tropical.
Jabiru. *Jabiru mycteria.* I6c3.   Jabirú
M-Pan. Resident near sea level sA (Tabasco+Chiapas to Quintana Roo); visitor sP
(s.Chiapas), cA (Veracruz). Very rare, local; in secluded portions of large fresh-water
or brackish marshes or secluded openings in extensive swamps, or large wet meadows.
*Pl.2. 52" Bill long, heavy, upturned, black; Ad: Red collar at base of black neck,
but plumage all-white. Im:Much duller, mostly grayish or whitish.* See Wood Stork.
Wood Stork. *Mycteria americana.* I6a1.   Cigüeñón
M-Pan. Resident near sea level, P, A, Y; cas.vis.BC. Rare+, irregular; in fresh-water
or brackish marshes or swamps, or lakes, pools, lagoons, or low-lying wet fields.
*Pl.3. 36" Long dark legs, rather long neck, long heavy bill; plumage mostly white;
tips and trailing edge of wing black; upper neck and head black; no* red on neck.

FLAMINGOS - PHOENICOPTERIDAE - FLAMENCOS
Very large; broad, rounded wings; short tail; bill inflated, bent down; mostly tropical.
American Flamingo. *Phoenicopterus ruber.* I7a1.   Flamenco
M. Resident Y (breeds ne.Yucatán; visitor additional coastal nw.+ne.Y). Abundant to
rare; brackish or salt-water lagoons, inlets, estuaries; wading; feeding with bill upside
down. (Almost all "flamingos" reported outside the Y Region are Roseate Spoonbills.)
*Pl.3. 45" Plumage pink, wings redder; tip and trailing edge of wing black; neck and
pink legs very long. Im: Plumage mostly dull brownish gray, usually partly pink.*

DUCKS, GEESE, SWANS - ANATIDAE - PATOS, ANSARES
Thirty-three species, mostly winter visitors, mostly northern and central Mexico; heavy body; short legs and tail, medium-long to very long neck, most have flattened bill; coastal or inland, fresh or salty water; strong fliers and swimmers; surface-divers or dabblers; world-wide; male and female plumages. Distinguish species by colors, patterns, size, body proportions, voice. **Plates 2, 8, and 9.**

Fulvous Tree-Duck (Whistling-D.). *Dendrocygna bicolor.* L2b3.   Chiquiote
US-M,G,H,CR-SAm. Resident up to 8000', ncP (Sonora to Guerrero), cH (Jalisco to México), ncA; winter visitor BC, sP, sA (Tabasco), Y. Rare; large wet grassy fields, fresh-water or brackish marshes, rice fields, meadows.   V: a shrill, whistled *kuh-wee*.
Pl.8. 21" Mostly rich tawny brown; black back and wings, with brownish feather tips; uptacs (and untacs) whitish, forming a white "V" on top of tail, in flight.

Black-bellied Tree-Duck (Whistling-D.). *Dendrocygna autumnalis.* L2b8.   Pijije
US-SAm. Resident up to 2000', P, A, Y. Common; marshes, swampy or marshy ponds, lakes, brackish lagoons, inlets, mangrove swamps.   V: a whistled *pe-he-he-he.*
Pl.8. 21" Ad: Tawny neck, breast, and lower back; black belly and rump; bill and legs red; large white patch on wing. Im: Paler and grayer .

Whistling (Tundra) **Swan.** *Cygnus columbianus.* L2c7.   Cisne Chiflador
AK-M. Winter visitor BC, nH (Chihuahua), nA. Very rare; flooded or dry fields, large lakes or marshes, lagoons, estuaries, salt-water bays and inlets. V: a melodious *whoo.*
Pl.8. 52" Very long neck. Ad: All white, except black bill. Im: Pale gray; lighter below; bill mostly grayish pink.

White-fronted (Gr.Wh.-fr.) **Goose.** *Anser albifrons.* L2c11.   Oca Salvaje
AK-M. Winter visitor BC, P, ncH (Chihuahua to México), A (Tamaulipas to Campeche), Y (Yucatán). Rare+; flooded fields, large marshes, lakes, lagoons or estuaries.
Pl.8. 29" White untacs; white uptacs form a "U" in flight. Ad: Dark gray; black belly-bands; white at base of bill. Im: No white on face; no black belly-bands.

Snow Goose. *Anser caerulescens.* L2c15.   Ansar Real
AK-M,H. Winter visitor nBC, nsP (Sonora+Sinaloa+Chiapas), ncH (Chihuahua to Guanajuato), A (Tamaulipas to Tabasco). Rare, irregular; (blue phase occurs only in ncA) grazing in moist or dry fields, large marshes; swimming in fresh or brackish water.
Pl.8. 28" Closed bill has noticeable gap; wing-tips black. Wh.ph.ad: Mostly white; pinkish legs and bill. Wh.ph.im: Pale gray above; bill, feet black. Bl.ph.ad: White head and upper neck; dark gray back and belly. Bl.ph.im: Dark, dull; bill, feet black.

Ross's Goose. *Anser rossii.* L2c16.   Ansar de Ross
AK-M. Winter visitor nBC, nP, nH (Chihuahua), nA. Very rare; lagoons,marshes.
Pl.8. 24" Like white phase Snow Goose, but bill short, no gap when closed. Bl.ph: Like "Blue" G., but neck all dark.

Brant. *Branta bernicla.* L2c21.   Ganso de Collar
AK-M. Winter visitor BC, NP (Sonora to Sinaloa). Common; on salt-water bays and inlets, brackish estuaries, lagoons, large tidal marshes; rarely inland lakes or marshes.
Pl.8. 26" Black bill, head, neck, and breast; small white marks on throat; white untacs; long white uptacs almost cover tail. Western race: Dark, not whitish, belly.

Canada Goose. *Branta canadensis.* L2c19.   Ganso de Cánada
AK-M. Winter visitor BC, P, ncH (Chihuahua to México), ncA (Tamaulipas to Veracruz). Rare+; in fresh-water marshes, lakes, or ponds, brackish lagoons and estuaries, salt-water bays, inlets and marshes; in flocks; often grazing in grassy fields.
Pl.8. 24"-38" Dark gray above; brownish gray below; black neck and head except white patch under chin; uptacs form white "U" in flight.. Races differ greatly, mainly in size, but also in color of underparts (from pale grayish to dark brownish gray).

Muscovy Duck. *Cairina moschata.* L2e2.   Pato Perulero
M-SAm. Resident, up to 3000', P (Sinaloa to Chiapas), A, Y. Rare+, irregular; mostly

large swamps, or quiet wooded rivers, or swampy borders of ponds, lakes, or lagoons.
Pl.2. 32", 26" M: Black, glossed green; wing-patch and <u>*under-wing-coverts*</u> *white; bill barred pale gray and black; facial caruncles mostly black. F: Much smaller.*
Wood Duck. *Aix sponsa.* L2e10.   <u>Pato de Charreteras</u>
Can-M. <u>Winter visitor nP, ncH, ncA</u>. Very rare; quiet lakes, ponds, swamps, marshes.
Pl.8. 18" Floppy nape-crest. M: White and black face, glossed green and purple; breast chestnut. F: Gray head, white tear-drop-shaped eye-patch; streaked below.
Green-winged Teal. *Anas crecca.* L2e23.   <u>Cerceta Común</u>
AK-M,B,H. <u>Winter visitor all sub-regions</u>. Rare+; ponds, lakes, marshes, lagoons.
Pl.9. 14" M: Reddish brown head, very large green eye-patch; spotted breast; gray sides. F: Streaked and mottled; green speculum, no blue patch on wing.
Mallard. *Anas platyrhynchos.* L2e30.   <u>Pato de Collar</u>
   Mottled group. *A. p. fulvigula.*   <u>Pato Moteado</u>
   US-M. <u>Resident, near sea level, nA; winter visitor csA (Veracruz to Tabasco)</u>.
   Rare+; in ponds, lakes, and fresh-water and brackish marshes, lagoons, estuaries.
   24" M+F: Like <u>female</u> *of Mallard group, but darker; tail brown; bill yellow.*
   Mallard group. *A. p. platyrhynchos.*   <u>Pato de Collar</u>
   AK-M,G,H,N-Pan. <u>Resident, 4000 to 6000', nBC; winter visitor BC, ncP, ncH, A</u>. Rare+, north; very rare, south; ponds, lakes, fresh-water or brackish marshes.
   Pl.8. 24" Tail white. M: Green head, white collar, yellow bill. F: Mottled yellowish brown; bill mostly dark, with reddish to yellowish base and tip.
   Mexican group. *A. p. diazi.*   <u>Pato Mexicano</u>
   US-M. <u>Resident, 4000 to 9000', ncH (Chihuahua+Coahuila to Jalisco+Puebla)</u>.
   Rare+; along shallow borders of ponds or lakes, or pools in fresh-water marshes.
   24" M+F: Like <u>female</u> *of Mallard group, but slightly darker; bill yellow to orange; and not much white in tail; even more like* Mottled group, *but paler;*
Northern Pintail. *Anas acuta.* L2e40.   <u>Pato Golondrino</u>
AK-SAm. <u>Transient or winter visitor all sub-regions</u>. Abundant to rare+; in fresh-water lakes, flooded fields, ponds, marshes, salty coastal waters, lagoons, estuaries, bays.
Pl.8. 28" Long neck, long tail. M: Brown head; neck mostly white. F: Mottled.
Blue-winged Teal. *Anas discors.* L2e47.   <u>Cerceta Aliazul</u>
AK-SAm. <u>Transient or winter visitor all sub-regions</u>. Abundant, but irregular; in ponds, lakes, rivers, and fresh-water or saltwater marshes, swamps, lagoons, estuaries.
Pl.9. 16" Green speculum, <u>*large blue patch*</u> *on wing. M: Head dark blue, with white crescent. F: Mottled grayish brown. See Cinnamon T. and Green-winged T.*
Cinnamon Teal. *Anas cyanoptera.* L2e48.   <u>Cerceta Café</u>
AK-SAm. <u>Resident, up to 8000', nBC, ncH (Chihuahua+Jalisco), nA (Tamaulipas); winter visitor sBC, P, csA, Y</u>. Common; lakes, ponds, marshes, lagoons, estuaries.
Pl.9. 16" Green speculum; <u>*large blue patch*</u> *on wing. M: Reddish brown head, neck, underparts. F: Browner than* female Blue-winged T. See Green-winged T.
Northern Shoveler. *Anas clypeata.* L2e52.   <u>Pato Cucharón</u>
AK-SAm. <u>Transient or winter visitor all sub-regions</u>. Common; in fresh or salty waters, such as ponds, lakes, lagoons, estuaries, large marshes, coastal bays, rivers.
Pl.8. 18" Dark, heavy, <u>*broad-tipped*</u> *bill; large blue patch on wing. M: Green head, white breast, reddish brown flanks. F: Mottled yellowish brown.* See female Teals.
Gadwall. *Anas strepera.* L2e21.   <u>Pato Pinto</u>
AK-M. <u>Winter visitor BC, P, ncH, A, Y</u>. Common; ponds, lakes, marshes, estuaries.
Pl.8. 20" Reddish brown wing-patch; speculum white. M: Breast and sides finely mottled gray; head brownish; untacs and uptacs black. F: Mottled brown; paler head.
American Wigeon. *Anas americana.* L2e18.   <u>Pato Chalcuán</u>
AK-SAm. <u>Winter visitor all sub-regions</u>. Common; lakes, marshes, lagoons, estuaries.
Pl.8. 20" M: Crown and wing-patch white; eye-patch green. F: Wing-patch and head grayish; sides not heavily mottled; breast tinged with reddish-brown.

Canvasback. *Aythya valisineria.* L2e59. Pato Coacostle
AK-M,G,H. <u>Winter visitor BC, P, ncH, A, Y</u>. Rare; on large lakes, or coastal waters.
Pl.9. 22" Forehead slopes into long, black, heavy-based bill. M: Red of head browner, back and sides whiter, than Redhead. *F: Head, back and sides pale gray.*

Redhead. *Aythya americana.* L2e61. Pato Cabeza Roja
AK-M,G. <u>Resident, about 5000', cH (Jalisco); transient or winter visitor all sub-regions</u>. Rare+; deep water of large lakes, salty lagoons, estuaries, bays, and inlets.
Pl.9. 21" White bar near tip of "normal" bill. M: Reddish brown head; black breast; F: Mostly brownish, some white on face. See Ring-necked D. and Canvasback.

Ring-necked Duck. *Aythya collaris.* L2e62. Pato Chaparro
AK-Pan. <u>Transient and winter visitor BC, P, ncH, A, Y</u>. Rare, in fresh or salty water, large lakes, lagoons, estuaries, usually in open areas where the water is relatively deep.
Pl.9. 17" White bar near tip of bill. M: Back black. F: Darker than Redhead; *area around base of bill whitish, but not contrasty.* See Greater and Lesser Scaup.

Greater Scaup. *Aythya marila.* L2e69. Pato Boludo
AK-M. <u>Winter visitor BC, nP (Sonora+Sinaloa)</u>. Very rare; mostly in coastal ocean waters, off beaches, in bays, lagoons, inlets and estuaries, usually in rather deep water.
Pl.9. 19" <u>Long</u> white wing-stripe shows in flight. M: Head, neck, breast black; <u>green</u> gloss on head; F: Darker than Redhead; *like* Lesser Scaup, *except wing-stripe.*

Lesser Scaup. *Aythya affinis.* L2e70. Pato Bola
AK-SAm. <u>Winter visitor BC, P, ncH, A, Y</u>. Common; lakes, lagoons, bays, estuaries.
Pl.9. 17" <u>Short</u> white wing-stripe shows in flight; <u>no</u> white bar on bill. M: Usually purplish, <u>not</u> greenish, gloss on head at close range; much paler on back (gray) than Ring-necked D. (black). *F: Dark brown; contrasty white area around base of bill.*

Oldsquaw. *Clangula hyemalis.* L2f7. Pato Viejo
AK-M. <u>Winter visitor nBC, nP (Sonora, Sinaloa, Jalisco)</u>. Very rare; usually ocean waters, sometimes inshore off beaches, or in bays or inlets, large estuaries.
Pl.9. 22", 16" M: Long slender pointed tail. Win.M: White neck and scapulars; black face-patch. Sum.M: Head, neck and breast black, but large white patch around eye. F:Short tail. Win.F: Head whitish, back scalloped gray. Sum.F: Dark face-spot.

Black Scoter. *Melanitta nigra.* L2f8. Negreta del Norte
AK-M. <u>Winter visitor BC</u>. Rare; off beaches, on bays, lagoons, estuaries and inlets.
Pl.9. 19" M: Plumage all-black; orange knob on bill. F: Blackish brown; pale patch on neck, head; black bill. Im.M: Like female, but less contrasty; yellow bill-knob.

Surf Scoter. *Melanitta perspicillata.* L2f9. Negreta de Marejada
AK-M. <u>Winter visitor BC, nP; casual nH</u>. Common; often in open ocean or deep bays.
Pl.9. 20" M: Black, with white patch on hind-neck and on forecrown; bill red, white, and black. F: Blackish brown,with black bill; whitish patches on face.

White-winged Scoter. *Melanitta fusca.* L2f10. Negreta Aliblanca
AK-M. <u>Winter visitor nBC, nP (Sonora)</u>. Very rare; off beaches or headlands, in bays.
Pl.9. 22" White wing-patch. M: Black, with white eye-patch; black-knobbed orange bill. F: Blackish brown, with whitish face-patches; bill dull.

Common Goldeneye. *Bucephala clangula.* L2f11. Pato Chillón Ojos Dorados
AK-M. <u>Winter visitor BC, nP (Sonora to Sinaloa), nH (Chihuahua to Durango), nA (Tamaulipas)</u>. Rare+; mostly ocean bays, inlets, lagoons, estuaries, also large lakes.
Pl.9. 21" Head appears puffy, bill short, dark. M: White below; black and white above; head dark <u>green</u>; rounded white patch below eye. F: Grayish above and below; white collar; head all dark brown. See Bufflehead and Common Merganser.

Bufflehead. *Bucephala albeola.* L2f13. Pato Chillón Jorobado
AK-M. <u>Winter visitor BC, nP, ncH, nsA, Y</u>. Rare+; ocean bays, estuaries, deep lakes.
Pl.9. 14" Head puffy. M: White below, black and white above; <u>large</u> white head-patch. F: Whitish below; brown back and head; white patch behind eye.

Hooded Merganser. *Lophodytes cucullatus.* L2f15.   <u>Mergo de Caperuza</u>
AK-M. <u>Winter visitor BC, ncH, ncA</u>. Very rare; lakes, ponds, coastal lagoons, bays.
Pl.9. 18" Slender, black bill. M: Black and white head and breast pattern; fan-shaped crest; tawny sides. F: Brown head; small tawny crest. See Bufflehead.

Common Merganser. *Mergus merganser.* L2f19.   <u>Mergo Común</u>
AK-M. <u>Resident, 4000 to 6000', nH (Chihuahua); winter visitor BC, nP, ncH, nA, Y</u>.
Very rare; coastal waters, bays, lagoons, estuaries; also deep ponds, large inland lakes.
Pl.9. 25" M: Rounded blackish green head; white breast and sides; slender red bill; large white wing-patch. F: Head and broad collar tawny; breast contrasty white.

Red-breasted Merganser. *Mergus serrator.* L2f17.   <u>Mergo Copetón</u>
AK-M. <u>Winter visitor BC, nP, ncA</u>. Rare+; coastal bays, estuaries, inlets, also lakes.
Pl.9. 23" Shaggy crest; red bill. M: Blackish green head; brownish breast; grayish sides; white wing-patch. F: Head brownish; throat, fore-neck, and breast whitish.

Ruddy Duck. *Oxyura jamaicensis.* L2g3.   <u>Pato Tepalcate</u>
AK-M,B,H,SAm. <u>Resident up to 8000', BC, ncH (Chihuahua to México); winter visitor P, A, Y</u>. Rare to abundant; open, rather deep lakes, lagoons, estuaries, inlets.
Pl.9. 16" Sum.M: Reddish brown; with black and white head; blue bill. Win.M: Grayish brown; head dark brown and white, less contrasty; bill dull bluish gray. F: Grayish brown above; much paler below; one dark streak on whitish face-patch.

Masked Duck. *Oxyura dominica.* L2g2.   <u>Pato Enmascarado</u>
US-SAm,x.N. <u>Resident near sea level, P (Nayarit to Chiapas), A</u>. Very rare; ponds, pools, lakes, lagoons, estuaries, sluggish rivers, often in or near beds of water plants.
Pl.9. 14" M: Black and reddish head, neck, and breast pattern; body mottled, reddish brown; bill blue. F:+Im: Crown brown; two dark lines on whitish face.

VULTURES - CATHARTIDAE - ZOPILOTES

Four residents, two mostly southern; short legs and neck, small head and bill, broad rounded wing, short or medium tail; coastal or inland, open country or forest; static soarers, carrion-feeders; New World temperate and tropical. Distinguish species by length of tail, color of head, white or pale on wing, manner of flight. **Plate 2.**

Black Vulture. *Coragyps atratus.* J1a1.   <u>Zopilote Común</u>
Can-SAm. <u>Resident up to 10,000', P, H, A, Y</u>. Common; tree-dotted pastures, beaches, rooftops in villages, *ranchos*, garbage dumps, roadsides, soaring overhead.
24" Like Turkey V. and Savanna V., *but tail short, wing-tips whitish below, head black. Soars with wings straight out, often flaps rapidly several times, then glides.*

Turkey Vulture. *Cathartes aura.* J1a2.   <u>Aura Común</u>
US-SAm. <u>Resident up to 15,000', all sub-regions</u>. Common; in situations similar to those favored by the Black V., but not as common in villages, corrals, close to people.
29" Head red; plumage black; tail longer than Black V.'s; <u>*no*</u> *white in wing. Soars with wings up at an angle, rocking, seldom flapping. Im: Head pale to dark gray.*

Savanna (Less.Yel.-head.)**Vulture.** *Cathartes burrovianus.* J1a3.   <u>Aura Chica</u>
M,B,H,N-SAm. <u>Resident near sea level, cP (se.Oaxaca), A, Y</u>. Rare; over large marshes, low-lying fields, gliding low, some slow flapping, rocking, appears buoyant.
Pl.2. 26" Closely resembles Turkey V., *but Ad: Head (close-up) yellowish with some red and blue; pale wing-patch <u>above</u> near tip. Im: Head dark with pale nape.*

King Vulture. *Sarcoramphus papa.* J1a7.   <u>Zopilote Rey</u>
M-SAm. <u>Resident up to 3500', P (Sinaloa to Chiapas), csA (Puebla to Quintana Roo), Y (Quintana Roo)</u>. Rare, local; dense humid forest, secluded clearings; high overhead.
Pl.2. 31" Tail very short, wings very broad. Ad: Tail, wing-tips, and broad trailing edge of wing black; rest of plumage white except gray collar; bare head and neck red, orange, blue. Im: Like Black V., *but much larger, and usually splotched with white.*

OSPREYS - PANDIONIDAE - GAVILANES PESCADORES
Osprey. *Pandion haliaetus.* J2a1. <u>Gavilán Pescador</u>
AK-SAm. <u>Resident near sea level, BC, np, Y; winter visitor csP, H, A.</u> Rare+; over
lakes, ponds, marshes, swamps, lagoons, bays, or on poles or in tree-tops near water.
*Pl.4. 23" Blackish above; white below; long wings angled at black-patched wrist;
head whitish with broad black line through eye (Y birds lack this black line).*

HAWKS, EAGLES, and KITES - ACCIPITRIDAE - GAVILANES
Thirty-six species, mostly residents, widespread in Mexico; very large to medium
small; mostly short legs, sharp-clawed feet; mostly broad wings, rather rounded; tail
short, square, to long and deeply forked; bill strong, hooked; mostly inland, humid
forest to semi-desert to wetlands, predators; world-wide; color phases and immature and
adult plumages, females larger. Distinguish species by size, colors, patterns, tail shape
and bands, under-wing markings, flight silhouette. **Plates 2, 4, 5, and 6.**
Cayenne (Gray-headed) **Kite.** *Leptodon cayanensis.* J4a6. <u>Gavilán Pantanero</u>
M-SAm. <u>Resident near sea level, A, Y.</u>Rare; in swamps, near lakes, or marsh-borders.
*Pl.2. 18" Ad: Blackish above; gray head; white below; two or three pale tail-bars.
Im: White face and underparts; blackish crown, back, and wings; or head black,
underparts streaked; tail as in adult.*
Hook-billed Kite. *Chondrohierax uncinatus.* J4a7. <u>Gavilán Pintado</u>
US-SAm. <u>Resident up to 7000', P (Sinaloa to Chiapas), cH (Guanajuato), A, Y.</u> Rare;
forests, patchy low woods or scattered trees, borders, river borders, often near water.
*Pl.2. 16" Spread wings narrow near body, broad near rounded tips; bill strongly
hooked; tail broadly barred. Ad.M: Medium to dark gray above; barred gray (may
show some brown) and whitish below; see Gray Hawk. Ad.F: Blackish above;
barred rufous and whitish below. Im: Blackish brown above; usually whitish with
some dark bars below; whitish collar. Bl.ph.Ad: Black, except broad white tail-bar.*
Swallow-tailed Kite. *Elanoides forficatus.* J4a14. <u>Milano Tijereta</u>
US-SAm. <u>Summer resident, near sea level, sA; transient up to 6000', csH, A, Y.</u>
Rare; swamps, marshes, humid forest; may maneuver overhead in small flocks,with
long, sweeping glides, occasional strong wing-beats, catching aerial insects in its feet.
*Pl.6. 24" Ad: Glossy black, except white head, underparts, and under-wing coverts;
deeply forked tail. Im: Similar, but spotted or streaked.*
White-tailed (Blk-should.) **Kite.** *Elanus leucurus.* J1a17. <u>Milano Maromero</u>
US-SAm. <u>Resident, near sea level, nBC, nsP, A; accidental Y.</u> Rare+; moist open
country with scattered trees, tree-dotted pastures, marshes, often hovers while hunting.
*Pl.6. 16" Tail appears virtually all-white. Ad: Mostly white head and underparts;
and pearl gray above, with black wrist-patch; iris red. Im: Mottled brown back; dark
wings; washed buffy below and on head with faint dark streaks.*
Everglade (Snail) **Kite.** *Rostrhamus sociabilis.* J4a22. <u>Gavilán Caracolero</u>
US-SAm,x.ES. <u>Resident sP, csA.</u> Common; large fresh-water or brackish marshes.
*Pl.6. 18" Bill very strongly hooked. Ad.M: Black, with white tail-base, untacs,
uptacs, and tail-tip; legs red. F+Im: Mottled and streaked dark brown and white.*
Double-toothed Kite. *Harpagus bidentatus.* J4a24. <u>Gavilán con Banda</u>
M-SAm. <u>Resident near sea level, cP (Guerrero to Oaxaca), sA.</u> Rare; humid forest.
*Pl.2. 13" Dark streak down center of white throat. Ad: Dark slaty gray above;
whitish below with rufous bars; chest and sides nearly plain rufous; three white bars
on black tail. Im: Blackish brown above; whitish below, with heavy black streaks.*
Mississippi Kite. *Ictinia misisippiensis.* J4a27. <u>Gavilán del Mississippi</u>
US-SAm. <u>Transient A.</u> Rare+; open country, borders; buoyant flight, much tail-motion.
*Pl.4. 14" Ad: Dark gray above, pearly gray below; whitish head, unbarred black
tail; slender, pointed dark wings. Im: Dark gray above; underparts and head whitish,
streaked with dark brown; tail dark with several pale gray bars. See Plumbeous Kite.*

Plumbeous Kite. *Ictinia plumbea.* J4a26. <u>Gavilán Plomizo</u>
M-SAm. <u>Summer resident up to 3000', sP, A, Y.</u> Rare+; in tree-tops, in river-border woods, swamps, borders, partial clearings, or flying buoyantly with much tail motion. *Pl.2. 15" Ad.+Im: Like* Mississippi Kite, *but two broad white bars on black tail.*

Bald Eagle. *Haliaeetus leucocephalus.* J4a40. <u>Aguila Cabeza Blanca</u>
AK-M. <u>Resident, near sea level, BC, nP; winter visitor nH.</u> Rare; in scattered trees in coastal areas, bay shores, lagoons, estuaries, or along wooded shores of inland lakes. *33" Ad: Blackish brown except white head and white tail. Im: Blackish brown; dull white tail-base; dull whitish mottling under wings.* See Golden Eagle.

Northern Harrier. *Circus cyaneus.* J4a75. <u>Gavilán Ratonero</u>
AK-SAm. <u>Resident nBC; winter visitor all sub-regions.</u> *M-P.* Rare+; tall-grass fields, large marshes, open grassy plains, flapping and gliding irregularly close to the ground. *Pl.4. 19" White rump-patch; long, barred tail; long wings. M: Medium gray above; whitish below. F.+Im: Dark brown above; more cinnamon (and streaked) below.*

Sharp-shinned Hawk. *Accipiter striatus.* J4a127. <u>Esmerejón Coludo</u>
Sharp-shinned group. *A. s. striatus.* <u>Esmerejón Coludo</u>
AK-Pan. <u>Resident, 4000 to 9000', ncH (Chihuahua+Nuevo León to Michoacán); winter visitor all sub-regions.</u> Rare+; in mountain forest, borders, or hedgerows. *Pl.4. 12" Long, barred, <u>square</u>-tipped tail; rounded wings. Ad: Dark gray above; narrow reddish bars below. Im: Dark grayish brown above; heavily streaked below.* See Cooper's Hawk.
White-breasted group. *A. s. chionogaster.* <u>Esmerejón Pechiblanco</u>
M,G,ES,H,N. <u>Resident, 4000 to 8000', sH (Chiapas).</u> Rare; in dense humid forest, or openings, flying rapidly among the trees, or perched in middle branches. *Pl.5. 13" Ad: Blackish gray above, white below. Im: Lightly streaked below.*

Bicolored Hawk. *Accipiter bicolor.* J4a128. <u>Esmerejón Bicolor</u>
M-SAm. <u>Resident up to 2000', A, Y.</u> Rare; in dense humid forest, and small openings. *Pl.2. 15" Ad: Dark gray above; pale gray below, reddish brown thighs; narrow whitish bars on blackish tail. Im: Dark grayish brown; <u>collar</u> and underparts buff.*

Cooper's Hawk. *Accipiter cooperii.* J4a129. <u>Esmerejón de Cooper</u>
Can-M,G,H,CR. <u>Resident up to 9000', nBC, nP (Sonora to Sinaloa), ncH (Chihuahua +Nuevo León to Michoacán); winter visitor sBC, csP, sH, A.</u> Rare; in dense to open woods, scattered trees, woodland borders, flies low (in forest) or overhead (in open). *Pl.4. 17" Ad: Dark gray above; narrow reddish bars below; tail long, barred, <u>rounded</u> at tip; wings rounded. Im: Dark brown above; heavily streaked below.*

Northern Goshawk. *Accipiter gentilis.* J4a133. <u>Gavilán Pollero</u>
AK-M. <u>Resident, 7000 to 11,000', ncH (Chihuahua to Guerrero); winter visitor, to sea level, nP.</u> Very rare; in secluded high mountain forest, small openings, partial clearings. *Pl.4. 22" Ad: Medium bluish gray above; finely barred pale gray below; white line over eye; black patch behind eye; long, barred tail. Im: Whitish line over eye; mottled dark brown above; whitish below, streaked and spotted blackish.* See Gray Hawk.

Crane Hawk. *Geranospiza caerulescens.* J4a144. <u>Gavilán Zancón</u>
M-SAm. <u>Resident up to 3000', P, A, Y.</u> Rare; swamps, forest and borders near water. *Pl.5. 19" Ad: Black; two broad white bars on long tail; legs long, orange. Im: Blackish, but white streaks on head; buffy bars on belly and flanks; whitish tail-base.*

White Hawk. *Leucopternis albicollis.* J4a152. <u>Gavilán Nevado</u>
M-SAm. <u>Resident up to 2000', sP, csA.</u> Rare; dense forest, partial clearings, openings. *Pl. 5. 22" Ad: (Mexico) Plumage all-white, except wing-tip (distal portion of outer primaries) and narrow tail-bar black. Im (and adults farther southeast): More black on wing (wing-tip, <u>and</u> secondaries, <u>and</u> coverts mostly black); <u>broad</u> black tail-bar.*

Common Black-Hawk. *Buteogallus anthracinus.* J4a157. <u>Aguililla Cangrejera</u>
US-SAm. <u>Resident up to 6000', P, nH (Chihuahua to Durango), A, Y; accidental nBC.</u>

Rare+; swamps, wooded river banks, tree-dotted fields, forest borders, partial clearings.
Pl.6. 21" Ad: Black; with broad white tail-bar, very narrow white tail-tip. Im: Heavily streaked brown and tawny; several rather distinct tail-bars.
Great Black-Hawk. *Buteogallus urubitinga.* J4a158.   Aguililla Negra
M-SAm. Resident up to 5000', P, A, Y. Rare+; forest borders, wooded river-banks.
Pl.5. 24" Ad: Black; but uptacs, narrow bar near tail-base, broad bar farther out, and very narrow tail-tip, white; may appear to have one white tail-bar and white rump-patch. Im: Heavily streaked brown and tawny; rather long tail with dull bars.
Harris's Hawk. *Parabuteo unicinctus.* J4a160.   Aguililla Cinchada
US-SAm,x.B,H. Resident up to 6000', BC, P, ncH (Zacatecas to Michoacán), ncA.
Rare; dry or semi-desert areas, in tops of low trees or large shrubs, or flying rather low.
Pl.6. 22" Ad: Black; with rufous wrist-patch and thighs; white untacs, uptacs, tail-base, and tail-tip. Im: Dark rich brown, and some tawny-brown, above; heavily streaked below; reddish wrist-patch and thighs; tail narrowly barred, white at base.
Chestnut (Black-collared) **Hawk.** *Busarellus nigricollis.* J4a161.   Gavilán Conchero
M-SAm. Resident, near sea level, P, csA. Rare; swamps, swampy river-edge woods, secluded wet woodlands; rather secretive, drops from branches to catch fish in its talons.
Pl.5. 19" Reddish brown; short-tailed, broad-winged. Ad: Head mostly whitish; black breast-patch; tips (broadly) and trailing edge of wings, and broad tail-tip, black. Im: Blotched and streaked below and on head; wings barred.
Solitary Eagle. *Harpyhaliaetus solitarius.* J4a163.   Aguililla Solitaria
M-SAm,x.ES,N. Resident, 2000 to 6000', csP, nH (Sonora+Coahuila), csA (Veracruz +Chiapas). Very rare; wooded foothills, mid-mountain slopes, soaring high overhead.
Pl.5. 27" Short tail; very broad wings. Ad: Short crest (not shown); black plumage; broad tail-bar and very narrow tail-tip whitish; finely "scaly" uptacs. Im: Blackish brown, with buffy belly and line over eye; tail paler at base; no white tail-bar.
Gray Hawk. *Asturina nitida.* J4a154.   Gavilán Gris
US-SAm. Resident up to 3000', P, A, Y. Rare+; open woods, river banks, borders.
Pl.6. 17" Smaller, shorter-tailed than N. Goshawk. Ad: Medium gray above; narrowly barred pale gray below; white tail-bars; paler than male Hook-billed Kite. Im: Streaked below, lacks belly-bars and large breast-patch of Roadside Hawk.
Roadside Hawk. *Buteo magnirostris.* J4a165.   Gavilán Lagartijero
M-SAm. Resident up to 3000', csP, A, Y. Common; in partial clearings, hedgerows, open woods, or borders; often perches on open branches, fence-posts, or utility poles.
Pl.5. 16" Several tail-bars. Ad: Gray or grayish brown above; broad grayish brown breast-streaks, may form breast-patch; belly barred. Im: Streaked breast, barred belly.
Red-shouldered Hawk. *Buteo lineatus.* J4a168.   Gavilán Ranero
Can-M. Resident up to 4000', nBC, ncA; winter visitor up to 7000', P, H, sA. Rare+; tree-dotted pastures, woods, hedgerows, swamps, on low branches, utility poles, posts.
Pl.4. 20" Ad: Mottled dark and white *above; narrow reddish bars below; chestnut wrist-patch; narrow white tail-bars on black. Im: Streaked below; hint of wrist-patch.*
Broad-winged Hawk. *Buteo platypterus.* J4a169.   Gavilán Aludo
Can-SAm. Transient up to 6000', sBC, P, sH, A. Common; often in flocks overhead.
Pl.4. 17" Ad. Dark grayish brown above, barred reddish below; broad white bars on black tail. Im: Streaked above, below; narrow tail-bands. See Red-shoulder. H.

Short-tailed Hawk. *Buteo brachyurus.* J4a170.   Gavilán Colicorto
US-SAm,x.ES. Resident, near sea level, P (Sinaloa to Chiapas), A, Y. Rare; in scattered trees, forest borders, scrubby woods, soaring overhead, hovers in updrafts.
Pl.6. 16" Several narrow tail-bands. Ad.d.ph: Black. L.ph: Throat and underparts white; sharp contrast with blackish sides of head and upperparts. Im: Blackish gray above; buff and blackish-brown-streaked or mottled below.

Swainson's Hawk. *Buteo swainsoni.* J4a171. <u>Gavilán Chapulinero</u>
Can-SAm. <u>Summer resident up to 6000', nP (Sonora), nH (Chihuahua to Durango); transient or winter visitor csP, csH, A; casual BC</u>. Rare+; dry sparsely-wooded terrain, among or over scattered trees, open woods, tall hedgerows; often migrating in flocks. *Pl.6. 21" All have throat whitish or buffy; chest dark brown or reddish brown, may be patchy; tail has narrow dark bands, broader sub-terminal band. Ad.d.ph: Mostly blackish brown. Ad.l.ph: Dark brown above; whitish below except chest-band. Im.l.ph: Brown above; heavy streaks on buff below; patchy dark brown chest-band.*

White-tailed Hawk. *Buteo albicaudatus.* J4a173. <u>Aguililla Coliblanca</u>
US-SAm. <u>Resident or visitor up to 9000', P, H, A, Y</u>. Rare; partly wooded mountain slopes, open dry grassy plains, extensive scrubby woods, borders, tree-dotted pastures. *Pl.6. 23" Ad: White below, dark tail-bar; gray above with reddish wrist-patch. Im: Splotchy dark streaks on white below, blackish above; tail faintly, narrowly, barred.*

Zone-tailed Hawk. *Buteo albonotatus.* J4a176. <u>Aguililla Cola Cinchada</u>
US-SAm. <u>Resident, 3000 to 7000', BC, H (Chihuahua+Coahuila to Chiapas); winter visitor P, csA</u>. Rare; tree-dotted shrubby fields, scrubby woods, borders, dry slopes. *Pl.6. 21" In flight resembles Turkey Vulture, but has tail-bars. Ad: Black, with three white tail-bars. Im: Several white tail-bars; breast speckled.*

Red-tailed Hawk. *Buteo jamaicensis.* J4a179. <u>Aguililla Ratonera</u>
AK-Pan. <u>Resident up to 13,000', BC, nP, H, nA (Nuevo León); winter visitor all sub-regions</u>. Rare+; grassy plains, forests, woodlands, open brushy country, borders. *Pl.4. 23" Races and phases differ - typical tail is rufous with narrow black band, but tail of blackish "Harlan's" is grayish with faint reddish wash near tip; tail of very pale "Krider's" is whitish basally and broadly pale rufous near tip. Typical Ad.L.ph: Dark above; rufous tail; white below, with patchy belly-band. Typical Ad.D.ph: Mostly blackish brown; paler under-wing; <u>rufous tail</u>. Im: Streaked below (less on upper belly); narrow black tail-bars on gray.*

Ferruginous Hawk. *Buteo regalis.* J4a185. <u>Aguililla Real</u>
AK-M. <u>Winter visitor nBC, nP, ncH</u>. Rare; open country, scrub woods, brushy plains. *Pl.4. 23" Flight-feathers white below. Ad.L.ph: Thighs, back, and large wing-patch mottled reddish brown; uptacs, untacs, and tail-base whitish; tail-tip broadly pale grayish brown. Ad.D.ph: Mostly very dark brown, including under-wing-coverts; tail grayish above, white below. Im: Brown above, buff below; tail mottled near tip.*

Rough-legged Hawk. *Buteo lagopus.* J4a186. <u>Aguililla Patas Asperas</u>
AK-M. <u>Winter visitor nH (Sonora+Chihuahua)</u>. Rare; open areas, open brushy plains. *Pl.4. 22" Broad dark sub-terminal tail-band; basally the tail is mostly white (female) or barred gray and white (male); flight feathers mostly white with black tips, from below; tarsi feathered. L.ph: Heavily streaked head, back, and breast; black belly and flanks. D.ph: Head, back, underparts, and under-wing-coverts blackish brown.*

Harpy Eagle. *Harpia harpyja.* J4a191. <u>Aguila Arpía</u>
M-SAm,x.ES. <u>Resident, near sea level, sA</u>. Very rare; in secluded dense humid forest. *Pl.2. 35" Very large; very broad wings, rather long tail. Ad: Ragged crest, hind-neck, upperparts and broad breast-band black; mostly white below; head mostly gray; heavy bill black; tail broadly barred black and pale gray. Im: Pale gray above, may be mottled; whitish below; crest dark and white; one broad black tail-band. Birds apparently acquire adult plumage in stages over several years.*

Golden Eagle. *Aquila chrysaetos.* J4a201. <u>Aguila Real</u>
AK-M. <u>Resident, 2000 to 6000', BC, nP (Sonora to Sinaloa), ncH (Chihuahua+Nuevo León to Guanajuato+Hidalgo)</u>. Rare; dry mountain slopes, open woods and brushland. *Pl.4. 34" Wings long, tail rather short; tarsi feathered. Ad: Dark brown with tawny head; grayish tail-bars. Im: Rather contrasty white patch at base of inner primaries below; tail white basally, broadly black-tipped.*

Black-and-white Hawk-Eagle. *Spizastur melanoleucus.* J4a210. <u>Guincho</u>
M-SAm,x.ES. <u>Resident, near sea level, sA, Y</u>. Very rare; in or near dense wet forest.
Pl.5. 24" Tail long, barred. Ad: Underparts, head, and hind-neck white, with short black crest; upperparts black. Im: Dark brown above; white below; white wing-bars.
Black Hawk-Eagle. *Spizaetus tyrannus.* J4a220. <u>Juan-de-a-pie Negro</u>
M-SAm,x.ES. <u>Resident up to 3000', A, Y</u>. Very rare; high branches, humid forest.
Pl.5. 27" Tail long, broadly barred. Ad: Mostly black; narrow white bars on thighs and untacs; speckles and bars on lower belly; white crest-streaks may be hidden. Im: Dark brown above; white below with black-barred thighs, belly, and untacs; may have faint streaks on breast; head white, may have some black on face and crest;
Ornate Hawk-Eagle. *Spizaetus ornatus.* J4a221. <u>Juan-de-a-pie Barrado</u>
M-SAm. <u>Resident up to 5000', cP (Jalisco+Colima), A, Y</u>. Rare; dense, humid forest.
Pl.5. 25" Tail rather long, broadly barred black and pale gray. Ad: Black crest and upperparts; rufous nape, sides of face and neck, and broad (usually partial) breast-band; white throat, black-bordered; underparts black-and-white barred. Im: Varies with age - Mostly white below, and on head and neck; sides, flanks, and thighs black-barred; usually dark brown above, with some black or brown in crest.

CARACARAS, FALCONS - FALCONIDAE - HALCONES

Twelve species, mostly residents; widespread in Mexico; mostly sharp talons, wing pointed (*Falco*) or rounded, tail medium-long, bill hooked; varied habitats, desert to rain forest; world-wide; color phases and immature and adult plumages. Distinguish species by silhouettes, colors, patterns, type of flight, and voice. **Plates 4, 5, and 6.**

Red-throated Caracara. *Daptrius americanus.* J5a2. <u>Comecacao</u>
M-SAm,x.B,ES. <u>Resident, near sea level, sP, sA (Veracruz)</u>. Very rare; dense forest, often in cackling groups in higher branches. V: a loud, harsh *cak, cak, cak, cak, cow.*
Pl.5. 22" Black, crested; legs, face, throat, and iris red; belly, thighs, untacs white.

Crested Caracara. *Polyborus plancus.* J5a8. <u>Quebrantahuesos</u>
US-SAm. <u>Resident up to 9000', all sub-regions</u>. Common in lowlands, rare+ in highlands; scrub woods, borders, farm fields, roadsides, often walks, eats carrion.
Pl.6. 23" Long-legged. Ad: Mostly blackish or dark brown, but throat, collar, untacs, tail-base, wing-patch white. Im: Like adult, but browner; streaked below.

Laughing Falcon. *Herpetotheres cachinnans.* J5a11. <u>Guaco</u>
M-SAm. <u>Resident up to 3000', P, A, Y</u>. Rare+; scrub forest, tree-dotted brushy fields; often perches in open. V: Musical *ah* or *ha* notes or series of notes like a human laugh.
Pl.5. 22" Crown, collar, and underparts creamy buff; face-patch to nape-bar, and upperparts, very dark brown; tail rather long, barred whitish and black.

Barred Micrastur (Forest-Falcon). *Micrastur ruficollis.* J5a12. <u>Guaquillo Selvático</u>
M-SAm. <u>Resident up to 4000', sP, csA, Y</u>. Very rare; dense humid forest or borders.
Pl.5. 14" Four narrow pale bars on long, rounded tail. Ad: Dark gray or brownish gray head, throat, and upperparts; narrow whitish and blackish bars below. Im: Dark brown above; pale buffy collar; buff below, more or less brown-barred; throat white.

Collared Micrastur (F.-F.). *Micrastur semitorquatus.* J5a16. <u>Guaquillo Collarejo</u>
M-SAm. <u>Resident up to 3000', P (Sinaloa to Chiapas), A, Y</u>. Rare+; open woods, swamps, forest borders, or partially open country. V: *Ow* or *wow*, loud and repeated.
Pl.5. 24" Blackish above; tail long, black with several white bars. Ad.L.ph: Underparts and collar white. Ad.Buff ph: Underparts and collar buffy or pale reddish brown. Ad.D.ph: Underparts and collar mostly blackish, like upperparts; belly may be barred whitish. Im: Buffy below; more or less barred with dark brown.

American Kestrel. *Falco sparverius.* J5b11. <u>Cernícalo Chitero</u>
AK-SAm. <u>Resident up to 10,000', BC, ncP (Sonora to Guerrero), H; winter visitor all sub-regions</u>. Rare+; usually in rather dry open areas, tree-dotted fields, tall hedgerows.
Pl.4. 11" Tail (barred in female; plain with black bar near tip in male), rump, and

barred back, reddish brown; two black lines down side of face; whitish or buffy below, spotted (male) or streaked (female); wings bluish (male), or rufous (female).

Merlin. *Falco columbarius.* J5b29. <u>Halconcillo</u>
AK-SAm. <u>Winter visitor all sub-regions</u>. Rare; large open areas, woodland borders. *Pl.4. 12" Streaked below. M: Bluish gray above; tail barred black and gray. F+Im: Brown above; tail dark brown and gray.* See American Kestrel.

Aplomado Falcon. *Falco femoralis.* J5b28. <u>Halcón Fajado</u>
M,G,B,N,P-SAm. <u>Resident up to 6000', nP (Sinaloa), H (Chihuahua, Oaxaca, Chiapas), csA (Tamaulipas to Chiapas), Y</u>. Rare; dry or humid areas, partial clearings, openings, forest borders, tree-dotted grassy fields, flies rapidly, sometimes erratically. *Pl.6. 16" Ad: Gray above; tail black with several fine white bars; pale line over black line behind eye; throat and breast white; sides and flanks broadly black, with white scaly marks; belly, thighs, and untacs tawny buff. Im: Like adult, but duller, browner; throat and breast buffy, streaked with blackish.*

Bat Falcon. *Falco rufigularis.* J5b30. <u>Halcón Garganta Blanca</u>
M-SAm. <u>Resident up to 3000', P, A, Y</u>. Rare+; humid forest borders, partial clearings. *Pl.5. 10" Ad: Black, except white throat, white bars on breast and tail, and rufous belly, thighs, untacs. Im: Duller, browner; unbarred dark brown breast and belly.*

Orange-breasted Falcon. *Falco deiroleucus.* J5b45. <u>Halcón Anaranjado</u>
M-SAm,x.ES. <u>Resident, near sea level, csA (Veracruz+Campeche)</u>. Very rare; in upper levels of dense, humid forest, small openings, secluded borders, partial clearings. *Pl.5. 14" Ad: Like* Bat F., *but upper breast rufous. Im: Paler; dark brown and buff.*

Peregrine Falcon. *Falco peregrinus.* J5b44. <u>Halcón Peregrino</u>
AK-SAm. <u>Resident (formerly?) up to 9000', BC, nP (Sonora), csH (Michoacán+ Chiapas), nA (Tamaulipas+San Luis Potosí); transient or winter visitor csP, csA, Y</u>. Very rare; on or near secluded cliffs or ledges in forest, or flying over various habitats. *Pl.4. 19" Dark bluish gray above; black crown with broad black ear-wedge down side of face; spotted and barred below, except whitish throat and breast; tail barred Im: Like adult, but dark brown; heavily* <u>streaked</u> *below.* See Prairie Falcon.

Prairie Falcon. *Falco mexicanus.* J5b38. <u>Halcón Café</u>
Can-M. <u>Resident up to 7000', BC; winter visitor nP, ncH, nA</u>. Rare; in open, arid or semi-arid country, usually hilly, rocky, brushy areas, and dry grassy tree-dotted plains. *Pl.4. 18" Mottled pale buffy brown above; heavy streaks below; not very contrasty tail-bars; black line down from eye; dark hind-border of ear-patch. Like* immature Peregrine F., *but much paler; not so heavily streaked below; face lines more delicate.*

GUANS, CHACHALACAS - CRACIDAE - FAISANES, CHACHALACAS
Seven residents; mostly lowlands; large; heavy-bodied; legs and neck medium-long, wings rounded, tail long, bill short; walk on branches, scrubby woods to humid forest; neotropical. Distinguish species by colors, calls, patterns. **Plates 7 and 47.**

Plain Chachalaca. *Ortalis vetula.* M2a1. <u>Chachalaca Común</u>
US-CR,x.ES. <u>Resident up to 4000', A, Y</u>. Very common; in thickets, hedgerows, borders, or scrubby woods, often in groups. V: a loud raucous chorus of *cha-cha-lac.* *24" Grayish olive above; grayish buff below; tail long, dark bronzy olive, whitish-tipped; head small, grayish; tail bronzy olive, whitish-tipped. Like* White-bellied Ch.*but more olive above; not* contrasty white and grayish below.

White-bellied Chachalaca. *Ortalis leucogastra.* M2a8. <u>Chachalaca Vientre Blanco</u>
M-N,x.B. <u>Resident up to 3000', sP</u>. Common; habitat like that of Plain Chachalaca. *Pl.47. 24" Dull olive-brown above; tail bronzy olive; head grayish; breast gray; belly, untacs, tail-tip white; bare skin of throat red in breeding season.* V: 4-noted.

Wagler's Chachalaca. *Ortalis poliocephala.* M2a6. <u>Chachalaca Occidental</u>
M. <u>Resident up to 9000', P</u>. Common; habitat and voice like those of Wh.-bellied Ch. *Pl.7. 24" (csP birds): Dark grayish olive above; tail greener; head grayish; breast*

somewhat darker, more olive gray; belly, untacs and tail-tip paler gray. (nP birds - shown in Plate 7) Similar but belly, untacs, and tail-tip dull rufous.

Black Chachalaca (Highland Guan). *Penelopina nigra.* M2a31. Pajuil
M-N,x.B. Resident, 2500 to 7000', sP, sH, sA (Oaxaca+Chiapas). Rare; on ground, or in lower branches of cloud forest or other humid forest. V: a high-pitched whistle. *Pl.7. 24" Long tail, small head. M: Glossy black, with red legs and throat. F: Rich brown with many narrow black bars.*

Crested Guan. *Penelope purpurascens.* M2a21. Ajol
M-SAm. Resident, 2500 to 5000', P (Sinaloa to Chiapas), A, Y. Rare+; arboreal, secluded portions of dense, usually humid, forest, usually in high branches or tree-tops. *Pl.7. 35" Very large; blackish all over; somewhat glossy; long, rounded tail; small head; bill and legs dark, but throat reddish; faint whitish streaks on breast.*

Horned Guan. *Oreophasis derbianus.* M2a32. Pavón
M,G. Resident, 7000 to 11,000', sH (Chiapas). Very rare; walking in small openings, or small partial clearings, or on higher branches in secluded portions of humid forest. *Pl.7. 35" Mostly black plumage, but white breast and bar on tail; red legs and vertical "horn" projecting from crown.*

Great Curassow. *Crax rubra.* M2a39. Faisán Real
M-SAm. Resident up to 3000', sP (Chiapas), A, Y. Rare; sometimes on ground under fruiting trees, usually middle to higher branches in secluded parts of dense humid forest. *Pl.7. 36" M: Mostly black, with curly black crest; yellow knob at base of bill; white belly and untacs. F (typical): Rich brown above; more rufous below; head, upper neck, and curly crest spotted black-and-white; tail broadly barred. F (barred phase): Barred black, brown, and white all over. Im: Like typical female.*

TURKEYS - MELEAGRIDIDAE - PAVOS
Very large; heavy body; small head, large tail; n.temperate, n.tropical, new world.

Common (Wild) Turkey. *Meleagris gallopavo.* M6a1. Guajolote
US-M. Resident, 1000 to 8000', ncH, nA (Nuevo León+Tamaulipas). Rare; in open pine or pine-oak woods, scrubby brushy areas, secluded borders, openings, clearings. *48, 34" Like Ocellated T. but tail bronzy, tipped buff or white; may have beard; lack blue subterminal spot on rump, uptacs, and tail feathers; less white on secondaries.*

Ocellated Turkey. *Agriocharis ocellata.* M6a2. Pavo Ocelado
M,G,B. Resident, near sea level, sA (Tabasco,Chiapas, Campeche), Y. Rare+; in or near dense forest or scrubby woods, secluded small openings, partial clearings, borders. *Pl.7. 46, 32" Mostly blackish brown, with green, purple, and bronze reflections; bronzy rufous greater wing-coverts; large white patch on secondaries; tail feathers and long uptacs grayish with blue subterminal spot and bronze tip.*

PARTRIDGES, QUAILS -PHASIANIDAE - CODORNICES
Fifteen residents; widespread Mexico; heavy body; short legs, neck, and bill; short, rounded wings; short to medium tail; walk on ground; semi-desert to humid forest; nearly world-wide; male and female plumages. Distinguish species by voice, colors, patterns, tail-length. **Plates 6 and 7.**

Long-tailed (Wood-) **Partridge.** *Dendrortyx macroura.* M5a2. Codorniz Coluda
M. Resident, 6000 to 12,000', cH (Jalisco+Veracruz to Oaxaca). Rare+; secluded mountain forest undergrowth. V: a loud, rollicking whistle, *whip-er-will-a*, repeated. *Pl.7. 15" Mottled rufous and gray; crest short; legs and tail rather long; bill, eye-ring, and legs bright red; face black with white malar streak and line over eye.*

Bearded (Wood-) **Partridge.** *Dendrortyx barbatus.* M5a2. Chiviscoyo
M. Resident, 3000 to 5000', cA (San Luis Potosí to Veracruz). Very rare; secluded dense cloud forest. V: A loud, rollicking, whistled *chee-vee-sco-yo*, repeated rapidly.

Pl.7. 11" Mostly rufous and grayish brown, mottled and streaked; throat broadly gray; breast mostly plain rufous; bill, legs, and eye-ring red; very short crest.

Highland (B-cr.W-) **Partridge.** *Dendrortyx leucophrys.* M5a3. Gallina de la Montaña
M-CR,x.B. Resident, 4000 to 7000', sH (Chiapas). Rare; undergrowth, borders, small openings of humid forest, or cloud forest. V: A loud, rollicking, repeated whistle.
Pl.7. 13" Streaked rufous, gray, and olive-brown; forehead, fore-crown, throat, and line over eye creamy buff; legs, eye-ring red; bill black above, orange below.

Spotted Wood-Quail. *Odontophorus guttatus.* M5a27.   Bolonchaco
M-Pan,x.ES. Resident, 1000 to 6000', sP, csA. Rare+; dense humid forest, often in groups. V: loud, rollicking, mellow call, *bo-lon-cha-co*; may add a chatter, *cha-cha-cha.*
Pl.7. 11" M: Floppy crest black with orange streaks; throat black with fine white streaks; dark olive-brown below, with small spotty streaks; blackish olive, or rufous olive-brown above; short tail; dark legs. F: Duller, darker; no orange crest-streaks.

Singing Quail. *Dactylortyx thoracicus.* M5a28.   Codorniz Dedilarga
M-N. Resident, 300 to 7000', csP, csH, A, Y. Rare+; varied habitats, dense humid forest to open woods. V: ascending series of loud notes, then *which-wheela*, repeated.
Pl.7. 9" Races vary. M: Grayish olive-brown, black-mottled, above; may be buffy brown or olive brown below; throat and long line over eye, tawny rufous. F: Like male above, but cinnamon to tawny-buff below; gray and dark brown head-pattern .

Mearns's (Montezuma) **Quail.** *Cyrtonyx montezumae.* M5a29.   Codorniz Pinta
US-M. Resident, 6000 to 10,000', ncH. Rare+; usually in open pine-oak woodland.
Pl.6. 9" M: Buff "pompadour" nape-crest; swirling black-and-white throat and head; white-spotted sides and flanks; chestnut brown medially below. F: Head mottled brown and buff; upperparts streaked brownish; cinnamon brown below.

Ocellated Quail. *Cyrtonyx ocellatus.* M5a30.   Perdiz Enmascarada
M-N,x.B. Resident, 4500 to 9500', sH. Rare+; in open woods, pine and pine-oak.
Pl.7. 9" Like Mearns's Q., but male has some bluish gray on face, less black; has fewer spots (buffy), and a black belly; and female is darker above.

Northern Bobwhite. *Colinus virginianus.* M5a10.   Cuiche Común
US,M,G. Resident up to 8000', P, csH, A. Rare to common; open shrubby or grassy areas, or woodland edge, pastures or cultivated fields. V: Loud *white* or *bob-white.*
Pl.6. 9" M: Birds of northeastern races are barred below; others mostly dark rufous below; most have white throat and superciliary, but the throat is black in northwestern birds, and the head (including throat) is all-black in southeastern birds. F: Streaked and spotted above; barred below, but throat and superciliary plain buff.

Yucatan (Black-thr.) **Bobwhite.** *Colinus nigrogularis.* M5a11.   Cuiche Yucateco
M-N,x.ES. Resident, near sea level, Y. Common; in semi-arid brushy areas, hedgerows, farm fields, borders, scrub woods. V: a loud whistled *white* or *bob-white.*
Pl.7. 8" M: "Scaly" black and white below; broadly black throat; white line over eye; ear-patch mostly white. F: Narrow bars below; throat and line over eye, buff.

Banded Quail. *Philortyx fasciatus.* M5a9.   Codorniz Listada
M. Resident up to 8000', cP (Guerrero), cH (Jalisco to Puebla). Rare+; scattered trees, hedgerows, thick brush. V: *Cleek* notes, a mellow *cwaw*, or barking *puck-cwa.*
Pl.7. 8" Ad: Black bands on white below; brown bands on brownish gray above; black crest, rufous-tipped, tilts back. Im: Throat and sides of head black.

Scaled Quail. *Callipepla squamata.* M5a5.   Codorniz Escamosa
US-M. Resident, 4000 to 7000', ncH (Sonora+Tamaulipas to Morelos). Common; in arid or semi-arid grassy areas, thick brush, roadsides. V: A harsh *puk-cwa* or *pe-co.*
Pl.6. 11" Mostly gray; short crest largely white; back and underparts appear scaly.

Elegant Quail. *Lophortyx douglasii.* M5a8.   Codorniz Gris
M. Resident up to 5000', nP. Rare+; in brushy areas, dry scrubby woods, hedgerows, thickets, shrubby borders. V: *Cleek* notes, also *puk-cwaw*, or *cwa-heet.*

Pl.7. *10" Head and neck finely streaked black, on gray and rufous; crest-plume rufous, tilts back; gray back and underparts; belly pale-spotted.* *F: Mostly dark brown, including crest; with pale spots below, and pale streaks on flanks and wings.*
Gambel's Quail. *Lophortyx gambelii.* M5a7. <u>Codorniz de Gambel</u>
US-M. <u>Resident, near sea level, nBC, nP (Sonora to Sinaloa).</u> Common; in dry brushy grassland, semi-desert, borders, thickets, hedgerows. V: loud *puk-cway-co-co.*
Pl.6. *11" M+F: Like* California Q., *but not scaly below; and male has black forehead, and creamy buff belly with black center-patch.*
California Quail. *Lophortyx californica.* M5a6. <u>Codorniz Californiana</u>
Can-M. <u>Resident, near sea level, BC.</u> Common; in arid to moist scrub, woods edge, hedgerows, borders, thorny semi-desert V: a loud, mellow *cwaw,* or *puk-cwaw-cuk.*
Pl.6. *10" Black crest-plume curves forward.* *M: Forehead broadly creamy buff; face and throat black, white-bordered; breast gray; belly "<u>scaly</u>", creamy with brown center-patch.* *F: Head mostly gray, brown, and buff, faintly streaked; breast gray; belly "scaly", creamy buff, but no darker center-patch.*
Mountain Quail. *Oreortyx picta.* M5a4. <u>Codorniz de Montaña</u>
Can-M. <u>Resident, 3500 to 8000', nBC.</u> Rare+; in moist woods, open pine forests, grassy borders, hedgerows, or drier scrub, brushy hillsides. V: Loud *wuk* or *cuh-wuk.*
Pl.6. *11" Long, slender back-tilted black crest-plume; white-barred chestnut flanks; throat chestnut, white-bordered; gray crown, hind-neck, and breast; brown back.*

RAILS, GALLINULES - RALLIDAE - GALLINETAS

Fifteen residents; widespread Mexico; medium-long legs, medium neck, rounded wings, very short tail, short to long bill; walkers or swimmers, coastal or inland marshes, swamps, ponds; world-wide, temperate and tropical. Distinguish species by voice, patterns, color of legs, bill, and plumage. **Plates 7 and 10.**

Yellow Rail. *Coturnicops noveboracensis.* N11b12. <u>Gallineta Amarilla</u>
Can-M. <u>Resident, 7000 to 9000', cH (México).</u> Rare; marshes,wet fields. V: *tick-tick.*
Pl.10. *6" Yellowish; spotted, barred, streaked above; flanks barred; bill short.*
Red Rail (Ruddy Crake). *Laterallus ruber.* N11b27. <u>Gallineta Rojiza</u>
M-CR. <u>Resident, near sea level, A, Y.</u> Rare+; freshwater or salty marshes, wet grassy or sedgy ditches or ponds; may call from only a few feet away. V: a chattering whinny.
Pl.7 . 6" Mostly rich reddish-brown, but most of head dark gray; legs greenish.
Black Rail. *Laterallus jamaicensis.* N11b34. <u>Gallineta Negra</u>
US-SAm,x.ES,N. <u>Resident, near sea level, nBC; visitor or resident ncA (San Luis Potosí+Veracruz).</u> Very rare, local; in fresh-water or saltwater marshes, or wet grassy fields, marshy pond borders. V: A metallic *tikee-too,* repeated, or a cooing *cro-cro-cro.*
Pl.10. *5" Blackish, spotted, barred; nape and upper back dark chestnut; bill black.*
Clapper Rail. *Rallus longirostris.* N11b54. <u>Rascón Picudo</u>
US,M,B,SAm. <u>Resident, near sea level, BC, nP, nA, Y.</u> Rare; usually coastal marshes.
Pl.10. *16" Grayer than* King R., *especially wrist-patch; duller streaks and bars.*
King Rail. *Rallus elegans.* N11b53. <u>Rascón Real</u>
Can-M. <u>Resident, 5000 to 9000', ncH (Nayarit+San Luis Potosí to Morelos+Puebla); winter visitor ncA.</u> Rare; usually large fresh-water marshes, sometimes brackish areas.
Pl.10. *17" Grayish brown above, black-streaked; large wrist-patch dark rufous; throat and breast bright rufous; flanks and untacs barred black and white; long bill.*
Virginia Rail. *Rallus limicola.* N11b58. <u>Rascón de Agua</u>
Can-M,G,SAm. <u>Resident up to 9000', nBC, nP (Sonora), csH (Tlaxcala+Puebla to Chiapas); winter visitor sBC, nH, ncA, Y.</u> Common, but irregular; mostly in fresh-water or brackish marshes, or marshy borders of ponds, lakes, and sluggish rivers.
Pl.10. *8" Ad: Like* King R., *but <u>much</u> smaller; has paler, duller brown throat and breast; gray sides of face. Im: Darker; blurred blackish streaks on throat and breast.*

Gray-necked (Wood-) **Rail.** *Aramides cajanea.* N11b70.   <u>Tutupana</u>
M-SAm. <u>Resident, near sea level, csP (Guerrero to Chiapas), A, Y</u>. Rare+; fresh-water
or salty swamps, wooded ponds, lakes and lagoons. V: A loud *tic-tic-tic-tic-tiree-tiree.*
*Pl.7. 16" Gray or greenish gray upperparts, crown, neck, and breast; rufous nape
and sides; black belly and untacs; bill red at base, yellowish near tip; red legs.*

Rufous-necked (W-) **Rail.** *Aramides axillaris.* N11b69.   <u>Gallineta de Collar Rojizo</u>
M,B,H,N,P,SAm. <u>Resident, near sea level, ncP (Sinaloa to Guerrero), Y</u>. Rare;
mostly flooded wooded areas, wooded brackish or salty lagoons, or mangrove swamps.
*Pl.7. 12" Grayish above, but head, neck, breast, and sides reddish brown; belly
and untacs black; bill yellowish; legs red.*

Uniform Rail (Crake). *Amaurolimnas concolor.* N11b75.   <u>Gallineta Café</u>
M-SAm,x.ES. <u>Resident, near sea level, sP (Chiapas), csA (Veracruz to Tabasco)</u>. Very
rare; in fresh-water swamps, undergrowth along forest streams, swampy pond-borders.
Pl.7. 8" Dark reddish brown above, bright rufous below; bill greenish; iris yellow.

Sora. *Porzana carolina.* N11b89.   <u>Gallineta de Ciénaga</u>
Can-SAm,x.ES. <u>Resident, near sea level, nBC; winter visitor all sub-regions</u>. Rare+;
fresh-water or salty marshes, swamps, rice fields. V: A descending chatter or whinny.
*Pl.10. 8" Ad: Brownish gray above, streaked; pale gray below, with black throat to
center of breast; flanks whitish-barred. Juv: Duller; brownish wash; no black throat.*

Yellow-breasted Rail (Crake). *Poliolimnas flaviventris.* N11b99.   <u>Gallineta Pálida</u>
M-SAm,x.H. <u>Resident up to 6000', cH (Michoacán to Puebla), csA (Veracruz to
Chiapas)</u>. Rare; mostly in large fresh-water marshes, marshy borders of lakes, ponds.
*Pl.7. 4 1/2" Like Yellow R., but much paler below, white with buff wash on breast;
black-barred flanks, untacs; sides of head gray; white line over eye; blackish crown.*

Spotted Rail. *Pardirallus maculatus.* N11b104.   <u>Gallineta Pinta</u>
M,B,CR-SAm. <u>Resident up to 8000', P (Nayarit to Chiapas), csH (Michoacán,
Puebla,Chiapas), csA (Veracruz to Chiapas), Y (Quintana Roo)</u>. Rare, range may be
expanding; secluded areas in large marshes, mostly fresh-water, or marshy lake borders.
Pl.7. 10" Blackish, with whitish streaks, spots, bars; bill long, green with red base.

Purple Gallinule. *Porphyrio martinica .* N11b114.   <u>Gallareta Morada</u>
US-SAm. <u>Resident up to 9000', P, csH, A, Y</u>. Rare+; in fresh-water to salty marshes
and swamps, or marshy borders of lagoons, lakes, ponds, sluggish rivers; often swims.
*Pl.10. 13" Ad: Head, neck, and underparts purplish, but lower belly and untacs
white; greenish olive above; pale blue frontal shield; red bill, yellow-tipped.
Im: Whitish to pale brown below; no white on head or* side. See Common Gallinule.

Common Gallinule (Moorhen). *Gallinula chloropus.* N11b122.   <u>Polla de Agua</u>
Can-SAm. <u>Resident up to 10,000', all sub-regions</u>. Rare+; ponds, marshes, swamps.
Pl.10. 13" Ad: Blackish gray above; dark bluish gray below; <u>*white side-stripe*;</u>
<u>*lateral*</u> *untacs white; frontal shield red; bill-tip yellow. Im: Grayish; white side-stripe.*

American Coot. *Fulica americana.* N11c3.   Gallareta Gris
Can-SAm. <u>Resident up to 10,000', all sub-regions</u>. Common; ponds, lakes, estuaries,
lagoons, large fresh-water or saltwater marshes or swamps; often walks on open shores.
Pl.10. 15" Ad: Mostly blackish gray; bill white. Im: Paler; bill whitish.

SUNGREBES - HELIORNITHIDAE

Sungrebe. *Heliornis fulica.* N10a3.   Pájaro Cantil
M-SAm,x.ES. <u>Resident up to 2000', sP (Chiapas), csA (San Luis Potosí to Quintana
Roo)</u>. Rare; swims in secluded ponds, lakes, lagoons, sluggish rivers, fresh or salty.
*Pl.13. 12" Mostly brownish gray above, pale gray below; heavy black stripes on
white to pale gray head and neck; bill rather long, reddish; toes broadly barred.*

SUNBITTERNS - EURYPIGIDAE - PAVITOS de AGUA

Sunbittern. *Eurypyga helias.* N9a1.   Pavito de Agua
M-SAm,x.B,ES. Resident, near sea level, sA (Tabasco and Chiapas). Very rare; on
ground in wet part of forest, near streams, ponds in dense forest, fresh-water swamps.
*Pl.13. 18" Head blackish, narrow white streaks; barred gray and black above; neck
and breast blackish; bill, legs, neck, long; two black and chestnut bars on gray tail;
spread wings show chestnut, yellow and black.*

LIMPKINS - ARAMIDAE - TOTOLACAS

Limpkin. *Aramus guarauna.* N5a1.   Totolaca
US-SAm. Resident, near sea level, sP, csA, Y. Rare+; wading in swamps, along
swampy or marshy rivers, extensive marshes, marshy or open shores of lagoons and
ponds. V: Loud, echoing, wailing or rolling *cyow,* or *cuk-cuk-cyow,* often at night.
*Pl.10. 28" Streaked dark brown and buff; legs, neck, and bill long; bill yellowish,
slightly decurved, rather blunt at end.*

CRANES - GRUIDAE - GRULLAS

Sandhill Crane. *Grus canadensis.* N4a4.   Grulla Cenicienta
AK-M. Resident up to 7000', nBC, nP, ncH (Chihuahua to México), ncA; accidental Y.
Rare+; large marshes, wet fields; neck extended in flight. V: a loud, rolling trumpeting.
*Pl.10. 45" Ad: Medium gray, may be stained brownish; crown red; throat whitish;
bill, neck, and legs long. Im: Mostly brown or grayish brown.*

STONE-CURLEWS (THICK-KNEES) - BURHINIDAE - ALCARAVANES

Mexican Stone-Curlew (Dou.-str.Th.-knee). *Burhinus bistriatus.* P9a5.   Alcaraván
M-SAm,x.P. Resident up to 2000', sP, csA (Veracruz to Chiapas+Tabasco). Rare+;
mainly nocturnal, rough, scrubby areas, grassy fields. V: Loud, echoing, cackling cries.
*Pl.13. 20" Like a giant plover; mostly brown, striped and mottled; crown broadly
striped; large yellow eye; extended wing striped; short, heavy bill; long greenish legs.*

PLOVERS - CHARADRIIDAE - PLUVIALES

Nine species, residents or winter visitors; mostly coastal; medium legs, short neck,
pointed wings, short tail, medium or short bill; walkers, mostly on beaches or mud-flats;
world-wide. Distinguish by colors of plumage, bill, legs; bill-size. **Plates 11 and 47.**

Black-bellied Plover. *Pluvialis squatarola.* P14b38.   Ave Fría
AK-SAm. Transient or winter visitor BC, P, cH, A, Y. Common on coastal beaches
or rocky shores and mud flats, shores of lagoons and estuaries; rare on ponds and lakes.
Pl.11. 12" Win.M: Mottled gray above; black patch under wing (shows in
flight); *pale gray below, faintly streaked; large head; thick black bill; black legs.
Sum.M: More contrasty above; black face and underparts; but belly and untacs white.*

Lesser Golden (-) Plover. *Pluvialis dominica.* P14b37.   Pluvial Dorado
AK-SAm. Transient or winter visitor BC; spring transient csP, cH. Rare to very rare;
grassy fields, coastal mud-flats, marshes, shores of lagoons, estuaries, ponds, or lakes.
Pl.11. 11" Like Black-bellied P., *but more yellowish above; and Win.M: buffier
below; no* black patch under wing; *and Sum.M: has mostly black belly and untacs.*

Collared Plover. *Charadrius collaris.* P14b19.   Chichicuilote de Collar
M-SAm. Resident, near sea level, P (Sinaloa to Chiapas), csA, Y. Rare+; coastal
beaches, mud flats, open shores of lagoons, estuaries, sometimes shores of large lakes.
*Pl.47. 6" Ad: White forehead and throat, black crown-patch and breast-band, all
bordered behind by rufous; white belly ; slender black bill; pinkish legs. Im: Crown
not* black; *breast-band duller, usually incomplete.*

Snowy Plover. *Charadrius nivosus.* P14b15. <u>Chichicuilote Nevado</u>
M-SAm,x.ES,N. <u>Resident, near sea level, BC, cP (Oaxaca), nA (Tamaulipas), Y;</u>
<u>winter visitor nsP, csA.</u> Rare+; coastal beaches, mud flats, lagoon shores, lake-shores.
   Pl.11. 6 1/2" <u>Pale</u> *brownish gray above; white below; black or blackish brown*
fore-crown; dark brown or black ear-patch and patch on side of chest; no breast
band; <u>legs and bill blackish</u>; *bill slender.*

Wilson's Plover. *Charadrius wilsonia.* P14b5. <u>Chichicuilote Piquigrueso</u>
US-SAm,x.N. <u>Resident, sea level, BC, P, A, Y.</u> Rare+; coastal beaches, mud flats.
   Pl.11. 8" M: Like summer Semipalmated P., *and F: like* winter Semipal. P.; *but*
larger; slightly paler above; bill much larger, heavier, and black; legs grayish.

Semipalmated Plover. *Charadrius semipalmatus.* P14b2. <u>Pluvial Frailecillo</u>
AK-SAm. <u>Transient or winter visitor BC, P, cH, Y.</u> Rare+; lake-shores, ocean beaches.
   Pl.11. 7" Medium brown above; white forehead, throat, collar, and most of
underparts; legs orange. Sum: Black fore-crown, eye-patch, and breast-band; bill
red-based, black-tipped. Win: Crown, eye-patch, and breast-band brown; bill dark.
Piping P. and Snowy P. are much paler above; Wilson's P. has a much larger bill.

Piping Plover. *Charadrius melodus.* P14b7. <u>Chichicuilote Chiflador</u>
Can-M. <u>Winter visitor nP, ncA.</u> Rare; coastal beaches and mudflats, shores of lagoons.
   Pl.11. 7" Like Snowy Plover, *but pale gray above; ear-patch much paler; legs*
orange-yellow; bill heavier; and Win: patch on side of chest much paler; and Sum:
partial or complete breast-band extends across hind-neck; bill orange with black tip.

Killdeer. *Charadrius vociferus.* P14b6. <u>Tildío Común</u>
AK-SAm. <u>Resident up to 8000', BC, ncP (Sonora to Guerrero), ncH (Chihuahua to</u>
<u>D.F.), nA (Tamaulipas); winter visitor all sub-regions.</u> Rare+; open shores of small
ponds, lakes, or rivers; wet fields or sandy areas, often nests on gravel or pebbles. V: a
loud, high-pitched, somewhat squeaky *kil-dee,* a musical *dee-it* and *dee-dee-dee-dee.*
   Pl.11. 11" Brown above; white forehead, throat, collar, and most of underparts;
two black breast-bands; rump, uptacs, and much of tail salmon-colored; bill black.

Mountain Plover. *Charadrius montanus.* P14b27. <u>Tildío Montañés</u>
Can-M. <u>Winter visitor BC, nP, nH, nA.</u> Rare+; farm fields, dry grassland, open plains.
   Pl.11. 9" Sum: Brown above; white forehead, throat and underparts; black
crown-patch and line through eye; breast washed with buff, no trace of breast-band.
Win: No black on crown or through eye; *usually buffier overall.*

OYSTERCATCHERS - HAEMATOPODIDAE - OSTREROS

American Oystercatcher. *Haematopus palliatus.* P10a6. <u>Ostrero Americano</u>
US-SAm,x.ES,N. <u>Resident, sea level, BC, P, A, Y; winter visitor sP.</u> Rare+; rocky
coastal headlands, gravel beaches, tidal mud-flats, rocks exposed at low tide.
   Pl.10. 17" Long red bill; black head, neck, and upper breast; wing-band, uptacs,
most of underparts, white . BC and ncP birds have black-spotted breast and sides.

Black Oystercatcher. *Haematopus bachmani.* P10a7. <u>Ostrero Negro</u>
AK-M. <u>Resident, sea level, nBC.</u> Rare+; rocky shores, headlands, beaches, mud-flats.
   Pl.10. 17" Has long red bill; black head, neck, and upper breast; dull pinkish legs;
like American Oystercatcher, *but rest of plumage dark olive-brown; no* white.

AVOCETS, STILTS-RECURVIROSTRIDAE-CANDELEROS, PIQUICURVOS

Black-necked Stilt. *Himantopus mexicanus.* P11a2. <u>Candelero</u>
US-SAm. <u>Resident or visitor up to 9000', all sub-regions.</u> Rare+; coastal mud-flats,
lagoons, estuaries, shallow marsh pools, shores of lakes, ponds; often in noisy flocks.
   Pl.10. 15" Black above; white below; slender black bill up-curved; long legs red.

American Avocet. *Recurvirostra americana.* P11a6. <u>Piquicurvo</u>
Can-CR,x.ES,N. <u>Resident up to 8000', nBC, nA (San Luis Potosí), cH (D.F.); winter</u>

visitor BC, P, ncH, cA, Y. Rare; lagoons, shallow ponds, wet meadows, marsh pools. *Pl.10. 19" Sum.Ad: Mostly black and white above; white below; head and neck cinnamon; bill slender, up-curved; legs gray. Win.Ad+Im: Head and neck pale gray.*

JACANAS - JACANIDAE - CIRUJANOS
Northern Jacana. *Jacana spinosa.* P15a7.   Cirujano
US-Pan. Resident up to 3000', P (Sinaloa to Chiapas), A, Y; resident or visitor up to 8000', cH. Common; marshes, swamps, ditches, ponds. V: a grating, cackling chatter. *Pl.10. 9" Ad: Chestnut above and below; black head and neck; spread wing mostly yellow. Im: Blackish above; face and underparts white; spread wing like adult's.*

SANDPIPERS - SCOLOPACIDAE - CHICHICUILOTES
Twenty-eight species, mostly transients and winter visitors; mostly BC, P, A, Y coasts; legs medium to long, neck short to medium, wings pointed, tail very short, bill short to very long; walkers or waders on beaches, mud flats, shallow waters; world-wide. Distinguish by patterns, bill and leg color, length, shape. **Plates 11, 12.**
Greater Yellowlegs. *Tringa melanoleuca.* P17a19.   Tingüís Grande
AK-SAm. Transient or winter visitor all sub-regions. Rare+; fresh or salt water, mud flats, small ponds, marshy fields, or lake shores. V: a loud, three-noted *hew-hew-hew.*
Pl.11. 14" Mottled gray above; white below with many fine neck-streaks; spots and bars on sides; bill long, black, very slightly up-curved; uptacs white. See Lesser Y.
Lesser Yellowlegs. *Tringa flavipes.* P17a20.   Tingüís Chico
AK-SAm. Transient or winter visitor all sub-regions. Common east, rare west and inland; coastal mud flats, lake shores, marshes, lagoons. V: one or two whistled notes.
Pl.11. 11" Like Greater Y., *but bill shorter, straighter; sides usually less barred.*
Solitary Sandpiper. *Tringa solitaria.* P17a21.   Chichicuilote Solitario
AK-SAm. Transient or winter visitor all sub-regions. Rare+; mud flats, ponds, streams.
Pl.11. 8" Dark grayish brown above, speckled with white; neck and upper breast finely streaked; legs dull greenish, not yellow; *much white on outer tail feathers.*
Willet. *Catoptrophorus semipalmatus.* P17a24.   Zarapico
Can-SAm. Resident, near sea level, nA (Tamaulipas), Y (Yucatán); transient or winter visitor BC, P, cH, A, Y. Common; coastal beaches and mud flats, rarely lake shores.
Pl.12. 15" Striking black and white wing-pattern in flight; bill long, stcraight, rather heavy. Win: Mostly unstreaked gray neck and upperparts; unstreaked whitish below. Sum: Mottled and streaked gray above; streaked neck and breast.
Wandering Tattler. *Heteroscelus incanus.* P17a29.   Agachadiza Vagabunda
AK-SAm,x.B. Winter visitor BC, ncP. Rare+; wave-washed rocks in coastal waters.
Pl. 12. 10" Win: Plain medium gray above, and on head and breast, white belly and untacs. Sum: Fine wavy bars below. Much longer bill than Surfbird.
Spotted Sandpiper. *Actitis macularia.* P17a27.   Alzacolita
AK-SAm. Transient and winter visitor all sub-regions. Rare+; "teeters" and bobs as it walks on shores of ponds, lakes, rivers, pools; flies with rapid stiff shallow wing-beats.
Pl.12. 7" White wing-stripe shows in flight. Win: Gray above; white below; dark bill. Sum: Heavy black spots below; bill orange, black-tipped; legs yellowish.
Upland Sandpiper. *Bartramia longicauda.* P17a13.   Ganga
AK-SAm. Transient csP, ncH, A, Y. Rare; open grassy, moist fields, or marshy areas.
Pl.11. 12" Mottled grayish brown above; neck buffy, finely streaked; belly and untacs white; long legs dull yellowish; short, straight, dark bill.
Whimbrel. *Numenius phaeopus.* P17a7.   Chorlo Real
AK-SAm. Winter visitor BC, P, A, Y. Common; coastal areas (rare on lakes, ponds).
Pl.11. 17" Mottled and spotted grayish brown above; whitish below, streaked on neck and upper breast; crown striped dark brown and whitish; bill long, decurved.

Long-billed Curlew. *Numenius americanus.* Pl7a12.   Picolargo
Can-CR,x.ES,N. Winter visitor BC, P, ncH, A, Y. Rare+; moist fields, open marshes.
Pl.11. 24" Rich buffy brown; mottled with black above, and streaked on head, neck, and breast; bill very long, decurved; legs long, grayish.
Hudsonian Godwit. *Limosa haemastica.* Pl7a2.   Agachona Café
AK-M,G,CR. Transient cP, ncA. Very rare; coastal beaches, mud flats, lagoon shores.
Pl.11. 16" Black tail; white uptacs; long, pinkish, black-tipped bill, slightly up-curved. Win: Medium gray above; pale gray to whitish below. Sum: Chestnut neck and underparts, with fine bars; black above with white spots or "scales".
Marbled Godwit. *Limosa fedoa.* Pl7a4.   Agachona Real
Can-SAm. Transient and winter visitor BC, P, cH, A, Y. Common; mostly on coastal beaches, or mud flats, lagoons, estuaries, marshes, also lake shores, wet fields, ponds.
Pl.11. 18" Mostly rich buffy brown, mottled and barred above, streaked on neck, and finely barred below; very long, pinkish-based bill slightly up-curved.
Ruddy Turnstone. *Arenaria interpres.* Pl7b1.   Chorlete Común
AK-SAm. Transient and winter visitor BC, P, cH, A, Y. Common; mostly coastal beaches, mud flats, sand bars, shores of lagoons and estuaries; also inland lake-shores.
Pl.12. 9" Bill short, black, with fine up-curved tip; legs orange; black-and-white wing, tail, and rump pattern. Win: Mottled brownish gray above; white below with whitish patch on side of blackish breast. Head paler than Black T.'s. Sum: Intricate black and white head-pattern; mostly bright rufous wings and back, with some black.
Black Turnstone. *Arenaria melanocephala.* Pl7b2.   Chorlete Negro
AK-M. Winter visitor BC, nP (Sonora). Common; rocky coastal shores, headlands.
Pl.12. 9" Bill, and black-and-white flight-pattern, like Ruddy T.'s, but legs dark gray. Win: Like Ruddy T., but much darker head and back; and no trace of pattern on dark gray throat and breast. Sum: Black back, head, and breast, with faint white streaks and bars; white over and before eye. See Surfbird.
Surfbird. *Aphriza virgata.* Pl7e1.   Chichicuilote de Marejada
AK-M,G,CR-SAm. Transient and winter visitor BC, P. Rare+; rocky shores, jetties.
Pl.12. 10" Bill yellowish at base, not fine-tipped; legs dull yellowish; black and white flight pattern, but rump and lower back gray, not white with black crossbar. Win: Upperparts, head, and breast dark gray; throat and line over eye whiter than Black T.'s. Sum: Gray; with streaked head, upperparts, and underparts.
Red Knot. *Calidris canutus.* Pl7e3.   Chichicuilote Canuto
AK-SAm,x.ES,N. Transient and winter visitor BC, nP, cA, Y. Rare+; beaches, flats.
Pl.12. 10" Sum: Streaked above; buffy reddish brown below; black-and-white barred rump and uptacs; faint white wing-bar; head rather large; bill medium-short, rather heavy, black; legs greenish. Win: Similar but grayish above; whitish below.
Sanderling. *Calidris alba.* Pl7e4.   Chichicuilote Blanco
AK-SAm. Transient and winter visitor BC, P, A, Y. Common; on sandy ocean beaches; running into receding water, then rapidly retreating from the incoming wave.
Pl.12. 7" Win: Whiter, less streaked than other "peeps". Underparts pure white; back gray, faintly streaked; legs black; bill medium length, black; white wing-stripe. Sum: Streaked head, neck, breast and upperparts, with reddish-brown wash.
Semipalmated Sandpiper. *Calidris pusilla.* Pl7e5.   Chichicuilote Semipalmeado
AK-SAm. Transient and winter visitor sP, ncA, Y. Rare+; ocean beaches, mud flats.
Pl.12. 6" Legs black; straight, short black bill; less brownish above; less streaked below than corresponding plumage of Western S. or Least S.
Western Sandpiper. *Calidris mauri.* Pl7e6.   Chichicuilote Occidental
AK-SAm. Transient and winter visitor all sub-regions. Common; ocean beaches, flats.
Pl.12. 6" Legs black; has longer, heavier (tip droops slightly) bill than Semipalmated S. or Least S. Win: Mottled gray above with slight brownish tinge;

faint streaks below. Sum: Mottled brownish gray above, with pale rufous wash on scapulars, ear-patch, and crown; many fine streaks below.
Least Sandpiper. *Calidris minutilla.* P17e11. Chichicuilote Mínimo
AK-SAm. Transient and winter visitor all sub-regions. Common; ocean beaches, flats.
Pl.12. 6" Legs dull yellowish; bill short, slender, slightly down-curved. Win: Brownish gray above; white below, with finely streaked brownish breast-band. Sum: Mottled black and brownish above; fine streaks on brownish neck and breast. Browner than Semipalmated S.; *more slender-billed than* Western S.
White-rumped Sandpiper.*Calidris fuscicollis.*P17e12.Chichicuilote Rabadilla Blanca
AK-SAm. Transient A, Y. Rare; coastal beaches, mud-flats; lake shores, marsh pools.
Pl.12. 7" Rump and uptacs white; legs blackish. Sum: Mottled brownish gray above; white below with streaked brownish gray breast. Win: Slightly grayer, paler.
Baird's Sandpiper. *Calidris bairdii.* P17e13. Chichicuilote de Baird
AK-SAm,x.H,N. Transient BC, P, ncH, cA, Y. Rare; fields near water, lake shores.
Pl.12. 7" Longer-billed and larger than Least S.; *bill and legs black; mottling above, black and buffy, suggests scales; pale grayish brown streaked breast; wings long.*
Pectoral Sandpiper. *Calidris melanotos.* P17e14. Chichicuilote Manchado
AK-SAm. Transient all sub-regions. Rare; lake shores, marsh pools, wet or dry fields.
Pl.12. 9" Mottled grayish brown above; belly and untacs white; breast appears dark and contrasty, with narrow black streaks on pale brown; legs dull greenish.

Dunlin. *Calidris alpina.* P17e18. Tingüís Lomo Rojo
AK-Pan,x.ES,H,N. Winter visitor BC, nP, nA, Y. Common; beaches, marshes, flats.
Pl.12. 8" Bill medium long (shorter than illustration) decurved near tip; legs black. Win: Faintly streaked gray breast and upperparts; white belly. Sum: Mottled rufous above; whitish below with fine black breast-streaks and large black belly-patch.
Stilt Sandpiper. *Micropalama himantopus.* P17e22. Chorlete Desconocido
AK-SAm. Transient P, ncH, nA, Y. Very rare; coastal mud flats, lagoons; lake shores.
Pl.11. 9" Rather long slender black bill; long grayish green legs; small head. Win: Gray above, and on breast; mostly white below; uptacs white. Sum: Mottled dark brown; streaked breast; barred belly and uptacs; trace of rufous on head.
Buff-breasted Sandpiper. *Tryngites subruficollis.* P17e23. Chorlete Canelo
AK-SAm. Transient cH, nA. Rare; moist grassy fields, dry upland fields, or mud flats.
Pl.12. 8" Entire underparts rich buff; "scaly" black and buff mottling above; bill short, black; legs yellowish; under-wings mostly white; head small. See Red Knot.

Short-billed Dowitcher. *Limnodromus griseus.* P17d18. Agachona Gris
AK-SAm. Transient and winter visitor BC, nP, Y. Rare+; lagoons, coastal marshes.
Pl.11. 11" Wedge-shaped long white rump-and-lower-back-patch; very long bill. Win: Gray upperparts and breast; whitish belly and untacs; faint bars on flanks. Sum: Mottled black and buffy brown above; reddish brown below, except whitish belly; spots and short bars on breast, sides, flanks; narrow black and white tail-bars. V: a loud *chew-chew-chew.* See Long-billed Dowitcher.
Long-billed Dowitcher. *Limnodromus scolopaceus.* P17d19. Agachona Piquilarga
AK-Pan,x.ES,H,N. Winter visitor BC, nP, ncH, nA. Rare+; lake shores, marshes.
Pl.11. 12" Like Short-billed D., *but bill averages longer; voice a weak tleek or tleek-tleek; and Sum: usually richer reddish brown below (including belly); more and longer bars (not spots) on breast, sides, flanks; tail blacker (broader black bars).*

Common Snipe. *Gallinago gallinago.* P17d9. Agachona Común
AK-SAm. Winter visitor all sub-regions. Common; marshes, wet fields, stream-banks.
Pl.12. 10" Bill very long; legs short; head striped; neck, back, and breast heavily streaked black and white; tail orange and black; erratic flight and rasping *crepe* note.

PHALAROPES - PHALAROPODIDAE - CHORLILLOS
Three transients or winter visitors; mostly coastal or offshore BC, P; medium legs, neck, bill, pointed wings, short tail; swim or walk, pond-shores or ocean; world-wide; female brighter. Distinguish by color of neck, breast, back, legs, bill, face. **Plate 12.**

Wilson's Phalarope. *Phalaropus tricolor.* P18a1.   Chorlillo Nadador
AK-SAm. Transient or winter visitor BC, P, ncH, nA. Rare+; walking near water's edge (in or out) or swimming in shallows of lakes, ponds, marsh pools; often far inland. *Pl.12. 9" Bill long, very slender. Win: Plain pale gray above; white below; pale gray eye-stripe and crown; tail whitish, uptacs white; no wing-stripes. Sum.F: Pale gray above; white below; black eye-patch joins reddish brown streak down side of neck onto back; pale rufous fore-neck. Sum.M: Duller; rufous wash on neck, back.*

Northern (Red-n.) Phalarope. *Phalaropus lobatus.* P18a2.   Chorlillo Norteño
AK-SAm,x.B,N. Transient or winter visitor BC, P, ncH. Common, ocean; rare inland. *Pl.12. 7" Win: Like Wilson's Ph., but bill shorter; central uptacs dark; whitish wing-stripe and back stripes; mottled upperparts; black crown and eye-patch. Sum.F: Dark gray above with buffy stripes; white below with pale gray sides; blackish crown to below eye; broadly white throat; rufous "bib". Sum.M: Slightly paler, duller.*

Red Phalarope. *Phalaropus fulicaria.* P18a3.   Chorlillo Rojo
AK-M,SAm. Transient BC, P, sA. Common at sea, rare near coast, very rare inland. *Pl.12. 8" Win: Like Northern P., but plain gray above; wing-stripe but no back-stripes; center-crown white, not black; bill thicker. Sum.F: Mottled black and buff above; black crown and throat; broadly white face; underparts and most of neck dark rufous; legs yellowish; bill yellowish, black-tipped. Sum.M: Paler and duller.*

SKUAS, JAEGERS - STERCORARIIDAE - SALTEADORES
Four transients or winter visitors; mostly offshore BC, P; short legs and neck; pointed, angled wings; short to long tail, medium-short bill; open ocean fliers; world oceans. Distinguish by white in wing, barring, breast band, tail-feathers. **Plate 1.**

Pomarine Jaeger. *Stercorarius pomarinus.* P3a5.   Salteador Marino
AK-SAm,x.B,H. Transient or winter visitor BC, P, Y; accidental nH. Common; over the open ocean, or around offshore islands, about 5 to 20 miles or more from shore. *22" Like Parasitic J., but larger, heavier, with heavier bill; more contrasty white at base of primaries above; and in Ad: central tail-feathers twisted, with broad rounded tip; and in L.ph.Ad: heavier barring on sides, darker breast band.*

Parasitic Jaeger. *Stercorarius parasiticus.* P3a6.   Salteador Parásito
AK-SAm. Transient or winter visitor BC, nP; accidental nH. Rare; often close to shore. *Pl.1. 20" Wings strongly angled. L.ph.ad: Dark grayish brown above; black crown; pale yellowish-and-whitish side of face and collar; mostly white below; with plain pale gray sides and breast-band; some white at base of primaries above, more below; central tail-feathers somewhat extended, narrow and pointed at tip. D.ph.ad: Very dark brown; with somewhat paler face and throat; black crown; some white at base of primaries. Im: Dark above; narrowly barred below; central tail feathers only slightly extended. Older light phase immatures may have black-and-white uptacs.*

Long-tailed Jaeger. *Stercorarius longicaudus.* P3a7.   Salteador Cola Larga
AK-SAm,x.B,H. Transient BC, csP. Rare+; open ocean, or just a few miles offshore. *23" Like Parasitic J., but grayer and more slender; paler below; less white in wings; more contrast between gray wing-coverts and blackish flight feathers above; and in Ad: central tail feathers much longer; and in L.ph.Ad: white collar wider; no breast-band; whiter below. Dark phase very rare.*

South Polar Skua. *Catharacta mccormicki.* P3a4.   Salteador Antártico
AK-M,P,SAm. Transient or summer visitor BC, nP. Very rare; offshore ocean waters. *22" D.ph: Nearly all blackish (and no extended tail-feathers) like older dark phase immature Pomarine Jaeger, but bulkier, heavier-billed, broader and more rounded*

wings; shorter, broader tail; and much more prominent white wing-patch. Blacker, less streaked than Great Skua. *L.ph.Ad: Pale gray head and underparts.*

GULLS, TERNS - LARIDAE - GAVIOTAS, CHARRANES
Twenty-seven residents or visitors; mostly coastal BC, P, A, Y; short legs and neck, pointed wings; tail short and square to long and deeply forked; bill medium-short, slender or stout; fliers, walkers, swimmers, mostly shores of oceans, lakes, rivers. Distinguish by head, tail, and wing patterns, bill and leg color, tail shape. **Plate 1.**

Laughing Gull. *Larus atricilla.* P5a7.   Gaviota Risqueña
Can-SAm. Resident, near sea level, nP (Sonora +Sinaloa); winter visitor BC, csP, cH, A. Common; mostly in coastal waters, along estuaries, bays, lagoons; or on large lakes.
Pl.1. 16" No white on wing-tip. Sum.Ad: Mostly white; head black; bill red; dark gray back and wings; black wing tips. Win.Ad: Black bill, head mostly white, with gray nape. Im: Dark brownish gray above, gray breast, white belly; white tail (with complete broad black tail-band first year.)

Franklin's Gull. *Larus pipixcan.* P5a40.   Apipizca de Franklin
Can-SAm. Transient BC, P, H, A, Y. Rare; near water; or migrating over open areas.
15" Like Laughing G., but Sum.Ad: redder legs, black bar on white wing-tip; and Win.Ad: larger dark area on crown, nape, around eye; and Im: grayer above; whiter breast and collar; black bar not on outer tail-feathers; some white on wing-tips.

Bonaparte's Gull. *Larus philadelphia.* P5a37.   Apipizca Blanca
AK-M,CR,P. Winter visitor BC, nP, cH, ncA. Rare+; coastal areas, and large lakes.
14" Like Laughing G., but Sum.Ad: much paler wings and back; very broadly white wing-tips, edged black; black bill; bright red legs; and Win.Ad: blackish spot behind eye; and Im: black tail-band on white; pinkish legs; white and black wing-tips.

Heermann's Gull. *Larus heermanni.* P5a6.   Apipizca de Heermann
Can-M,G. Resident, near sea level, BC, ncP (Sonora to Nayarit). Common; in coastal areas and near-shore areas, large bays, lagoons, estuaries, sandy beaches, rocky coasts.
Pl.1. 17" Ad: Dark pearly gray, paler below; with white head (mottled in winter); blackish flight feathers; black tail with white tip-band; red bill. Im: Blackish brown.

Mew Gull. *Larus canus.* P5a12.   Gaviota Pico Corto
AK-M. Winter visitor nBC. Very rare; coastal strands, rocky shores, bays, lagoons.
16" Like Ring-billed G., but Ad: slender bill with no black mark; more white between black patches on wing-tip; and Im: Back, wings, and tail darker;

Ring-billed Gull. *Larus delawarensis.* P5a14.   Apipizca Pinta
Can-CR,x.N. Winter visitor BC, P, ncH, A, Y. Rare+; coastal areas, and inland lakes.
Pl.1. 18" Sum.Ad: White head, tail, and underparts; black spot on yellow bill; black wing-tips with two white spots; legs yellow. Win.Ad: Crown and hind-neck lightly mottled. Im: Profusely small-spotted or mottled head, breast, and wing-coverts; tail mottled with broad black tail-band, or white with narrow black band.

California Gull. *Larus californicus.* P5a15.   Gaviota Californiana
Can-M. Winter visitor BC, ncP, cH. Common; coastal beaches, lagoons, or offshore.
21" Like Ring-billed G., but larger, slightly darker; and Sum.Ad: bill has small red and black spot near tip; and Win.Ad: more and heavier streaks on head and neck; and Im: much darker, browner, and more mottled; tail blackish brown. See Herring G.

Herring Gull. *Larus argentatus.* P5a24.   Gaviota Plateada
AK-Pan. Winter visitor BC, P, A, Y. Rare+; sandy or rocky seashores, lagoons; lakes.
24" Like California G., but larger; legs and feet pink at all ages; and Sum.Ad: red bill-spot but no black bill-spot; even less white in wing-tip; and Win.Ad: more heavily mottled on head, neck, upper back and breast.

Thayer's Gull. *Larus thayeri.* P5a23.   Gaviota de Thayer
AK-M. Winter visitor BC, nP. Rare+; coastal areas, such as bays, lagoons, beaches.

23" Like Herring G., but slightly smaller, and all plumages paler, grayer; and Sum.Ad: more white and little black on pale gray wing-tips.
Cortez (Yellow-footed) **Gull.** *Larus livens.* P5a18.   Gaviota de Cortez
US-M. Resident, near sea level, BC, nP; winter visitor cP. Common; mostly coastal, bays, lagoons, beaches, rocky areas; also on and near nest islands in Gulf of California.
23" Like Western G., but Ad: yellow legs and feet; and Im: much whiter head and underparts with much less mottling.
Western Gull. *Larus occidentalis.* P5a19.   Gaviota Occidental
Can-M. Resident BC, nP (Sonora); winter visitor ncP. Rare+; coasts, bays, lagoons.
23" Ad: White, with blackish gray mantle; one white spot in black wing-tip; red spot on yellow bill; pinkish legs. Im: Head, back, and underparts heavily mottled dark grayish brown; legs dull pinkish; bill mostly black ; tail black.
Glaucous-winged Gull. *Larus glaucescens.* P5a20.   Gaviota de Alas Glaucas
AK-M. Winter visitor BC, ncP; accidental cP. Rare+; ocean bays, shores, and lagoons.
24" Like Herring G., but immature plumages much paler, grayer; and Ad: paler mantle; white-spotted wing-tips pale gray like rest of mantle.
Glaucous Gull. *Larus hyperboreus.* P5a21.   Gaviota Glauca
AK-M. Winter visitor BC, nP. Very rare; rocky, sandy shores; coastal bays, lagoons.
25" Like Glaucous-winged G., but all plumages much paler; appear white or nearly so, overall; immatures have whitish, black-tipped bill; adults have white wing-tips.
Black-legged Kittiwake. *Larus tridactylus.* P5a43.   Rissa
AK-M. Winter visitor BC, nP. Rare; over open ocean waters, or near offshore islands.
17" Ad: White; except pale gray mantle and black wing-tips (Win.ad. has grayish nape and smudge behind eye.); black legs; yellow bill; tail notched.. Im: Blackish band across hind-neck; black-mottled wing-coverts; black tail-tip-band; black bill.
Sabine's Gull. *Larus sabini.* P5a45.   Gaviota de Sabine
AK-SAm,x.B,H. Transient BC, P. Rare+; off-shore ocean and islands; buoyant flight.
14" Tail forked; dark M-pattern on spread wings; legs black. Ad: Mostly white, but bill black with yellow tip; head blackish slate (white with gray nape-smudge in winter); wing-coverts mostly gray; long black patch from wrist to wing-tip. Im: Hind-crown, hind-neck, back, and most wing-coverts dark grayish brown; black tail-tip band; pale gray legs; all-black bill.
Gull-billed Tern. *Gelochelidon nilotica.* P5b6.   Pico de Gaviota
US-SAm. Summer resident BC (or visitor), nP (Sonora to Sinaloa); resident ncA; transient or winter visitor csP. Rare, local; coastal marshes, lagoons, tidal pools, flats.
14" Ad: Mostly white, but crown, legs, and heavy bill black (in winter hind-crown and nape grayish); mantle, and notched tail, pale gray. Im: Head and back mottled. (in win. hind-crown and nape grayish).
Caspian Tern. *Hydroprogne caspia.* P5b7.   Charrán Cáspica
Can-SAm,x.ES. Resident BC, nP (Sinaloa); winter visitor cP, nA, Y. Rare+; coastal beaches, sand-bars, bays, lagoons, estuaries; also fresh-water situations, lakes, ponds.
22" Like Royal Tern, but bill heavier, redder; outer primaries darker below; legs longer; tail less deeply forked. Win: Forehead, fore-crown, eye-patch, mottled dark.
Royal Tern. *Sterna maxima.* P5b8.   Charrán Real
US-SAm. Resident BC, nP, Y; transient or visitor csP, A. Rare+; mostly coastal areas.
Pl.1. 20" Sum: Mostly white; with black forehead, crown, and nape; pale gray mantle; but outer primaries dark gray above; wing mostly white below; legs short, black; bill rather heavy, orange. Win: Forehead, fore-crown white; black nape-crest.
Elegant Tern. *Sterna elegans.* P5b14.   Charrán Elegante
US-SAm,x.B,H. Resident BC, nP (Sonora to Nayarit); transient or winter visitor cP. Common to rare; coastal mainland or islands, beaches, sand-bars, lagoons, estuaries.
17" Like Royal T., but has slender bill; longer ragged crest; and dark on hind-neck in

winter extends farther forward (to front of crown).

Sandwich Tern. *Sterna sandvicensis.* P5b12.   Charrán de Cabot
US-SAm. Resident, near sea level, Y; winter visitor csP, cA. Rare; coast, open ocean.
16" Like Royal T., *but bill slender, black with yellow tip; very short rounded crest.*

Common Tern. *Sterna hirundo.* P5b19.   Charrán Común
AK-SAm. Transient and winter visitor BC, P, A, Y. Rare+; mostly coastal waters.
*15" Mostly white, with pale gray mantle, and some blackish on wing-tips; black
forehead, crown and nape (summer adult); deeply forked tail; red legs; and red bill
with black tip. Win.Ad.+Im: Bill black; black on head from eye to hind-crown to
nape; blackish strip on upper side of leading edge of wing from wrist to shoulder.*

Arctic Tern. *Sterna paradisaea.* P5b20.   Charrán Ártico
AK-M,SAm. Winter visitor ncP. Very rare; beaches, tidal flats, lagoons, and estuaries.
16" Like Common Tern, *but bill rich red (no black tip); legs shorter; tail longer;
wings plain gray above (no dark wedge on primaries); show narrowly black-tipped
primaries below; wing-tips seem translucent; chest, throat, and sides of neck grayer.*

Forster's Tern. *Sterna forsteri.* P5b23.   Charrán de Forster
Can-CR. Winter visitor BC, P, nA. Rare+; ocean beaches, rocky shores, and lagoons.
15" Like Common T., *but tail grayish, more deeply forked; primaries whitish; and
Win.Ad: no* black wing-bar shoulder to wrist; *black patch through eye, not* on nape.

Least Tern. *Sterna antillarum.* (P5b33).   Charrán Mínimo
US-SAm,x.N. Resident, near sea level, BC, P; resident, transient, or visitor A, Y.
Rare; ocean beaches, shores of lagoons and estuaries; also lake shores, sandbars, rivers.
9" Ad+Im: Like Common T., *but much smaller; outer primaries black; forehead
white; and Sum.Ad: bill yellow, black-tipped; legs yellow; and Im: legs can be black.*

Sooty Tern. *Sterna fuscata.* P5b30.   Charrán Oscuro
Can-SAm. Resident, near sea level, sBC (visitor only?), ncP (Nayarit to Revillagigedo
Is.), Y. Rare; over open ocean, on or near nest-islands, or along rocky or sandy shores.
*16" Black above, except white forehead, and white edges of deeply forked black tail;
white below; bill and legs black. Im: Blackish brown; pale spotty bars on mantle.*

Black Tern. *Chlidonias niger.* P5b4.   Charrán Negro
Can-SAm. Transient all sub-regions. Common; near-shore ocean waters, lakes, rivers.
*Pl.1. 10" Pale gray mantle and (notched) tail; black bill. Sum.Ad: Black head and
underparts, except white untacs. Win.Ad: Mostly white, with black hind-neck to eye;
Im: Like win. ad., but back brown. Patchy molting or sub-adult birds are common.*

Brown Noddy. *Anous stolidus.* P5b41.   Charrán Pardelo
US-SAm. Resident, sea level, ncP (Nayarit to Guerrero), Y. Rare+; off-shore islands.
*15" Dark brown; with pale gray to whitish nape to forehead; wedge-shaped tail long,
tip slightly notched. Im: Brown; with narrow whitish line over eye.*

SKIMMERS - RYNCHOPIDAE - RALLADORES

Black Skimmer. *Rynchops nigra.* P4a1.   Rallador Negro
US-SAm. Resident, sea level, P, A, Y; winter visitor or resident nBC. Common; quiet
coastal waters, lagoons, estuaries; buoyant flight, lower mandible in water as it feeds.
*Pl.1. 18" Mostly black above; white below; bill long, blade-like, red with black
tip, lower mandible longer than upper; legs red. Im: Mottled brown and gray above.*

AUKLETS, MURRES - ALCIDAE - ALCUELAS, PATOS NOCTURNOS

Three residents, two visitors; off BC, nP; heavy body; short legs, neck, and tail;
small, pointed wings; short tail, short to medium bill; mostly oceanic swimmers, divers;
widespread northern oceans. Distinguish by size patterns, bill shape and size. **Plate 1.**

Common Murre. *Uria aalge.* P1a1.   Alcuela Grande
AK-M. Winter visitor nBC. Very rare; in the open ocean or waters around nest islands.

17" Sum: Black above, white below, with all-black head and upper neck. Win: Throat, and sides of head and neck, white; narrow black line from eye through cheek.
Xantus's Murrelet. *Endomychura hypoleuca.* P1a10.   Pato Nocturno
Can-M. Resident, near sea level, BC; winter visitor nP. Rare+; swimming in open ocean waters or near offshore islands; nests on ground or in rock crevices, on islands.
Pl.1. 10" Chunky, stubby-tailed; short-billed; black sides and upperparts; lower side of face, under-wings, and underparts (except sides) white.
Craveri's Murrelet. *Endomychura craveri.* P1a11.   Pato de Craveri
US-M. Resident, sea level, BC, nP (Sonora). Rare+; open ocean, or offshore islands.
10" Like Xantus's M., but dark under-wings; more black on sides of breast.
Cassin's Auklet. *Ptychoramphus aleuticus.* P1a15.   Alcuela Norteamericana
AK-M. Resident, sea level, BC. Rare+; open ocean, rocky coasts, or on nest islands.
9" Compact, stub-tailed; blackish gray above; dark gray throat, breast, sides, and flanks; belly and untacs white; bill short, thick, pale spot basally; eye-crescents white.
Rhinoceros Auklet. *Cerorhinca monocerata.* P1a20.   Alcuela Rinoceronte
AK-M. Winter visitor BC. Rare; offshore ocean waters, surface-diving, seldom flying.
14" Win.Ad: Blackish brown; grayish throat and breast; whitish belly; thick yellowish bill. Sum.Ad: Two white face-plumes; brighter bill, with basal knob.

PIGEONS, DOVES - COLUMBIDAE - PALOMAS

Twenty-four residents; mostly P, A, Y; short legs and neck; broad, pointed to slightly rounded, wings; medium-short to medium tail; medium-short bill; walkers to strong fliers, dry to humid, ground to tree-tops; world temperate, tropical. Distinguish by plumage colors, patterns, tail shape and size, and voice. **Plates 13 and 16.**

Rock Dove. *Columba livia.* Q3a1.   Pichón de las Rocas
AK-SAm. Resident up to 12,000', all sub-regions. Common; in cities, towns, farms.
13" Variable; white to nearly black, variegated or uniform; many individuals are close to the wild type - mostly medium bluish gray, with iridescent green and purple collar; two broad black wing-bars; white rump; and broad black tail-tip band; legs red.
Rufous (Pale-v.) **Pigeon.** *Columba cayennensis.* Q3a41.   Pepencha Rojiza
M-SAm,x.ES. Resident up to 2000', csA. Rare; tree-tops, or flying over, dense forest.
Pl.13. 13" M: Purplish red; shading to dark bluish gray on rump; hind-neck bronzy green; sides of head gray; throat, belly, untacs whitish. F: Duller. See Short-billed P.
Scaled Pigeon. *Columba speciosa.* Q3a34.   Paloma Escamosa
M-SAm. Resident up to 3000', csA, Y. Rare+; tree-tops, or flying over dense forest.
Pl.13. 13" M: Head and upperparts purplish and chestnut; upper back, collar, and breast scaled black and rufous; belly and untacs scaled white and purplish; legs purplish. F: Duller; more reddish brown above; less reddish tinge below.
White-crowned Pigeon. *Columba leucocephala.* Q3a32.   Torcaz de Cabeza Blanca
US-M,B,H,Pan. Resident near sea level, Y (Cozumel I.). Common; mangroves, scrub.
Pl.16. 13" M: Blackish-purple; but crown and forehead white; barred green of hind-neck often not noticed; bill red, pale-tipped. F: Crown whitish. Im: Crown dark.
Red-billed Pigeon. *Columba flavirostris.* Q3a42.   Torcaz Morada
US-CR. Resident P, A, Y. Common; woodlots, forest edge, hedgerows, scrub woods.
Pl.16. 13" Head, neck, breast purplish rufous; shading to grayish brown back, to dark bluish gray wings, rump, belly, untacs, tail; bill red, with yellow tip; legs red.
Band-tailed Pigeon. *Columba fasciata.* Q3a38.   Paloma Ocotera
Can-SAm,x.B. Resident, 4000 to 10,000', BC, H. Common; pine or pine-oak woods.
Pl.16. 14" Dark bluish gray and paler gray above, with greenish scaled upper back; white band across nape; head and breast purplish gray; tail black, with very broad gray tail-tip band; belly and untacs white; legs, and black-tipped bill, yellow.

Short-billed Pigeon. *Columba nigrirostris.* Q3a47.   <u>Torcaz Piquinegra</u>
M-SAm,x.ES. <u>Resident up to 3000', csA, Y</u>. Rare+; tree-tops, in dense humid forest.
*Pl.13. 12" Dull grayish purple head and underparts, no white; tail and upperparts
dark grayish brown; bill black; iris red; legs dull red.* V: like human voices
murmuring *waddle, wat-wat-waddle;* last *waddle* may be higher (pitch), or lower.

Spotted Dove. *Streptopelia chinensis.* Q3a59.   <u>Torcaz Pintada</u>
US-M. <u>Resident, near sea level, nBC</u>. Rare+; suburban gardens, borders, hedgerows.
12" Like Mourning Dove, *but darker above; has more contrasty maroon breast and
pale gray head; more rounded tail with broader white feather-tips; and Ad: hind-neck
and neck-sides black with many small white spots. Im: Faint spotting on hind-neck.*

White-winged Dove. *Zenaida asiatica.* Q3a111.   <u>Tórtola</u>
US-SAm. <u>Resident up to 8000', all sub-regions</u>. Abundant, irregular; semi-desert,
scrub woods, woodlots, hedgerows. V: Hoo-<u>hoot</u>-hoo-hoo-oo ("who cooks for you").
*Pl.16. 12" Grayish brown above; paler, buffier head and underparts; white patch
shows on folded and extended wing; tail broadly white-cornered; bill black.*

Zenaida Dove. *Zenaida aurita.* Q3a110.   <u>Torcaz Zenaida</u>
M. <u>Resident near sea level, Y (Yucatán+Quintana Roo)</u>. Rare+; scrub and palm groves.
Pl.13. 11" Like Mourning D., *but has white wing-bar; shorter, rounded tail, which
is gray-tipped, not* white-tipped. *Like* White-winged D., *but more reddish brown;
has white wing-bar, but no* white wing-patch; *tail-corners gray, not* white.

Mourning Dove. *Zenaida macroura.* Q3a108.   <u>Huilota Común</u>
Mourning group. *Z. m. macroura.*   <u>Huilota Común</u>
Can-Pan. <u>Resident up to 9000', BC, ncP (Sonora+Tres Marias Is.+Revillagigedo
Is.), ncH; winter visitor all sub-regions</u>. Common; scattered scrubby trees,
hedgerows, patchy farmlands, semi-desert scrub, grassy brushy plains, borders.
*12" Brownish gray above, with darker wings; grayish buff below; long,
narrow-wedge-shaped tail, with tail-feathers gray-based, white-tipped. Like*
Socorro group, *but much paler, duller, grayer; has* <u>white</u> *tail-feather-tips.*
Socorro group. *Z. m. graysoni.*   <u>Huilota de Socorro</u>
M. <u>Was resident cP (Socorro I. of Revillagigedo Is.); now extinct in the wild</u>.
Pl.13. 12" Brown above; rufous below; pointed tail; grayish tail-feather-tips.

Inca Dove. *Scardafella inca.* Q3a127.   <u>Coquita Común</u>
US-CR,x.B,ES. <u>Resident up to 10,000', P, H, A</u>. Common; gardens, farms,borders.
*Pl.16. 8" Brownish gray above; paler below; liberally "scaled" above and below;
sides and tip of long tail white; rufous wing-patch.* V: Abrupt *coo-cote* ("no hope").

Common Ground-Dove. *Columbina passerina.* Q3a113.   <u>Mucuy</u>
US-SAm. <u>Resident up to 10,000', all sub-regions</u>. Common; scrub, borders, *ranchos.*
*Pl.16. 6 1/2" Grayish; paler on head and below; scaly head and breast; tail short,
rounded, little white; rufous and black flight-feathers; folded wings spotted; red bill
black-tipped. M: Bluish on nape, pinkish on face and below.* V: Repeated *hoo-ut.*

Plain-breasted Ground-Dove. *Columbina minuta.* Q3a114.   <u>Torcacita</u>
M-SAm,x.H. <u>Resident up to 2500', csP (Oaxaca to Chiapas), csA (Veracruz to
Campeche)</u>. Rare, irregular; rather humid areas, in hedgerows, moist savannas,borders.
Pl.13. 6" Plumage and voice like Common Gr.-D.'s, *but has no scaly marks or
spots on head or breast; few spots on folded wing.*

Ruddy Ground-Dove. *Columbina talpacoti.* Q3a116.   <u>Tortolita</u>
M-SAm. <u>Resident up to 4000', P (Sinaloa to Chiapas), A, Y</u>. Common; parks,
gardens, woodland borders, farms, orchards, hedgerows, open brushy grassy fields.
Pl.13. 7" Like Plain-breasted and Common Gr.-D.s, *but much more rufous, and
lacks* breast-marks of the latter. *M: Rich reddish brown with bluish head. F: Paler,
more grayish brown; head not bluish; wing-spots* <u>black.</u> ncA birds are paler, duller.

Blue Ground-Dove. *Claravis pretiosa.* Q3a120.   <u>Coquita Plomiza</u>
M-SAm. <u>Resident, sea level to 4000', A,Y</u>. Rare; patchy humid forest and fields; flies

rapidly near ground, usually paired. V: from tree-tops, quiet *hoot* - long pause - *hoot*.
***Pl.13.** 8" M: Pale blue-gray, with black tail-sides and wing-spots. F: Brownish; like female Ruddy Gr.-D., but wing-spots reddish-brown; seldom apart from male.*

Mondetoura Dove. *Claravis mondetoura.* Q3a122.   Chicuquita
M-SAm,x.B,N. Resident, 6000 to 10,000', sH. Very rare; cloud forest undergrowth.
***Pl.13.** 8" Like Blue Gr-D. but tail broadly white-cornered; and M: purplish breast; gray sides and flanks; white belly; and F: dark purplish wing-spots.*

White-fronted (-tipped) **Dove.** *Leptotila verreauxi.* Q3a130.   Paloma Morada
US-SAm. Resident up to 6000', P, A, Y. Rare+; undergrowth, from scrubby woods to dense forest. V: a very low-pitched, unobtrusive, mournful *oo-ooo*, ascending slightly.
***Pl.16.** 11" Grayish brown above; pinkish buff breast and sides of head; whitish belly and untacs; forehead pale pinkish, to pale purplish gray crown, to iridescent purplish hind-neck; tail-corners white; bill black; legs red.* See other *Leptotila spp.*

Gray-headed Dove. *Leptotila plumbeiceps.* Q3a133.   Paloma Cabezigris
M-SAm,x.ES. Resident up to 3000', A, Y. Rare; undergrowth, woods to dense forest.
***Pl.13.** 10" Like White-fronted D., but forehead pale bluish gray; and crown and hind-neck medium gray; belly and untacs whiter.*

Caribbean Dove. *Leptotila jamaicensis.* Q3a136.   Torcaz de Caribe
M. Resident, near sea level, Y. Rare (common, Cozumel I.); scrub woods, thickets.
***Pl.13.** 10" Like Wh.-fr.D., but whiter belly and untacs; more broadly iridescent purplish on hind-neck and sides of neck.* Best distinguished by voice, which is four-noted, slow, last note higher, *hoo-hoo hoo-hoo* ("Who, who, poor Pooh?").

Cassin's (Gray-ch.) **Dove.** *Leptotila cassinii.* Q3a137.   Torcaz Pecho Vinoso
M-SAm,x.ES. Resident, near sea level, sA (Tabasco and Chiapas). Very rare; on the ground in the undergrowth, dense humid lowland forest, usually well inside the forest.
***Pl.13.** 10" Like White-fronted D., but upper belly, breast neck, and head much darker, medium purplish gray not pinkish buff; flanks brownish; less white on tail.*

White-faced Quail-Dove. *Geotrygon albifacies.* Q3a147.   Paloma Codorniz
M-N,x.B. Resident, 4000 to 9000', csP, sH, csA (San Luis Potosí to Chiapas). Rare; ground or low shrubs in dense cloud forest or overgrown coffee plantations or orchards.
***Pl.13.** 12" Rich reddish brown to purplish above; crown and nape pale bluish gray; forehead, chin, sides of face whitish; lines of "scales" on sides of neck; bill black.*

Lawrence's (Pur.-b.) **Quail-Dove.** *Geotrygon lawrencii.* Q3a140. Paloma Morena
M,CR,P. Resident, 4000 to 7000', cA (se.Veracruz). Rare; undergrowth, cloud forest.
***Pl.13.** 10" Above olive-brown and violet; gray crown to dark greenish hind-neck; forehead and black-rimmed ear-patch white; breast bluish gray; bill red with black tip.*

Ruddy Quail-Dove. *Geotrygon montana.* Q3a154.   Paloma Montañes
M-SAm,x.ES. Resident up to 3000', P (Sinaloa to Chiapas), A, Y. Rare; usually on the ground or in low shrubs in dense humid forest undergrowth. V: a rasping *wa-a-ah*.
***Pl.13.** 9" M: Rich rufous above; pinkish buff below; ear-patch buff outlined dark reddish brown; streaked reddish-brown and buff below eye. F: Like male, but duller and more olive above; duller and somewhat darker than male below.*

PARROTS, MACAWS - PSITTACIDAE - COTORRAS, GUACAMAYAS
Nineteen residents; mostly P, A, Y; small to medium-large size; short legs and neck, rounded wing, short to very long tail; short, heavy, arched, hooked bill; strong fliers; clamber among branches; scrubby woods to humid forest; world tropical and adjacent temperate. Distinguish by head-colors, other colors, patterns, tail shape. **Plate 17.**

Green Parakeet. *Aratinga holochlora.* R1d109.   Periquito Verde
  Green group. *A. h. holochlora.*   Periquito Verde
  M-N,x.B. Resident up to 5500', ncP (Sonora+Chihuahua+Sinaloa+Revillagigedo Is.), cH (Guanajuato+México), A (Tamaulipas to Chiapas). Common; in patchy

farms and woods, open forest, borders, river-border woods, or tree-dotted fields.
Pl.17. 11" Green, may be tinged yellowish below; tail long, pointed.
Pacific group. *A. h. strenua.* Periquito Pacífico
M-N,x.B. Resident up to 4000', csP (Oaxaca+Chiapas). Rare+; woods, borders.
11" Like Green group., *but bill thicker and legs heavier.*
Aztec Parakeet. *Aratinga astec.* R1d119. Periquillo Alcaparrero
M-SAm,x.ES. Resident up to 2000', A, Y. Common; forest, farms, and open woods.
Pl.17. 10" Smaller than Green P.; *flight feathers blue and black; breast brownish.*
Orange-fronted Parakeet. *Aratinga canicularis.* R1d121. Periquillo Común
M-CR,x.B. Resident up to 5000', P (Sinaloa to Chiapas). Common; arid scrub, farms.
Pl.17. 9" Forehead orange; whitish eye-ring; flight feathers blue and black.
Military Macaw. *Ara militaris.* R1d127. Guacamaya Verde
M,SAm. Resident, 1000 to 8000', P, ncH, nA. Rare; *barrancas,* forest, and river-edge.
Pl.17. 30" Mostly dull yellowish green; forehead red; flight feathers, untacs, uptacs,
and tail-tip (above) blue; basal half of tail red above; bill black.
Scarlet Macaw. *Ara macao.* R1d129. Guacamaya Roja
M-SAm,x.ES. Resident up to 2500', sA (Tabasco?,Campeche?,Chiapas). Very rare; in
secluded dense forest, and nearby openings; disappearing in most of Middle America.
Pl.17. 36" Red; some wing-coverts yellow; flight feathers, untacs, and uptacs, blue.
Thick-billed Parrot. *Rhynchopsitta pachyrhyncha.* R1d102. Cotorra Serrana
M. Resident or visitor, 5000 to 10,000', ncH (Sonora+Chihuahua to Jalisco+
Veracruz). Rare+; secluded mountain pine-oak or pine forests, or flying high overhead.
Pl.17. 16" Green; but forehead, short superciliary line, wrist-patch, and thighs red;
under-wing patch yellow; medium-long pointed tail; black bill.
Maroon-fronted Parrot. *Rhynchopsitta terrisi.* R1d103. Cotorra Frente Purpurea
M. Resident, 5000 to 8000', nH (Coahuila+Nuevo León+Tamaulipas). Rare, local;
mountain pine-oak or pine forests; often in flocks. V: a loud high-pitched rolling *cra-ak.*
Pl.17. 16" Like Thick-billed P., *but forehead maroon; under-wing patch gray.*
Barred Parakeet. *Bolborhynchus lineola.* R1d4. Catarina Listada
M,G,H,CR,P,SAm. Resident, 4000 to 7000', csP, csH, csA (Puebla+Guerrero+
Oaxaca+Chiapas). Very rare, local; tree-tops in secluded cloud forest; or high overhead.
Pl.17. 6 1/2" Green; heavy black bars above, narrow bars below; tail short, pointed.
Mexican (Bl.-r.) **Parrotlet.** *Forpus cyanopygius.* R1d6. Catarinita
M. Resident up to 4000', ncP (Sonora to Colima). Common, but very irregular;
scrubby woods, orchards, borders, large parks; often in flocks. V: a thin,tinkling *cree.*
Pl.17. 5 1/2" M: Green; rump and wing-patch, blue; tail very short. F: Has no blue.
Tovi (Or.-ch.) **Parakeet.** *Brotogeris jugularis.* R1d17. Periquito Colicorto
M-SAm,x.B. Resident, near sea level, csP (Guerrero to Chiapas). Rare+; farms,
woodlots, borders, parks; rapid flight in flocks - flaps then sails. V: *scree,* and *ji-ji-ji-jit.*
Pl.17. 7" Shades of green; more brownish and bluish above, more yellowish below;
orange chin; brown wrist-patch; tail short, pointed.
Brown-hooded Parrot. *Pionopsitta haematotis.* R1d31. Perico Orejirojo
M-SAm,x.ES. Resident up to 3000', csA. Rare; tree-tops, humid forest, forest edge.
Pl.17. 8" Mostly green; with mostly olive-brown and dark gray head, with red
ear-patch; breast yellow-olive; red sides under wing.
White-crowned Parrot. *Pionus senilis.* R1d45. Loro Chilillo
M-SAm,x.ES. Resident, 1000 to 5000', A, Y. Rare; feeds quietly in tree-tops in
secluded forests, flies strongly high overhead. V: rasping *cleek,* or *scree, culey, culey.*
Pl.17. 9" Green; but back, breast, and head very dark bluish, except white crown
and throat, and red eye-ring; wing-patch brown; untacs red.
White-fronted Parrot. *Amazona albifrons.* R1d51. Perico Frentiblanco
M-CR. Resident up to 3000', P, sA, Y. Rare+; on farms, open forest, scrub, borders.

Pl.17. 10" Green with white forehead, red lores and eye-ring; somewhat "scaly" breast, back, hind-neck. M: Red wing-patch. F: No red on wing. See Yucatan P.

Yucatan (Yel.-lored) **Parrot.** *Amazona xantholora.* R1d52.   Loro Yucateco
M,B,H. Resident, near sea level, Y. Rare+; in patchy forest and clearings, or overhead.
Pl.17. 10" M+F: Like White-crowned P.*, but more "scaly" appearance; blackish ear-patch, yellow lores; and M: has less red on wing (alula green, not* red*); and F: blue, not* white*, on head; no* red *around eye or on wing.*

Red-crowned Parrot. *Amazona viridigenalis.* R1d57.   Cotorra Cabeza Roja
US-M. Resident up to 3000', ncA (Tamaulipas to n.Veracruz). Common; river-border woods, forest-edge, *ranchos,* second-growth. V: *clee-u,* then harsh *crack-crack-crack.*
Pl.17. 12" Mostly dull yellowish green, somewhat "scaly"; crown red and forehead red; cheeks pale green; red wing-patch; tail short, rounded.

Lilac-crowned Parrot. *Amazona finschi.* R1d58.   Cotorra Guayabera
M. Resident up to 7000', ncP, ncH. Common in lowlands, in patchy farms, orchards, woodlots, scrubby open woods; rare in highlands, pine-oak or pine forest, or openings.
Pl.17. 12" Mostly green; forehead dark red; crown pale bluish; and red wing-patch.

Red-lored Parrot. *Amazona autumnalis.* R1d59.   Loro Frentirrojo
M-SAm,x.ES. Resident up to 2000', A. Rare+; forest, patchy woods, farms, borders.
Pl.17. 12" Mostly green; forehead and lores red; yellow cheek-patch (north of Costa Rica); *pale bluish-green crown; red wing-patch; bill gray; tail short, rounded. Im: No* yellow. V: loud, harsh *be-brick,* or *she-currick;* soft, rasping "petulant" *ca-crra-cra.*

Mealy Parrot. *Amazona farinosa.* R1d69.   Loro Verde
M-SAm,x.ES. Resident, near sea level, sP (Chiapas), csA. Rare; middle branches, humid forest near openings; flies above forest crown. V: quiet *crack or sreek;* loud *rack.*
Pl.17. 15" More grayish *green than other Amazona spp.; broadly pale blue crown; dark bill; tail rather short, rounded, with broadly yellowish green tip; red wing-patch.*

Yellow-headed Parrot. *Amazona ochrocephala.* R1d66.   Cotorra Cabeza Amarilla
Yellow-headed group. *A. ochrocephala oratrix.*   Cotorra Cabeza Amarilla
M,B. Resident up to 3000', ncP (Tres Marias Is.+Colima to Oaxaca), and A.
Rare, local; patchy forest, river borders. V: loud *wow* or *ow,* like a human voice.
Pl.17. 14" Mostly green; but entire head yellow; bill pale yellowish; two red wing-patches. Im: Head all-green or nearly so; no red *on wings; bill dark.*
Yellow-naped group. *A. o. auropalliata.*   Cotorra Nuca Amarilla
M-CR,x.B. Resident up to 3000', sP. Rare, local; patchy humid forest, clearings.
14" Like Yellow-headed group, *but head green, except broadly yellow hind-neck and sometimes crown; bill dark; one red wing-patch.*

CUCKOOS, ANIS - CUCULIDAE - PLATEROS, GARRAPATEROS

Twelve residents or transients; mostly P, A, Y; short or medium legs and neck, rounded wings, long to very long tail; medium bill, normal or high-arched; walkers or arboreal, open dry areas to humid woods; world temperate, tropical. **Plates 14, 15.**

Black-billed Cuckoo. *Coccyzus erythropthalmus.* S2b3.   Platero Piquinegro
Can-SAm,x.ES. Transient P, csH, A, Y. Rare+; borders, hedgerows, scrubby woods.
Pl.15. 12" Like Yellow-billed C.*, but bill black; eye-ring red; no* rufous *on wing; white tips on tail feathers very* narrow; *form narrow bars across tail.*

Yellow-billed Cuckoo. *Coccyzus americanus.* S2b4.   Platero Piquiamarillo
Can-SAm. Summer resident up to 5000', BC, nP (Sonora to Sinaloa), nH (Chihuahua+Coahuila), ncA, Y (Yucatán); transient all sub-regions. Rare, local; patchy thickets, trees, and overgrown fields, brushy borders, hedgerows, scrubby woods.
Pl.15. 12" Brown above; white below; bill black above, buffy yellow below, slightly decurved; inner webs of primaries rufous, forming a wing-patch in flight; tail graduated, black with long white feather-tip spots.

Mangrove Cuckoo. *Coccyzus minor.* S2b6. Platero Manglero
US-SAm. Resident up to 3000', P (Sinaloa to Chiapas), A, Y. Rare; patchy woods
and thickets, river-edge woods, mangrove swamps. V: a slow *cuk-cuk-cuk, co, co, co.*
Pl.15. 12" *Like* Yellow-billed C., *but has black mask; tawny-buff belly and untacs;
no rufous markings on wing.*

Squirrel Cuckoo. *Piaya cayana.* S2b12. Vaquero
M-SAm. Resident up to 7500', P, ncH, A, Y. Rare+, up to 4000', very rare higher;
river-border woods, tree-dotted fields, borders, woodlots. V: sharp *peek* or *peek-purr-rr.*
Pl.14. 19" *Races vary. ncP birds: Rich rufous above, including top of very long
graduated tail; throat broadly pale pinkish brown; lower breast, belly and untacs pale
gray; tail-feathers mostly chestnut, with sub-terminal black bar, broad white tip; iris
red; bill and eye-ring green. sP, A, Y birds: Like ncP birds, but lower breast, belly
and untacs blackish gray; tail feathers (from below) mostly blackish, with white tip.*

Striped Cuckoo. *Tapera naevia.* S2d1. Chiflador Rayado
M-SAm. Resident, near sea level, sP (Chiapas), csA. Rare; pastures, scrub, borders.
Pl.14. 11" *Brownish above; back heavily streaked, and crown (slightly crested)
finely streaked, with black; face striped whitish and brown; white below except
broadly pale buff throat . V: a deliberate far-carrying whistle, of 2 or 3 to 5 notes.*

Pheasant Cuckoo. *Dromococcyx phasianellus.* S2d3. Cuco Faisán
M-SAm. Resident up to 5000', sP (Chiapas), csA, Y. Very rare; humid forest, thickets.
Pl.14. 15" *Blackish brown above, spotted and scaled; white below, except
black-spotted buffy throat and breast ; head small, with short dark brown crest; white
line behind eye; tail long, graduated; uptacs very long, plume-like. V: a slow, loud,
clear haw-haw-ha-ha, haw, or tremolo ho-haw-ho-o-o-o.*

Lesser Ground-Cuckoo. *Morococcyx erythropygus.* S2d2. Cuclillo Chiflador
M-CR,x.B. Resident up to 4000', P (Sinaloa to Chiapas). Rare+; scrubby woods,
thickets, borders, brushy fields, hedgerows. V: one rasping hoot; or several, slowing.
Pl.14. 11" *Green-glossed grayish brown above, with blackish-and-rufous rump;
tawny-rufous below, with blackish untacs; face-lines buff and black; blue eye-ring.*

Lesser Roadrunner. *Geococcyx velox.* S2d6. Correcamino Veloz
M-N,x.B. Resident up to 8000', P, csH, csA, Y. Rare+; habitat like that of Greater R.
Pl.14. 18" *Like* Greater R., *sides of neck streaked, but underparts not streaked.*

Greater Roadrunner. *Geococcyx californianus.* S2d5. Correcamino Californiano
US-M. Resident up to 8000', BC, nP (Sonora to Sinaloa), ncH, ncA. Rare+; usually
dry areas, brushy fields, scrubby borders, mesquite-grassland, roadsides, semi-deserts.
Pl.15. 22" *Heavily streaked above and on lower throat, neck, and upper
breast; ragged crest; long tail, with white feather-tips. V: low "mournful" coo or hoot.*

Greater Ani. *Crotophaga major.* S2c1. Garrapatero Grande
M,Pan-SAm. Resident, near sea level, nA (s.Tamaulipas). Very rare, known only
from a small area along the Río Tamesí; river-border woods, brushy fields, hedgerows.
18" *Like* Groove-billed Ani, *but much larger; glossier; has white iris; and basal half
of the bill has an extra flange on top which is nearly straight, not highly arched.*

Smooth-billed Ani. *Crotophaga ani.* S2c2. Pijón
US-SAm,x.G,ES. Resident, near sea level, Y (is. off Quintana Roo). Common;
scrubby woods, orchards, thickets, tree-dotted pastures, brushy fields. V: harsh *peu-ut.*
Pl.15. 13" *Like* Groove-billed Ani, *but bill-arch higher, no grooves on bill.*

Groove-billed Ani. *Crotophaga sulcirostris.* S2c3. Garrapatero
US-SAm. Resident up to 6000', P, A, Y. Abundant; brushy fields, gardens, borders.
Pl.15. 12" *Black all over, appears scaly; tail rather long, rounded, floppy; bill
laterally compressed, very high, sides grooved. V: a somewhat musical pee-clue.*

BARN-OWLS - TYTONIDAE - LECHUZAS
Common Barn-Owl. *Tyto alba.* K1a2.   Lechuza Mono
Can-SAm. Resident up to 10,000', all sub-regions. Rare; old buildings, towers, wells.
Pl.15. 15" Buffy brown above, mottled and barred; white or buff below, with scattered small spots; face heart-shaped, white or buff. V: a raspy, hiss-like screech.

OWLS, SCREECH-OWLS - STRIGIDAE - TECOLOTES, LECHUZAS
Twenty-five residents, one winter visitor; widespread Mexico; short legs, strong feet, very short neck, large head, rounded wings, short to medium tail, hooked bill; nocturnal predators; forest, borders, and open areas, dry to humid; world-wide. Distinguish by voice, patterns, ear-tufts, tail-bars, spotting, eye-color. **Plates 14 and 15.**

Flammulated Owl. *Otus flammeolus.* K2a9.   Tecolotito de Flámulas
Can-M,G,ES. Resident, 7000 to 10,000', ncH; winter visitor sH. Rare; highland forest.
Pl.15. 7" Like Western Screech-Owl, *but iris dark brown; ear-tufts very short; facial disk redder than other feathers.* V: low *hoot,* or paired hoots, repeated slowly.

Eastern Screech-Owl. *Otus asio.* K2a31.   Tecolotito Chillón
Can-M. Resident up to 5000', nA. Rare+; dry woods, river borders, pine-oak or pine.
Pl.15. 8" Gray phase: Pale to medium gray all over; streaked, mottled, barred, and spotted; facial disk has black border and white "V" above bill, leading to prominent ear-tufts; iris bright yellow. Red phase: Like gray phase, *but rufous replaces most of gray; less heavily streaked.* V: mellow or wailing tremolo, descending or not.

Western Screech-Owl. *Otus kennicottii.* K2a32.   Tecolotito Occidental
AK-M. Resident to 8000', BC, nP (Sonora to Sinaloa), ncH. Rare+; dense pine or pine-oak woods, semi-desert, openings. V: "bouncing" *hoot, hoot, hoot-hoo-hoo-oo-o.*
8" Like E.Screech-Owl, *but "red" phase dull brown, not* rufous. The "Vinaceous" Screech-Owl, *(Pl.14), has a pinkish wash above and below, and has fewer dark streaks, but nevertheless is now considered a race of the* Western Screech-Owl.
Balsas Screech-Owl. *Otus seductus.* K2a33.   Tecolotito de Balsas
M. Resident up to 4000', cP (Colima to Guerrero). Rare+; scrub woods and cactus.
8" Like gray phase Western Screech-O., *but eyes* brown; and V: rougher.

Pacific Screech-Owl. *Otus cooperi.* K2a34.   Tecolotito Manglero
M-CR,x.B. Resident, near sea level, csP (Oaxaca to Chiapas). Rare; palm groves, open woods, mangrove swamps. V: a rather rough, uniformly low-pitched, short trill.
8" Like W.Screech-O., *but toes and lower tarsus not* feathered; voice differs.

Whiskered Screech-Owl. *Otus trichopsis.* K2a35.   Tecolotito Manchado
US-N,x.B. Resident, 4000 to 9000', ncH. Rare+; dry oak, pine-oak, or pine woods.
8" Like E. Screech-Owl, *gray phase and bright red phase, but facial bristles longer, and* V: low-pitched hoots on one pitch - *hoohoohoo, hoo, hoo,* or *hoohoohoo, hoo.*

Vermiculated Screech-Owl. *Otus guatemalae.* K2a39.   Tecolotito Guatemalteco
M-SAm. Resident up to 5000', P, A, Y. Rare; river-woods, low forest, forest-edge.
Pl.14. 8" Like W. Screech-Owl, *but fewer dark streaks, more narrow bars, below; eye-brow lines not as contrasty; toes not* feathered; and V: a long rather low-pitched trill on one pitch, beginning quietly, gradually becoming louder, ending abruptly.

Bearded Screech-Owl. *Otus barbarus.* K2a43.   Tecolotito Ocotero
M,G. Resident, 4500 to 6000', sH. Rare; mid-mountain pine or pine-oak woodlands.
Pl.14. 7" Like Western Screech-Owl, *but smaller; more contrasty black-streaked on white below; eyebrow marks and whisker marks more contrasty white; toes and lower tarsus not* feathered; and V: a short, quiet, high-pitched trill.

Crested Owl. *Lophostrix cristata.* K2a90.   Tecolote Cuerniblanco
M-SAm,x.B. Resident up to 3000', sP (Oaxaca to Chiapas), csA (Veracruz to Chiapas). Rare; humid lowland forest, woodlots, partial clearings, and forest on low mountain slopes.
Pl.14. 16" Brown above, with large white wing-spots; vermiculated dark brown

(breast) and paler tawny brown below; face dark reddish brown, with white eye-brow lines extending into long white ear-tufts.

Spectacled Owl. *Pulsatrix perspicillata.* K2a91. <u>Tecolote de Anteojos</u>
M-SAm. <u>Resident, near sea level, sP, csA</u>. Rare; in dense humid lowland forest, forest borders, openings, partial clearings. V: a rapid series of low-pitched, thumping notes. *Pl.14.* 19" No ear-tufts; *blackish brown above and on breast; belly and untacs tawny; face blackish brown, with white throat, whisker marks, and eye-brow lines.*

Great Horned Owl. *Bubo virginianus.* K2a53. <u>Tecolote Cornudo</u>
AK-SAm. <u>Resident up to 9000', all sub-regions</u>. Rare+; semi-desert to moist forest. *Pl.15.* 20" *Races vary greatly; most are brownish, streaked and mottled above, mostly barred below; face rufous with black border; white throat; medium ear-tufts.*

Northern Pygmy-Owl. *Glaucidium gnoma.* K2b3. <u>Picametate</u>
Can-M,G,H. <u>Resident, 5000 to 12,500', sBC, H</u>. Rare+; upland forest, scrub woods. V: a <u>long</u> slow series of high piping notes on one pitch - *ho, ho, ho, ho, ho, ho, ho,* etc. *Pl.15.* 7" *Gray or reddish above, with pale spots; mostly white below with blackish streaks; 2 eye-spots on nape; 5 or 6 bars on tail; tiny <u>spots</u> on crown.*

Least Pygmy-Owl. *Glaucidium minutissimum.* K2b5. <u>Tecolotillo Mínimo</u>
M-SAm,x.ES,N. <u>Resident up to 6000', ncP, cH (Oaxaca), A</u>. Rare; wooded barrancas, pine-oak forest, cloud forest, borders. V: Like N.P.-O. but higher, much shorter series. *Pl.14.* 6 " *Like* Northern Pygmy-Owl, *but has only 2 or 3 bars on its short tail.*

Ferruginous Pygmy-Owl. *Glaucidium brasilianum.* K2b7. <u>Tecolotillo Rayado</u>
US-SAm. <u>Resident up to 4000', P, A, Y</u>. Common; humid forest-edge, scrub woods, river-bank forest, thickets. V: Like N.P.-Owl, but faster; may begin with *cwirt* notes. *Pl.15.* 7" *Like* N. and L. Pygmy-Owl, *but has faint crown-<u>streaks</u>, 6 to 8 tail-bars.*

Elf Owl. *Micrathene whitneyi.* K2b19. <u>Tecolote Enano</u>
US-M. <u>Resident up to 6000', BC, ncP, ncH</u>. Rare; semi-desert scrub with large cacti. *Pl.15.* 6" *Grayish brown above, with white nape-band; whitish and buffy brown below; no ear-tufts; tail much shorter than* Pygmy-Owl's.

Burrowing Owl. *Athene cunicularia.* K2b23. <u>Lechucilla Llanera</u>
Can-SAm,x.B,N. <u>Resident or winter visitor, up to 6000', BC, P, ncH, ncA, Y</u>. Rare; usually on ground or post in grassy plains, dry brush, rocky areas; often active by day. *Pl.15.* 9" *Reddish to grayish, spotted above; whitish below, with barred sides and flanks; black band across white throat; legs long; tail short.* V: a loud piping *toot-too.*

Wood (Mottled) **Owl.** *Ciccaba virgata.* K2a85. <u>Mochuelo Café</u>
M-SAm. <u>Resident up to 7000', P, ncH (Chihuahua to México), A, Y</u>. Rare+, lowlands; very rare, highlands; humid forest, openings, and partial clearings, borders, orchards, plantations, woods. V: a slow descending, burred *hroot, hroot, hroot, hroot.* *Pl.14.* 14" *Blackish brown above, mottled and dotted; buffy or tawny below, with heavy streaks; white- or buff-rimmed facial disks; eyes brown; tail 4-or-5-barred.*

Black-and-white Owl. *Ciccaba nigrolineata.* K2a86. <u>Mochuelo Zarado</u>
M-SAm. <u>Resident up to 4000', csA (San Luis Potosí to Quintana Roo)</u>. Rare; dense humid forest, tall river-border woodlands, small openings, borders, or partial clearings. *Pl.14.* 15" *Black above, but hind-neck barred with whitish; narrowly barred black-and-white underparts; usually only 4 or 5 narrow white tail-bars; no ear tufts.*

Spotted Owl. *Strix occidentalis.* K2a79. <u>Tecolote Manchado</u>
Can-M. <u>Resident, 4000 to 8000',ncH (Sonora+Nuevo León to Michoacán)</u>. Rare; highland pine or pine-oak forests. V: like the first three or four notes of Barred Owl's call. *Pl.15.* 19" *Like* Barred O., *but has large whitish spots above, not* bars; *and is barred and spotted below, not* streaked.

Barred Owl. *Strix varia.* K2a80. <u>Tecolote Listado</u>
  Barred group. *Strix varia varia.* <u>Tecolote Listado</u>
  AK-M. <u>Resident, 5000 to 8000', ncH (Durango + San Luis Potosí to Oaxaca)</u>.

Rare; pine or pine-oak forests. V: a loud *ho-hoo ho-hoo, ho-hoo ho-hoo-ah.*
Pl.15. 20" *Brownish gray, barred above and on upper breast; rest of underparts heavily streaked; no* ear-tufts; *iris brown.*
Fulvous group. *Strix varia fulvescens.* Lechuzón
M,G,ES,H. Resident, 7000 to 10,000', sH. Rare; open pine, or humid pine-oak forest. V: a loud four-noted *huho, huhoo;* may be repeated a second time quickly.
Pl.14. 17" *Like* Barred group, *but much more reddish-brown and buff or tawny above and below.*
Long-eared Owl. *Asio otus.* K2c5. Lechuza Barranquera
Can-M. Resident up to 6000', nBC, nh (Coahuila), na (Nuevo León); winter visitor cP, ncH. Rare; river valleys, pine or pine-oak forest. V: often three low-pitched hoots.
Pl.15. 15" *Like* Great Horned O., *but smaller and more slender; ear-tufts proportionally longer, and attached closer to the center of the (reddish) face.*
Stygian Owl. *Asio stygius.* K2c4. Lechuza Fusca
M,G,B,N,SAm. Resident, 5000 to 10,000', H; and near sea level Y (Quintana Roo: Cozumel I.). Very rare; dense mountain forest; dense low woods. V: *hoo*, or *hoo-hoo.*
Pl.14. 17" *Like* Striped O., *but is duller buff and has heavier black streaks below; and its head, ear-tufts, and upperparts are blackish, with some buff spots and streaks.*
Short-eared Owl. *Asio flammeus.* K2c7. Tecolote Orejas Cortas
AK-M,G. Winter visitor BC, nP, ncH, ncA. Rare; grassy, open country; marshy, grassy, or sedgy fields; often hunts in daylight, flight buoyant and somewhat erratic.
Pl.15. 16" *Streaked tawny and brown above and below; but whitish belly and untacs; sooty around eyes; white between eyes; ear-tufts very short, close together.*
Striped Owl. *Rhinoptynx clamator.* K2c1. Tecolote Gritón
M-SAm. Resident up to 3000', csA (Veracruz, Oaxaca, Chiapas). Rare; patchy trees, thickets, dense humid forest. V: rapid series of rather rough notes, *ho-ho-ho-ho-ho-ho.*
Pl.14. 14" *Streaked dark brown and tawny above; tawny buff below, with "sharp" brown streaks; face white, black-bordered; ear-tufts long, near center of face.*
Northern Saw-whet Owl. *Aegolius acadicus.* K2b25. Tecolotito Cabezón
AK-M. Resident, 6000 to 9500', ncH. Very rare, local; mountain forest of fir, pine-oak or pine. V: like Ferruginous Pygmy-Owl's, but slightly slower, more mellow.
Pl.15. 7" *Ad: Dark brown above, with white spots; whitish below, with rufous streaks; head appears square; tail short, barred. Juv: Reddish brown above, spotted; head and breast chocolate brown; belly and untacs tawny rufous; white between eyes.*
Unspotted Saw-whet Owl. *Aegolius ridgwayi.* K2b26. Tecolotito Volcanero
M,G,ES,CR. Resident, 7000 to 10,000', sH. Very rare; pine, pine-oak or cloud forest.
Pl.14. 7" *Like* Northern Saw-whet Owl, *but no spots on upperparts; no bars on tail; toes partly bare. Juv: Rich brown above, buffy below.*

NIGHTJARS - CAPRIMULGIDAE - TAPACAMINOS, PACHACUAS
Eleven species, mostly residents; widespread Mexico; very short weak legs, short neck, large head, pointed wing, tail medium, bill very short and weak, but mouth large; fliers, catch insects in flight; semi-desert to humid forest borders; world temperate, tropical. Distinguish by voice, white in tail or wings. **Plates 14 and 15.**
Lesser Nighthawk. *Chordeiles acutipennis.* T4a4. Tapacamino Halcón
US-SAm. Resident up to 8000', sBC, ncH, P (Sinaloa to Chiapas), csA, Y; summer resident nBC, nA. Common; scrub woods, semi-desert. V: low-pitched, quiet tremolo.
Pl.15. 8" *M: Mottled grayish above; buffy-gray-barred below; white throat, barred tail; white bar near wing-tip crosses 4 outermost primaries. F: Wing-tip-bar buffy.*
Common Nighthawk. *Chordeiles minor.* T4a5. Tapacamino Zumbón
US-SAm. Summer resident up to 6000', sP, nH(Sonora to Durango), A, Y; transient csH. Rare+; open areas, brushy short-grass fields; flies high. V: a nasal, rasping *peent.*
Pl.15. 9" *Like* Lesser N., *but darker and grayer; white bar farther from wing-tip,*

crosses 5 outermost primaries; may have unbarred whitish lower belly and untacs;
Pauraque. *Nyctidromus albicollis.* T4b8. <u>Pochocuate</u>
US-SAm. <u>Resident up to 4000', P, A, Y</u>. Common; patchy farms, brushy fields,
hedgerows, dirt roads, borders. V: a repeated, rasping whistle, *pur-weer* or *wee-o.*
*11" M: Mottled grayish brown, buff, and black above; barred blackish and dull tawny
below; white patches on tail; white bar on wing. F: little white in tail; wing-bar buff.*

Common Poorwill. *Phalaenoptilus nuttallii.* T4b9. <u>Pachacua Común</u>
Can-M. <u>Resident up to 8000', BC, nP (Sonora), nH, nA</u>. Rare+; scrub, semi-desert,
open rocky, grassy, brushy plains, borders. V: a mellow whistle, *pur-will* or *cor-yillup.*
*8" Mostly mottled gray above and below. M: Broad white bar on blackish throat and
upper breast; white tail-corners. F: Throat-bar buff; tail-patches buff or whitish.*

Eared Poorwill. *Nyctiphrynus mcleodii.* T4b12. <u>Pachacua Orejón</u>
M. <u>Resident, 4000 to 6000', Chihuahua to Oaxaca (ncP, ncH)</u>. Rare, local; mountain
pine woods and pine-oak forest, open woods and borders. V: a loud, abrupt, *pyeeoo.*
*Pl.14. 7" M: Mostly dark brown and tawny above and below; with black-spotted
scapulars, white-spotted wing-coverts, and white band on throat; tail-corners white;
feathers of upper breast and side of crown elongated. F: Similar but more reddish.*
Yucatan Poorwill. *Nyctiphrynus yucatanicus.* T4b13. <u>Zumbador</u>
M,G,B. <u>Resident, near sea level, Y</u>. Rare; farms, fields, thorny woods, borders. V:
may <u>not</u> be the rolling*whee-o-wee* or *puh-ree-uh-ree* usually attributed to this species;
<u>may be</u> the abrupt *whee-oo* or *will,* long thought to be the call of the Yucatan form of the
Chip-Willow (see Pierson, J.E. MBA "Bulletin Board". Vol. 1, No.86-1:pp.3-4.)
Pl.14. 7" Like Eared P., *but much darker and more mottled above and below.*

Chuck-will's-widow. *Caprimulgus carolinensis.* T4b15. <u>Pachacua de Norte</u>
US-SAm,x.B. <u>Transient and winter visitor cP, ncA, Y</u>. Rare; thickets, undergrowth in
humid forest or woods, river-edge woods, borders, hedgerows. Seldom calls in winter.
*11" Mottled dark buffy reddish brown; white throat-bar; two large tail-patches white
above, buffy below. F: No tail-patches. V: a loud whistle yuc-wheeoo-witto.*
Chip-willow (Tawny-collared Nightjar). *Caprimulgus salvini.* T4b19. <u>Papavientos</u>
M,G,B,N. <u>Resident, near sea level, A, Y</u>. Rare+; semi-desert, dry scrubby woods; or
patchy farms, fields, thickets and borders in more humid areas. V: a clear, loud,
yip-willow, or (Yucatan form) may be a rolling *yip-willo-ree.* See Yucatan Poorwill.
*Pl.14. 9" M: Mostly mottled rich blackish brown; hind-neck collar reddish buff; tail
blackish with broadly white corners. F: Similar but tail all-dark.*
Tucuchillo (Buff-coll. Nightj.). *Caprimulgus ridgwayi.* T4b21. <u>Préstame-tu-cuchillo</u>
US,M,G,H,N. <u>Resident up to 6000', P, H</u>. Rare; thickets, borders, brushy fields,
pine-oak forest. V: rapid chatter, *cu-cu-cu-cu-cu-cu-whee-o,* rising then falling sharply.
*9" M: Mostly dark grayish brown above, paler below; reddish buff hind-neck collar;
tail barred, with large white corner-patches. F: Similar but no white tail-patches.*
Whip-poor-will. *Caprimulgus vociferus.* T4b22. <u>Cuerporruín</u>
Can-Pan. <u>Resident, 5000 to 10,000', H; resident or visitor sBC, nP, A</u>. Rare+;
hedgerows, forest borders. V: a loud, rythmic, repeated whistle, *whip-pur-wee-o.*
*10" M: Mottled grayish brown above; barred brownish gray below; throat-bar and
very <u>large</u> tail-corner-patches white. F: Throat-bar and very <u>small</u> tail-patches buffy.*
Pit-sweet. *Caprimulgus maculicaudus.* T4b28. <u>Tapacamino Enano</u>
M,H,N,SAm. <u>Resident or summer resident up to 1500', sA (Veracruz, Oaxaca,
Chiapas)</u>. Rare; small-tree-dotted savannas. V: a single, very high-pitched *keep-sweep.*
*Pl.14. 7" M: Mottled blackish brown above; reddish nape-collar; mottled buff and
black below, but plain buff lower belly and untacs; tail black with
white tail-corners and white spots below. F: Similar, but no white on tail.*

POTOOS - NYCTIBIIDAE - JOJUS
Jamaican Potoo. *Nyctibius jamaicensis.* T3a4.   Jojú
M-CR. Resident up to 3000', P (Sinaloa to Chiapas), A. Rare; borders, shrubby
fields, pastures; perches upright on posts, snags. V: a loud *baw*; loud rasping notes.
*Pl. 14. 14" Mottled, blotched and streaked brownish gray and blackish; more
blackish blotches on breast; head striped black, brown, and whitish; tail long; mouth
large, but bill small; iris yellow, but eye glows red in light-beam.*

SWIFTS - APODIDAE - VENCEJOS
Nine residents or visitors; widespread Mexico; small to medium small; very short
legs, weak feet, short neck, pointed wings, short to long tail; short bill; fliers, over
many habitats; world temperate and tropical. Distinguish by pattern, voice, tail. **Pl.21.**
Black Swift. *Cypseloides niger.* U3a8.   Vencejo Negro
AK-CR,x.B,ES. Summer resident, 5000 to 11,000', H (Durango to Chiapas);
transient nBC, nP. Rare; over open areas, dry rocky slopes, shrubby grassy plains.
Pl.16. 7" M: Black; tail medium, notched or square. F: Belly scalloped with white.
Chestnut-collared Swift. *Cypseloides rutilus.* U3a1.   Vencejillo Cuellicastaño
M-SAm,x.B,N. Summer resident, 5000 to 8000', H (Durango to Chiapas); visitor nP
(Sinaloa). Rare; over open or wooded slopes or deep ravines. V: a rasping *zee-zee-zee.*
*Pl.21. 6" Blackish-brown; appears round-headed. M: Has inconspicuous broad,
dark reddish brown full-collar. F: No reddish brown collar.*
White-collared Swift. *Streptoprocne zonaris.* U3a10.   Vencejo Listado
M-SAm. Resident up to 4500', P (Nayarit to Chiapas), A. Rare+; cliffs, caves, over
wet fields, stream valleys, humid forest, partial clearings. V: a loud *cleek, cleek, cleek.*
Pl.21. 8" Blackish, except white full-collar (broader below); tail medium, notched.
White-naped Swift. *Streptoprocne semicollaris.* U3a12.   Vencejo Nuquiblanco
M. Resident or visitor up to 11,000', P (irregular Sinaloa to Chiapas), H (irregular
Chihuahua to Chiapas). Rare; over deep ravines, wooded slopes, or brushy flatlands.
Pl.21. 9" Blackish; except white nape-band; tail square or slightly notched. V: a
harsh, extended *chi-ik, chi-ik.*
Chimney Swift. *Chaetura pelagica.* U3b43.   Vencejillo de Chimenea
Can-SAm. Transient A,Y. Rare+; varied habitats. V: notes louder than Vaux's S's.
Pl.16. 5" Blackish brown; throat pale gray; tail short, square, spiny. See Vaux's S.
Vaux's Swift. *Chaetura vauxi.* U3b44.   Vencejillo Común
AK-SAm. Resident up to 4000', P (Sinaloa to Chiapas), A, Y; transient or winter
visitor nBC, H. Common; over most habitats, especially clearings, openings, orchards.
Pl.16. 4" Like Chimney S., *but paler below and on rump; throat whitish (but both*
Chimney S. and Vaux's S., *may be blackened with soot); tail short, square, spiny.*
White-throated Swift. *Aeronautes saxatalis.* U3b48.   Vencejo Listado
Can-ES+H. Resident up to 9000', BC, nP (Sonora to Sinaloa), H. Rare; over variety
of habitats, usually in rugged terrain, deep ravines, wooded or open mountain slopes.
Pl.16. 6 1/2" Black-and-white like Geronimo S., *but has white line over eye; breast
and center of belly are white; and tail is much shorter, only* slightly *forked.*
Cayenne (L.Sw.-t.) Swift. *Panyptila cayennensis.* U3b55.   Vencejo Gola Blanca
M-SAm,x.ES. Resident, near sea level, sP (Chiapas), csA (Veracruz to Chiapas). Very
rare; high over humid forest, clearings, borders, and openings; long fibrous tube nest.
Pl.21. 5" Like Geronimo S., *but much smaller;* flight more like that of *Chaetura sp.*
Geronimo (Gr.Sw-t.) Swift. *Panyptila sanctihieronymi.* U3b54. Vencejo Tijereta
M,G,H,N. Resident, 2000 to 6000', P (Nayarit to Chiapas). Very rare; most often in
very acrobatic flight over rugged terrain - canyons, steep slopes. V: a plaintive *tyee-ew.*
*Pl.21. 8" Glossy black; but throat, sides of neck, upper breast, flank-patch and
narrow stripe on hind-border of long slender wing, white; tail long, deeply forked.*

HUMMINGBIRDS - TROCHILIDAE - CHUPAFLORES

Fifty-four species, almost all residents; widespread; very small size; very short legs, weak feet, short neck, large head, pointed wings, short to long tail; short to long, slender, bill, straight or decurved; fliers, semi-desert to humid forest; new world termperate, tropical; male and female plumages in some. Distinguish by colors, patterns, tail length and shape, bill length and shape and color. **Plates 16, 18, 19.**

Long-tailed Hermit. *Phaethornis superciliosus.* U1a16.   Ermitaño Grande
M-SAm,x.ES. Resident up to 4000', P (Nayarit to Chiapas), csA. Rare+; undergrowth of humid forest, river-edge woods, ravines, often near streams. V: a rasping *creep.*
Pl.18. 6" Greenish back; blackish ear-patch; buffy eye-line and malar streak; mostly buffy below; grayer on throat and breast; bill very long, decurved; tips of feathers of very long graduated tail form a whitish "Y". See smaller Little Hermit.

Little Hermit. *Phaethornis longuemareus.* U1a36.   Ermitaño Chico
M-SAm,x.ES. Resident up to 3000', csA. Rare+; undergrowth, dense humid forest.
Pl.18. 3 1/2" Crown and back bronzy; rump and uptacs dark rufous; tawny buff below; blackish ear-patch with buffy border above and below; bill very long, slightly decurved; tail graduated, long-wedge-shaped. See Long-tailed Hermit.

Cuvier's (Scaly-br.) Hummingbird. *Phaeochroa cuvierii.* U1a38.   Colibrí de Cuvier
M-SAm,x.ES. Resident or visitor, sA (Chiapas). Very rare; woods-edge, river borders.
Pl.18. 5" M: Greenish above; throat, breast scaled dull greenish; tail black below, broadly white-cornered; belly buff. F: Belly whitish. See White-necked Jacobin.

Wedge-tailed Saberwing. *Campylopterus curvipennis.* U1a41.   Fandanguero Gritón
Wedge-tailed group. *Campylopterus c. curvipennis.*   Fandanguero Gritón
M,G,B,H. Resident up to 4000', A, Y. Rare+; humid forest, borders, gardens.
Pl.18. 5 to 5 1/2" Greenish above, with violet forehead; pale gray to whitish below; tail blackish, rather long, wedge-shaped; bill long straight. Smaller, shorter-tailed than Long-tailed group.
Long-tailed group. *Campylopterus c. excellens.*   Fandanguero Cola Larga
M. Resident up to 4000', cA (s.Veracruz). Rare; dense forest, borders, openings.
5 1/2 to 6" Like Wedge-tailed S., *but larger, and longer-tailed.*

Rufous Saberwing. *Campylopterus rufus.* U1a43.   Fandanguero Rojizo
M,G,ES. Resident, 3000 to 6000', sP. Rare; cloud-forest, openings, coffee fincas.
Pl.18. 5" Greenish above; dark patch through eye; rufous below; tail square, rufous from below, black bar near tip; bill long, slightly decurved, black. See Little Hermit.

Violet Saberwing. *Campylopterus hemileucurus.* U1a46.   Fandanguero Morado
M-Pan. Resident, 1500 to 6000', csP (Guerrero to Chiapas), csA. Rare; dense undergrowth of humid forest, overgrown coffee plantations, small shrubby openings.
Pl.18. 5 1/2" Bill medium-long, strongly decurved. M: Dark purple, appears black in poor light; blackish tail with very broad white corners. F: Greenish above; pale gray below; small violet throat-patch; tail black below with prominent white corners.

White-necked Jacobin. *Florisuga mellivora.* U1a52.   Chupaflor Coliblanco
M-SAm,x.ES. Resident, near sea level, csA. Rare; humid forest, borders, lush thickets.
Pl.18. 4 1/2" Bill medium, black, straight. M: Dark blue head, throat, and chest; white hind-neck band; bright green back and rump; white belly, untacs, most of tail. F: Like female Cuvier's H., *but more contrastingly scaled blackish or greenish on white; and white tail-corners much smaller, on greenish, not black, tail.*

Green Violet-ear. *Colibri thalassinus.* U1a55.   Verdemar
M-SAm,x.N. Res., 6000 to 10,000', H (Guanajuato+San Luis Potosí to Chiapas). Rare+; humid mountain pine-oak, fir, or pine forest, small openings or partial clearings.
Pl.18. 4 1/2" Bill medium, slightly decurved. M: Mostly dark iridescent green, with purplish ear-patch and center-breast-patch; buffy untacs; dull blackish band on bluish tail. F: Like male, but duller; may not have purplish center-breast-patch.

Prevost's (Gr.-br.) **Mango.** *Anthracothorax prevostii.* U1a59.   Mango de Prevost
M-SAm. Resident up to 4000', sP, A, Y. Rare+; humid open woods, borders, gardens.
*Pl.18. 4 1/2" Bill black, medium long, slightly decurved. M: Mostly bright
green, with darker ear-patch; black throat- and breast-streak; tail bright purple. F:
Like male, but white below, with jagged black median stripe; dark tail white-tipped.*
Abeille's (Em.-ch.) **Hummingbird.** *Abeillia abeillei.* U1a70.   Colibrí de Abeille
M,G,ES,H,N. Resident or visitor, up to 6000', sP, sA. Very rare;humid forest, edges.
*Pl.18. 3" White spot or short line behind eye; dark, square tail gray-tipped; short,
straight, black bill. M: Iridescent green; throat brighter green; breast black. F: Bright
greenish above; whitish or pale gray below.*
Rufous-crested Coquette. *Lophornis delattrei.* U1a75.   Chupamirto Penachudo
M,CR-SAm. Resident, 1000 to 5000', cP (Guerrero).   Very rare; dense humid forest.
*Pl.18. 2 1/2" Bronzy above; short, straight bill; buff or whitish bar on lower back.
M: Elongated rufous crest-feathers; red bill, black-tipped; grayish below, bright green
gorget; square, rufous tail. F: Mostly grayish buff below, but throat white; crown
rufous, not crested; bill dark; tail square, blackish, with cinnamon tip.*
Black-crested Coquette. *Paphosia helenae.* U1a79.   Chupamirto Cornudo
M-CR,x.ES. Resident up to 4000', sA.   Rare; humid forest, second growth, borders.
*Pl.18. 2 1/2" Bronzy above; bill short, straight; white bar on lower back. M: Long
black crest; chin broadly green with buff and black throat-plumes; bronzy rufous
speckles on white breast and belly; tail short, reddish brown. F: No crest; buffy
below with many dark breast-speckles; tail reddish brown, with broad black bar.*
Fork-tailed Emerald. *Chlorostilbon canivetii.* U1a89.   Esmeralda Verde
M-CR. Resident up to 6000', P, H (Durango to Chiapas), A, Y. Common; humid to
rather dry forest, partial clearings, borders, gardens, orchards; often perched in open.
*Pl.18. 3 1/2" M: Bright iridescent green, with brighter throat; bill short, straight, red
at base; black-tipped; tail black, deeply forked. F: Dull greenish above; whitish
below; tail slightly forked, with white corners; white line behind eye; black ear-patch.*
Dusky Hummingbird. *Cynanthus sordidus.* U1a99.   Chupamirto Prieto
M. Resident, 5000 to 8000', cH (Jalisco+Hidalgo to Oaxaca).   Rare+, irregular;
river-border woods, tree-dotted fields, gardens, parks, orchards, overgrown vacant lots.
*Pl.18. 3 1/2" Like female Broad-billed H., but has slender bill; darker underparts;
and duller, more bronzy green, not blackish blue, tail; and M: no small gray
tail-corner-patches; and F: rather large white tail-corners.*
Broad-billed Hummingbird. *Cynanthus latirostris.* U1a100. Chupaflor Piquiancho
US-M. Resident up to 7000', P, ncH, nA. Rare+; gardens, woods-edge, thickets.
*Pl.16. 3 1/2" Bill mostly broad (and red), with black tip; tail blackish blue. M:
Iridescent green; gorget greenish blue; untacs pale gray or whitish; tail forked. F:
Greenish above; pale gray below; tail square, with small gray corners.*
Blue-crowned Woodnymph. *Thalurania colombica.* U1a102.   Ninfa del Bosque
M-P,x.ES. Resident, 1000 to 4000', ncP (Nayarit to Colima).   Rare; low in woods.
*Pl.18. 4" Bill medium, black, slightly decurved; tail slightly notched. M: Dark
iridescent green above, but forehead and fore-crown violet-blue; blackish below, but
gorget to center of breast bright bluish green; tail blackish. F: Greenish above; pale
grayish below, with dull gray-green breast; tail dark with whitish tail-corners.*
Blue-throated Goldentail. *Hylocharis eliciae.* U1a114.   Chupaflor Colidorado
M-P,x.B. Resident up to 3000', sP; visitor csA. Rare; forest, river-border woods.
*Pl.18. 3 1/2" Iridescent green; with reddish bronze uptacs; cinnamon-brown untacs;
iridescent greenish gold tail; purplish blue throat; bill straight, red with black tip.*
White-eared Hummingbird. *Hylocharis leucotis.* U1a113.   Chupaflor Orejiblanco
US-N,x.B. Resident, 4000 to 12,000', H.   Common; gardens, woods, dense forest.
*Pl.16. 3 1/2" Square tail; slender bill red with black tip; white line behind eye. M:
Iridescent green; crown broadly dark purple; blackish ear-patch; bright green throat;*

pale gray untacs. F: Similar, but crown and upperparts dull greenish; whitish below, with variable green-speckling on throat, sides, and flanks.
Xantus's Hummingbird. *Hylocharis xantusii.* U1a113.   Chuparrosa de Xantus
M. Resident up to 6000', BC. Common; semi-desert, gardens, borders, open forest.
Pl.18. 3 1/2" Like White-eared H.*, but M: forehead and chin black; breast, belly, untacs, and tail rich rufous below; and F: all-rufous underparts; tail rufous below, with dull black bar near tip.*
White-bellied Emerald. *Amazilia candida.* U1a134.   Esmeralda Petiblanca
M-CR,x.ES. Resident up to 4000', sP, csA, Y. Rare+; humid forest, openings, edge.
Pl.18. 3 1/2" Greenish crown and upperparts; clear white below, except mottled green sides; tail grayish, dull dark band near tip; bill medium-short, dark above, red below. See Azure-crowned H.
Azure-crowned Hummingbird. *Am.cyanocephala.* U1a146. Chupaflor Cabeza Azul
M-N. Resident, 2000 to 6000', A. Common; mostly cloud forest, gardens, borders.
Pl.18. 4" Like White-bellied Emerald, *but crown iridescent blue; sides more broadly (and more grayish) green; no dark tail-band; and bill darker, mostly blackish.*
Berylline Hummingbird. *Amazilia beryllina.* U1a148.   Chupaflor de Berilo
M,G,ES,H. Resident, 3000 to 10,000', P, H, csA. Common; pine woods, borders.
Pl.18. 3 1/2" M: Iridescent green; folded wings, uptacs, and tail rufous; lower belly and untacs dull rufous; bill reddish below, dark above. F: Belly and untacs grayish.
Blue-tailed Hummingbird. *Amazilia cyanura.* U1a149.   Chupaflor Coliazul
M-CR,x.B. Resident up to 5000', sP (Chiapas). Common; humid forest, *cafetales.*
Pl.19. 3 3/4" Bright iridescent green above and below; with coppery rump; blackish blue tail and uptacs; dark purplish folded wings with rufous patch (secondaries); untacs whitish; bill medium long, straight, pinkish below, blackish above.
Rufous-tailed Hummingbird. *Amazilia tzacatl.* U1a156.   Chupaflor Pechigris
M-SAm,x.ES. Resident up to 4000', A, Y. Rare+; borders, gardens, thickets, forest.
Pl.18. 3 1/2" Iridescent green, but lower breast and belly gray; untacs, uptacs, and tail rich reddish brown, the tail tinged purple; wings blackish; red bill black-tipped.
Buff-bellied Hummingbird. *Amazilia yucatanensis.* U1a155.   Chupaflor Yucateco
US,M,G,B,H. Resident up to 4000', sP, A, Y. Common; woods, *ranchos*, gardens.
Pl.16. 3 1/2" Like Rufous-tailed H., but buffy rufous (not gray) lower breast, belly, and untacs; and slightly notched tail tinged bronzy green, not purplish.
Cinnamon Hummingbird. *Amazilia rutila.* U1a154.   Chupaflor Canelo
M-CR. Resident up to 4000', P (Sinaloa to Chiapas), Y. Common; scrub, borders.
Pl.19. 4" Dull greenish above; uptacs, tail (darker near tip), sides of face, and underparts rich reddish brown; bill bright red, black-tipped.
Violet-crowned Hummingbird. *Amaz.violiceps.* U1a161. Chupaflor Corona Azul
US-M. Resident, 1000 to 7000', ncP, ncH. Rare+; scrubby open woods, river borders.
Pl.16. 4" Contrasty white below, dull greenish bronze above (tail greener); crown broadly violet (dull in some immatures); bill red, black tipped. See Green-fronted H.
Green-fronted Hummingbird.*Amazilia viridifrons.*U1a160.Chupaflor CoronaVerde
M. Resident, 2000 to 5000', csP (Guerrero to Chiapas). Rare+; open woods, parks.
Pl.19. 4" Like Violet-crowned H., *(especially dull-crowned immatures) but crown green or blackish; uptacs and tail rufous-bronze, not greenish; sides gray or reddish.*
Stripe-tailed Hummingbird. *Eupherusa eximia.* U1a163.   Chupaflor Cola Rayada
M-P,x.ES. Resident, 1000 to 4000', csA. Rare+; dense forest, deep humid ravines.
Pl.19. 3 1/2" Bill black, medium; rufous patch (secondaries) on folded blackish wing; tail (from below) contrasty white-based, black-tipped. M: Iridescent green; lower belly buff; untacs white. F: Pale gray below; greenish sides. See Oaxaca H.
Oaxaca (Blvc.) **Hummingbird.***Eupherusa cyanophrys.* U1a164.   Chupaflor de Oaxaca
M. Resident, 2500 to 7000', s.Oaxaca (cP,cH). Common; a few areas of humid forest.

Pl.19. 3 1/2" Like Stripe-tailed H*., but M: crown iridescent blue; belly all green, not partly buffy; tail mostly whitish below, shading to gray tip; and F: paler gray below; tail appearing all-white or whitish below.*
Guerrero (Wh.-t.) **Hummingbird.** *Euph.poliocerca.* U1a162. <u>Chupaflor de Guerrero</u> **M.** <u>Resident, 4000 to 6000', cP (Guerrero+w.Oaxaca).</u> Rare+, local; humid forest.
Pl.19. 3 1/2" Like Oaxaca H*., but crown <u>green,</u> in male and female.*
Green-throated Mountain-gem.*Lampo.viridipallens.*U1a174. <u>Chupaflor Montañero</u>
M,G,ES,H. <u>Resident, 4000 to 10,000', sH.</u> Rare+; high pine-oak or cloud forest.
Pl.19. 4" M: Bright green crown, to greenish back, to coppery rump to black uptacs and tail; underparts whitish, throat speckled green; sides mottled green; ear-patch black; line behind eye white; bill medium, straight. F: Similar, but uniformly bright green above; tail has white sides; no speckles on throat.
Cazique (A.-th.) **Hummingbird.***Lampornis amethystinus.*U1a173.<u>Chupaflor Amatista</u>
M,G,ES,H. <u>Resident, 3500 to 12,000', H (Nayarit+Tamaulipas to Chiapas); winter visitor P, A.</u> Rare+; lower levels in humid pine-oak, fir, or cloud forest, or openings.
Pl.19. 5" Bill medium-short, black, straight. M: Iridescent green above and on sides; black ear-patch; bright red throat; blackish gray breast, belly, untacs; gray-cornered black tail. F: Similar, but paler below; throat rich buff.
Blue-throated Hummingbird.*Lampo.clemenciae.* U1a172. <u>Chupaflor GargantaAzul</u>
US-M. <u>Resident, summer resident, or winter visitor, 3000 to 13,000', ncP, ncH, ncA.</u>
Rare+, local; high-mountain meadows, brushy ravines, borders, open pine forest.
Pl.16. 5" Bill medium-long, slightly decurved, black. M: Mostly bronzy green above; large white corners on rounded black tail; blue throat; gray breast and belly; white line behind eye; black ear-patch. F: Similar, but throat pale gray.
Garnet-throated Hummingbird.*Lamprolaima rhami.* U1a178. <u>Chupaflor Alicastaño</u>
M,G,ES,H. <u>Resident, 4000 to 10,000', csH (México to Chiapas).</u> Rare; dense forest.
Pl.19. 4 1/2" Shiny green above; rufous wings; short black bill; blackish purple tail; underparts and border of red throat, black; chest violet. F: Duller; tail gray-cornered.
Rivoli's (Magnif.) **Hummingbird.** *Eugenes fulgens.* U1a194. <u>Chupaflor Magnífico</u>
M-P. <u>Resident, 5000 to 10,000', H.</u> Rare+; dry rocky slopes, pine-oak or pine woods.
Pl.16. 4 1/2" M: Dark green above; crown purple, tail and wings blackish; throat bright green; mostly blackish below, but bright green throat. F: Dull greenish above; tail greenish, black bar near tip, gray corners; underparts pale gray; throat speckled.
Purple-crowned Fairy. *Heliothrix barroti.* U1a278. <u>Chupaflor Pechiblanco</u>
M-SAm,x.ES. <u>Resident near sea level, sA (Tabasco+Chiapas).</u> Very rare; dense forest.
Pl.19. 5 or 6" Shining pale bluish green above, but black central tail-feathers; underparts and tail (below) clear white; black patch through eye; short, straight, black bill. M: Crown purple. F: Similar, but crown green; tail much longer, graduated.
Long-billed Starthroat. *Heliomaster longirostris.* U1a284. <u>Chupaflor Piquilargo</u>
M-SAm,x.B. <u>Resident up to 5000', csP (Oaxaca to Chiapas), csA.</u> Rare+; dense forest.
Pl.19. 4 1/2" Like Plain-capped S*., but white line behind eye shorter; tail shorter; folded wings shorter, not reaching end of tail; base of tail (below) greenish, blending to black, with small pale tail-corners; untacs sharply scalloped white on blackish; and M: crown bright blue; not as much black on chin and lower throat; and F: throat blackish, may have some purplish speckles.*
Plain-capped Starthroat. *Heliomaster constantii.* U1a283. <u>Chupaflor Pochotero</u>
M-CR,x.B. <u>Resident up to 5000', P.</u> Rare+; scrubby dry woods, borders, hedgerows.
Pl.19. 4 1/2" Bill long, rather stout, straight, black; tail rather long, pale gray at base, then contrasty black bar, and prominent whitish corners; folded wings reach beyond end of tail; untacs scalloped whitish on gray. M: Greenish above, bill to tail, with a whitish streak down center of rump; white malar streak and line behind eye; black ear-patch; blackish chin and upper throat; bright red lower throat; grayish breast and belly. F: Similar, but entire throat may be mostly blackish, with little or no red.

Slender Sheartail. *Doricha enicura.* U1a291. Chupaflor Tijera
M,G,ES,H. Resident, 4000 to 7000', sH. Rare+; humid forest, lush borders, *cafetales.*
Pl.19. 4 1/2 or 2 1/2" Bill medium somewhat decurved, black. M: *Shiny green above; very deeply forked tail all-black; white below, except violet gorget and bronzy green sides.* F: *Buff below, and line behind eye; black mask; slightly forked tail rufous at base, then a black bar, and white tip.* See Dupont's H.

Mexican Sheartail. *Doricha eliza.* U1a292. Chupaflor Cola Hendida
M. Resident, near sea level, cA (c.Veracruz), Y (Yucatán and Quintana Roo). Very rare (cA), common (Y); coastal: low thorny woods, brushy fields, hedgerows, gardens.
Pl.19. 4 or 2 1/2" Bill long, slightly decurved, black. M: *Shiny green above; white below with broadly green sides, and purplish red gorget, with pointed corners; tail-feathers square-tipped, black with brown stripe.* F: *Greenish above; mostly white below; rounded tail buffy at base (below), then broadly black, with white corners.*

Dupont's (Sp.-tail.) Hummingbird.*Tilmatura dupontii.* U1a293. Chupaflor Moscón
M-N,x.B. Resident, 3000 to 7000', P (Sinaloa to Chiapas), csH (Jalisco+Veracruz to Chiapas). Rare; parks, gardens, open pine-oak woods, humid-forest openings, *cafetales.* Drifting, super-smooth flight is like that of a large bee; tail of male "sparkles".
Pl.19. 4" or 2 1/2" Bill short, straight, black. M: *Mostly shiny green; white side-of-rump patch; blue throat; white chest; tail very deeply forked, feathers black, some brown, and white-tipped.* F: *Greenish above; buff patch each side of rump; darker rufous below, and straighter-billed than female* Slender or Mexican Sheartail, or Lucifer or Beautiful H.; *tail notched, black (below) with white corners.*

Lucifer Hummingbird. *Calothorax lucifer.* U1a295. Chupaflor de Golilla
US-M. Resident, 5000 to 8000', ncH (Chihuahua+Nuevo León to D.F.), casual winter visitor nP, sH. Rare; dry brushy grassland, open pine or pine-oak woods, borders.
Pl.16. 3 1/2 or 3" Greenish above; bill medium, black, decurved. M: *Whitish below with long-cornered gorget; broadly grayish green sides and flanks; tail black, medium long, deeply forked.* F: *Pale buffy below; whitish untacs; tail double-rounded, with rufous base (below) then broadly black, then white corners; pale streak behind eye.* See Beautiful H., female Dupont's H., and Slender Sheartail.

Beautiful Hummingbird. *Calothorax pulcher.* U1a296. Chupaflor Barbón
M. Resident, 4500 to 8000', csH (Guerrero+Morelos to Chiapas). Rare; brushy areas.
Pl.19. 3 1/2 or 3" Like Lucifer H. (Pl.16), *but bill shorter, more slender, nearly straight; and M: tail longer, outer feathers broader, more rounded-tipped; and F: folded wings longer (reach end of tail -* Lucifer's *do not).*

Ruby-throated Hummingbird. *Archilochus colubris.* U1a297. Chupaflor Rubí
Can-Pan. Winter visitor P, H, A, Y. Rare; mixed farms, gardens, woodlots, borders.
3 1/2" Greenish above; bill medium, slender, black, straight; tail-feathers pointed. M: *Tail forked, blackish; front of face blackish; whitish below, but gorget iridescent red and sides broadly greenish.* F: *Black tail double-rounded, white-tipped; underparts whitish, sides tinged brownish* See Black-chinned, Broad-tailed, and Anna's H.

Black-chinned Hummingbird.*Archilochus alexandri.*U1a298.Chupaflor Barbinegro
Can-M. Resident or summer resident, near sea level to 4000', nBC, nP (Sonora), nA (Tamaulipas); winter visitor cP, ncH. Rare; gardens, dry brushy areas, stream borders.
Pl.16. 3 1/2" Like Ruby-throated H., *but M: gorget black and (lower part) violet; and F: may be less brownish below; crown less greenish.* See Costa's H.

Anna's Hummingbird. *Calypte anna.* U1a299. Chupaflor Cuello Escarlata
Can-M. Resident, sea level to 4000', nBC; winter visitor nP, nH. Common; open areas with scattered trees, semi-desert, gardens, overgrown fields, river-border woods.
Pl.16. 4" Bill black, short, straight. M: *Greeenish above, with red forehead and crown; dull greenish gray below; with white chest and short-cornered red gorget; tail notched, black.* F: *Greenish above; pale gray below; red and gray specks on throat; dark ear-patch; tail rounded, greenish (below) to black, with white tips.* See

Broad-tailed and Costa's H.

Costa's Hummingbird. *Calypte costae.* U1a300.   Chupaflor Garganta Violeta
US-M. Resident, sea level to 4000', BC, nP (Sonora); winter visitor nP (s.to Sinaloa).
Common; scrubby thorny semi-desert, scattered trees and shrubs, gardens, dry streams.
*Pl.16. 3 1/2" Like Anna's H. but not as much greenish gray below; and M: crown
and longer-cornered gorget violet, not red; and F: white underparts, no* specks *on
throat.* See Black-chinned H.

Calliope Hummingbird. *Stellula calliope.* U1a305.   Chupaflor Rafaguitas
Can-M. Summer resident, 4000 to 8000', nBC; winter visitor ncP, ncH. Rare;
woodland edge, open pine-oak or pine woods, low river-border woods, thickets, brush.
*Pl.16. 2 1/2" Greenish above; mostly whitish below. M: Gorget ragged, streaked
white and violet-red; tail short, blackish. F: Whitish below; red and gray
throat-specks; tinged cinnamon on sides, flanks, and untacs; little rufous on tail,
which is short, rounded, green at base (below) to black, with white corners.* See
Broad-tailed and Anna's H.

Bumblebee Hummingbird. *Atthis heloisa.* U1a306.   Chupaflor Violada
M. Resident, 4500 to 10,000', ncH. Rare; cloud forest, open pine or pine-oak woods.
*Pl.19. 2 1/2" Greenish above, mostly white below; bill short, straight, black; tail
rounded, rufous at base, to contrasty black, with white corners. M: Sides greenish;
gorget violet-red, corners medium long. F: Gray specks on throat; pale rufous sides,
buffy untacs, white line behind eye.* See Elliot's, and larger Allen's and Rufous H.

Elliot's (Wine-thr.) **Hummingbird.** *Atthis ellioti.* U1a307.   Chupaflor de Elliot
M,G,ES,H. Resident, 5000 to 10,000', sH. Rare; cloud forest, woods, openings.
2 1/4" Like Bumblebee H., but slightly smaller, bill shorter; and M: gorget redder.

Broad-tailed Hummingbird.*Selasphorus platycercus.*U1a316.Chupaflor Cola Ancha
Can-M,G. Resident, 6000 to 13,000', H. Common; mountain meadows, open grassy
pine woodlands, large openings in oak woods; often perches on tall flower stalk.
*Pl.16. 3 1/2" Greenish above; mostly whitish below; bill straight, medium, black.
M: Gorget bright red; sides broadly grayish green; tail black (below). Wings produce
high-pitched trill in flight. F: Gray throat-specks; buffy wash on sides and flanks; is
much larger, has more rufous on (rounded) tail above, than Calliope H., has less
rufous than Allen's or Rufous H.* See Ruby-throated Hummingbird.

Rufous Hummingbird. *Selasphorus rufus.* U1a317.   Chupaflor Dorado
AK-M. Transient BC; winter visitor ncP (Sinaloa to Oaxaca), ncH. Common; open,
shrubby pine woods, gardens and parks, or open terrain with scattered trees and shrubs.
*Pl.16. 3 1/2" White below, but pale rufous sides, flanks, and untacs; bill
medium-short, straight, black. M: Rich rufous above; short-cornered gorget dark red.
(Young males and some adults have much green on back and crown, somewhat like*
Allen's H.) *F: Greenish above; tail has much rufous at base, then black, then
white-corners; gray or red throat-specks.* See Allen's, Calliope, and Broad-tailed H.

Allen's Hummingbird. *Selasphorus sasin.* U1a318.   Chupaflor Petirrojo
US-M. Transient nBC; winter visitor ncP, cH. Common; open woods, thickets, brush.
3 1/2" Like Rufous H., *but male has green back, nape, and crown; female is
virtually identical to* RufousH. *in the field (Allen's has much narrower outer
tail-feathers); has more rufous on rounded tail than* Calliope and Broad-tailed H.

TROGONS - TROGONIDAE - TROGONES
Nine residents; all except BC; legs and neck short, feet weak, wings rounded; tail
mostly square-tipped, medium; bill short, stout; arboreal, fliers, dry woods to humid
forest; mostly tropical. Distinguish by under-tail patterns, belly color. **Pl. 20, 23.**

Black-headed Trogon. *Trogon melanocephalus.* Y1a16.   Trogon Cabeza Negra
M-CR. Resident up to 2000', A, Y. Rare; river-borders, woods-edge, humid forest,
orchards, hedgerows. V: like that of Citreoline T. See also Barred Antshrike voice.

11" Like Citreoline T. (Pl.20), *but tail (below) usually shows two black bars across white (broad white tips of graduated tail-feathers do not overlap); iris <u>brown</u>; eye-ring lighter blue; and male has blacker head and chest, and <u>bluish</u> tail (above) and back.*

Citreoline Trogon. *Trogon citreolus.* Y1a15. Trogón Amarillo
M. <u>Resident up to 2000', P (Sinaloa to Chiapas)</u>. Common; dense thorny woods, borders, thickets, hedgerows, dry river-border woods. V: accelerating series of croaks, ending in a rattle, *co - co - co - co - co-co-co-kr-r-r-r.* See Barred Antshrike voice.

Pl.20. 11" M+F: Tail white below, except black base and tip; untacs, belly yellow; iris yellow; eye-ring bluish. M: Tail (above) and back green; head blackish. F: Head slaty gray; tail (above) and back blackish. See Black-headed and Violaceous T.

Violaceous Trogon. *Trogon violaceus.* Y1a25. Trogón Violáceo
M-SAm. <u>Resident up to 4000', sP, A, Y</u>. Rare; dense forest, open humid woods, river-border forest, dense scrubby woods. V: a musical series - *cyo, cyo, cyo, cyo,* etc.

Pl.20. 10" Like Citreoline T., *but eye-ring greenish yellow; and M: upper breast, back, tail (above) more purplish, and most of tail narrowly barred black and white below; and F: tail black below, with narrow white feather-tips, and barred margins.*

Mexican (Mountain) Trogon. *Trogon mexicanus.* Y1a17. Trogón Mexicano
M,G,H. <u>Resident, 4000 to 10,000', H</u>. Common; in open or dense pine-oak or pine or fir forest, cloud forest. V: a regular ringing series *co, co, co,* etc., or *cah-oo,* etc.

Pl.20. 12" Red belly; white breast-bar. M: Tail black below, with 3 broad white bars; black-tipped bluish green above; head and back iridescent greenish; bill yellow. F: Tail-feathers black below, with white-tips, barred margins; upperparts and tail (above) brown. See Elegant and Collared Trogon.

Elegant Trogon. *Trogon elegans.* Y1a18. Trogón Elegante
US-CR,x.B. <u>Resident up to 8000', ncP, ncH, ncA</u>. Common, irregular; rocky ravines, in dry oak or pine-oak woods, or thorny scrub, humid river-border woods, low dry woodland. V: a hoarse, clucking, croaking series, *co-wy, co-wy, co-wy, co-wy.*

Pl.23. 11" Like Mexican T. *and Collared T., but tail gray (finely vermiculated black-and-white) below, with white feather tips; and M: tail copper-color above, with black tip; and F: tail brown above with black tip; white patch behind and below eye.*

Collared Trogon. *Trogon collaris.* Y1a19. Trogón de Collar
M-SAm. <u>Resident up to 7500', csP (Guerrero to Chiapas), csA (San Luis Potosí to Quintana Roo), Y</u>. Common; dense humid forest, river-border woods, dense scrub woods, overgrown *cafetales.* V: a slightly descending musical two-noted call, *cyo-cyo.*

Pl.20. 10" Like Mexican T., *but M: back more golden green; tail black below with fine white bars, golden green above with black tip; and F: tail dull grayish below with narrow dark bar near feather-tips, and brown above with black tip.*

Massena (Slaty-tailed) Trogon. *Trogon massena.* Y1a9. Trogón Grande
M-SAm. <u>Resident, near sea level, csA</u>. Rare; humid forest. V: loud barking notes.

Pl.20. 13" Red belly, no white breast-bar; tail black below. M: Orange bill and eye-ring; head, chest, and upperparts, including tail, bluish green. F: Similar, but slaty gray head, chest, upperparts, and tail; and upper mandible is partly dark.

Eared Trogon. *Euptilotis neoxenus.* Y1a6. Trogón Orejón
US-M. <u>Resident, 6000 to 10,000', ncH (Chihuahua to Michoacán)</u>. Rare, irregular; mountain pine or open pine-oak forest. V: a slow *co, co, co, co,* like sound of a bell.

Pl.20. 14" M+F: Like Massena T., *but bill dark gray; filmy ear-tufts; and M: tail mostly white below, blackish blue above; and F: bluish green above, not slaty gray.*

Resplendent Quetzal. *Pharomachrus mocinno.* Y1a1. Quetzal
M-Pan. <u>Resident, 4000 to 7000', sH</u>. Very rare; cloud forest, other dense humid forest.

Pl.20. 35",15" Red lower belly and untacs; wing-coverts and uptacs form plumes. M: Tail mostly white below; uptacs up to 2 or more feet in length. F: Tail barred below; uptacs reach tip of tail; back and breast-band green, some green on head.

MOTMOTS - MOMOTIDAE - PAJAROS RELOJ

Six residents; mostly lowlands; short legs and neck, rounded wings; short to medium-long tail, may be racket-tipped; bill medium; dry woods and borders to humid forest; Neotropical. Distinguish by colors, patterns, tail structure, voice. **Plate 20.**

Tody Motmot. *Hylomanes momotula.* X4a1.   Bobito
M-SAm. Resident up to 5000', sP, csA. Rare; undergrowth and low branches of dense humid forest, rarely tree-tops; sits quietly, flies rapidly, directly, with rapid wing-beats, as would a Shrike or Pygmy Owl. V: a slow series of *cwook* or *cwonk* notes.
Pl.20. 7" Tail not racket-tipped; *no black breast-spot; suggests* Brown Puffbird (Pl.22), *but crown rufous, back and wings green, not* spotted; *faint streaks below.*

Blue-throated Motmot. *Aspatha gularis.* X4a2.   Bobo Garganta Azul
M,G,ES,H. Resident, 5000 to 10,000', sH. Very rare; humid pine or pine-oak forest, or cloud forest, near secluded bank suitable for nest. V: *coot* or *took*, singly or series.
Pl.20. 11" Green with pale blue throat; small black ear-patch; small black breast-spot; tail long, graduated, but not racket-tipped.

Blue-crowned Motmot. *Momotus momota.* X4a9.   Turco Real
M-SAm. Resident up to 4000', sP, A, Y. Rare; river-border woods, dry or humid forest, orchards, near dirt bank; switches tail side to side. V: low-pitched *hoot, hoot.*
Pl.20. 16" Green above (or with some rufous); olive green (or rufous) below; crown pale blue with black border (nA, n. cA), or crown has black center then blue circle then black border (s. cA, sA, sP, Y); short bare space on tail; black breast-spot.

Russet-crowned Motmot. *Momotus mexicanus.* X4a8.   Pájaro Reloj
M-G. Resident up to 6000', P, ncH (Chihuahua to Oaxaca). Common, low; rare, high; open arid country, stream border woods, low thorny woodland, semi-desert scrub, near dirt bank for nest; switches tail from side to side. V: a burred, low-pitched *h-rr-oot.*
Pl.20. 13" Pale olive-green above; pale bluish green below; crown rufous.

Keel-billed Motmot. *Electron carinatum.* X4a4.   Gallinola
M-CR,x.ES. Resident, near sea level, sA (Veracruz, Tabasco, Chiapas). Very rare; dense humid forest. V: like part of cackle of chicken, a loud, nasal *donk* or *conk.*
Pl.20. 13" Olive green above, dull brownish below; bill broad, flat, keeled on top.

Turquoise-browed Motmot. *Eumomota superciliosa.* X4a5.   Pájaro Raqueta
M-CR,x.B. Resident, near sea level, sP, sA, Y. Common; dry woods or humid-forest edge, mixed farms, orchards, gardens, archaeological sites, road cuts, caves, *cenotes;* often switching tail from side to side. V: mellow or harsh, *toke*, or *tuck* or *tuck-a-loke.*
Pl.20. 14" Brownish green above, with dull rufous back-patch; greenish breast, with long black streak down throat to chest; rufous belly and untacs; pale blue plume-like stripe over eye; broad black line through eye; long bare space on tail.

KINGFISHERS - ALCEDINIDAE - PESCADORES

Four residents, one winter visitor; mostly lowlands; chunky body, large head; short, weak legs; short neck and tail; long, straight, sharp bill; near water, coastal or inland; world temperate, tropical. Distinguish by breast bands, back color. **Plates 20, 23.**

Ringed Kingfisher. *Megaceryle torquata.* X1a3.   Pescador Gigante
US-SAm. Resident up to 4000', P (Sinaloa to Chiapas), A. Rare; rivers, canals, ponds, estuaries, lagoons, marshes, swamps, brackish or fresh-water; near dirt banks.
Pl.20. 17" M+F: Gray-blue above (collar white); reddish brown below; ragged crest; bill stout. M: Untacs whitish. F: Blue collar, white breast-band. See Belted K.

Belted Kingfisher. *Megaceryle alcyon.* X1a4.   Pescador Norteño
AK-SAm. Transient and winter visitor all sub-regions. Rare; rivers, lakes, ponds, lagoons, marshes and swamps with open water, coastal bays and estuaries.
13" Like Ringed K. (Pl.20), *but M: white below with blue breast-band; and F: three breast-bands - blue upper, white middle, rufous lower; belly and untacs white.*

Amazon Kingfisher. *Chloroceryle amazona.* X1a6.   <u>Pescador Verde</u>
M-SAm. <u>Resident up to 3000', P (Sinaloa to Chiapas), A.</u> Rare; wooded rivers, ponds, lakes, lagoons, estuaries, mangrove swamps, or marshes, near dirt banks. *Pl.20. 11" Like* Green K.*, but larger, with heavier bill; larger and shaggier crest; less white on wing and sides of tail; and streaked, not* spotted*, on sides. M: No* spots <u>across</u> breast. *F: Single patchy green breast-band, may be incomplete.*

Green Kingfisher. *Chloroceryle americana.* X1a7.   <u>Pescador Americano</u>
US-SAm. <u>Resident up to 7000', P, H, A, Y.</u> Common (rare H); streams, rivers, ponds, lagoons, lakes, marshes, and swamps; fresh, brackish or salty; near dirt banks. *Pl.23. 8" Dark green above, slightly crested, white spots and spotty bars on wings and tail. M: Flank spots may go across breast. F: Usually two spotty breast-bands.*

Pygmy (, American) Kingfisher. *Chloroceryle aenea.* X1a9.   <u>Pescador Mínimo</u>
M-SAm. <u>Resident, near sea level, sP, csA, Y.</u> Rare; wooded stream banks, small ponds, mangrove swamps, marsh pools; "buzzy" wing-beats; eats insects, small fish. *Pl.20. 5" Dark green above; much smaller than* Green K.*, M: Throat (and sides of neck, more or less), breast, sides, and flanks, tawny buff to rufous; belly and untacs white. F: Similar, but not as much rufous below, and has dark green breast-band.*

PUFFBIRDS - BUCCONIDAE - BOCONES

White-necked Puffbird. *Notharchus macrorhynchos.* V2a1.   <u>Bocón</u>
M-SAm. <u>Resident up to 1500', sP, csA.</u> Rare; upper branches at humid-forest edge, river-border forest, trees in partial clearings; perches upright, catches flying insects. *Pl.22. 9" Large head; heavy black bill; crown, back, wings black; forehead, cheeks, collar, and underparts white (except broad black breast-band); short, graduated tail.*

Brown (Wh.-whiskered) Puffbird. *Malacoptila panamensis.* V2a19.   <u>Barbón</u>
M-SAm,x.ES. <u>Resident up to 1500', sA (Chiapas+Tabasco).</u> Very rare; lower branches or undergrowth at humid-forest edge, trees and hedgerows in partial clearings. *Pl.22. 8" Streaked below, spotted above; whitish shaggy whisker-mark; heavy bill; graduated tail. M: Brown head and upperparts; rufous below; buffy untacs. F: Brownish gray head and upperparts; pale buffy and whitish below.*

JACAMARS - GALBULIDAE - PICOLARGOS

Rufous-tailed Jacamar. *Galbula ruficauda.* V1a11.   <u>Picolargo</u>
M-SAm, x.ES. <u>Resident, near sea level, csA.</u> Rare; forest, stream-banks, lush borders; perches quietly, catches flying insects. V: a loud, clear *wheet* or *tyoop,* or a trill. *Pl.20. 9" Top and sides of head, breast, and upperparts (including top of tail) shiny green; belly, untacs, and tail (below) rufous; throat white (male), or rufous (female).*

TOUCANS - RAMPHASTIDAE - TUCANES

Three residents; mostly se.Mexico; medium-large; legs short, neck medium-short, wings rounded, tail medium-short, bill very long and thick; arboreal, mostly humid forest; Neotropical. Distinguish by voice, plumage and bill colors and patterns. Pl.22.

Emerald Toucanet. *Aulacorhynchus prasinus.* V4a1.   <u>Tucán Verde</u>
M-SAm. <u>Resident or winter visitor up to 9000', sP, csH (Guerrero to Chiapas), csA</u> <u>(San Luis Potosí to Quintana Roo).</u> Common in cloud forest above 4000'; occurs in dense forest, openings, partial clearings. V: a long, slow series - *wok, wok, wok,* etc. *Pl.22. 14" Bright green, darker above; throat white; tail graduated, feathers blackish below with broad rufous tip; bill mostly yellow above, black below, very large.*

Collared Toucan (Aracari). *Pteroglossus torquatus.* V4a16.   <u>Pitorreal</u>
M-SAm. <u>Resident up to 4000', sP, csA, Y.</u> Rare, irregular; dense humid forest, river-border forest, large trees in partial clearings. V: abrupt whistle - *see-ah,* or *pee-ah.* *Pl.22. 16" Blackish green above; red rump; patchy bright yellow, red, and black below; bill very large, whitish above, black below, appears many-toothed; iris white.*

Keel-billed Toucan. *Ramphastos sulfuratus.* V4a35.   Pico Canoa
M-SAm,x.ES. Resident up to 3000', csA, Y. Rare, irregular; humid forest, partly cleared areas, forest-edge. V: a croaking series, *r-rak, r-rak, r-rak,* or *crak, crak,* etc. *Pl.22. 20" Mostly black; throat, face, sides of neck, and chest yellow; untacs bright red; uptacs and rump white; very large bill greenish, with orange patch and red tip.*

WOODPECKERS - PICIDAE - CARPINTEROS

Twenty-two residents, four winter visitors; widespread Mexico; medium-large to small; legs and neck short and strong, wings rounded; tail short, pointed, stiff; bill medium, straight, strong; mostly tree-trunks and branches, semi-desert to humid forest; world temperate, tropical. Distinguish by patterns, colors, size. **Plates 22 and 23.**

Lewis's Woodpecker. *Melanerpes lewis.* V6c2.   Carpintero de Lewis
Can-M. Winter visitor nBC, nP (Sonora), nH (Chihuahua). Rare, very irregular; scattered trees and brush, woods in dry river valleys, open pine woods or oak woods. *10" Front of face maroon-red; rear of face (and upper throat) black; collar and breast silvery gray; belly deep pink; untacs blackish; upperparts black with greenish gloss.*

Acorn Woodpecker. *Melanerpes formicivorus.* V6c6.   Carpintero Encinero
US-SAm. Resident up to 10,000', BC, nP, H, A. Common; often in groups, oak, pine-oak or pine woods, pine ridges, grass-palmetto-pine areas; pack acorns into rows of holes drilled in trees. V: nasal rythmic *wick-y, wick-y, wick-y,* or a single *crenk.* *Pl.23. 8" M: Black; but has white rump, uptacs, forehead, cheek-patch, throat-band (tinged yellowish), and small wing-patch; crown red; belly and untacs white with some black streaks. F: Similar, but crown-center black (hind-crown red).*

Black-cheeked Woodpecker. *Melanerpes pucherani.* V6c11. Carpintero Selvático
M-SAm,x.ES. Resident up to 3000', csA. Rare; dense humid forest, forest-edge. *Pl.22. 7 1/2" Darker-backed than similar species, has black eye-streak. M: Narrow white bars on black back; dark bars on pale gray sides and untacs; throat and breast pale gray; reddish belly-patch; white rump; red crown. F: Crown only partly red.*

Golden-cheeked Woodpecker.*Melan. chrysogenys.* V6c15. Carpintero Cariamarillo
M. Resident up to 5000', ncP. Common; woods-edge, river borders, low woods. *Pl.22. 8" Black-and-white barred back, rump, and untacs; mostly pale gray underparts with yellow-tinged belly; small black eye-patch; yellowish cheeks; red crown; yellow forehead and nape. F: Similar, but crown gray, not red.*

Balsas (Gr.-br.) Woodpecker.*Melanerpes hypopolius.* V6c16. Carpintero del Balsas
M. Resident, 3000 to 6000', cP (Morelos+Guerrero to Oaxaca). Common; desert or semi-desert with saguaro-type cactus, or scrubby, thorny woods. V: a harsh *cherr.* *Pl.22. 10" M+F: Like Gila W. (male has round red crown-patch), but pale red on cheek, short black line over eye, and is much darker, grayer, below and on head.*

Yucatan (Red-vent.) Woodpecker. *Melanerpes pygmaeus.* V6c19. Carpintero Enano
M,B,H. Resident, near sea level, Y. Rare, to rare+; scrubby woods, woods-edge. *Pl.22. 6" Like*Yucatan form of Golden-fronted W., *but is smaller, smaller-billed, somewhat darker, has more yellow around base of bill, and more white on forehead.*

Gila Woodpecker. *Melanerpes uropygialis.* V6c17.   Carpintero del Gila
US-M. Resident up to 5000', rarely higher, BC, nP, nH (Zacatecas+Aguascalientes). Common; mostly desert or semi-desert, with cactus, thorny shrubs, and scrubby trees. *Pl.23. 9" Paler than Balsas W. Barred back and rump; grayish below, and on face, with barred untacs. M: Round red crown-patch. F: Crown pale brownish gray.*

Golden-fronted Woodpecker. *Melanerpes aurifrons.* V6c21.   Cheque
US-N. Resident up to 8000', sP, ncH (Chihuahua+Coahuila to Hidalgo), A, Y. Common; scrubby woods, humid forest borders, river-edge woods, gardens, orchards. *Pl.23. 9" Wide-barred type: M: Barred black-and-white above, the white bars about as wide as the black bars; rump and uptacs white; tail black, or barred black and white; forehead pale gray or whitish; crown red; nape or hind-crown gray; hind-neck*

yellow or orange; pale gray below, with yellow or orange wash on belly; white patch on extended wing. F: Similar (has yellow hind-neck), but entire crown gray, no red.
Narrow-barred type: *Similar to wide-barred type, but white bars noticeably narrower than black bars; tail usually black, but may be barred with white; has yellow orange or red wash on belly; and M: has large red patch on crown, nape, and hind-neck; and F: has red hind-neck, but entire crown is gray, not red.*

Yellow-bellied Sapsucker. *Sphyrapicus varius.* V6c24.   Chupasavia Común
AK-Pan. Transient and winter visitor up to 11,000', all sub-regions. Rare; in wooded habitats except very dry, or very dense humid forest; digs small holes in bark, eats sap.
9" M: Crown and throat red; black breast-band; black with white spots above, long white patch on wing; rump-patch white. F: Like male but chin and throat white. Im: Like adult, but browner, and has little or no red on throat and crown.

Red-naped Sapsucker. *Sphyrapicus nuchalis.* V6c25.   Chupasavia Nuca Roja
Can-M,G,H. Winter visitor up to 8000', BC, nH. Rare; same habitat as Yel.-bellied S.
9" M+F: Like M+F Yellow-bellied S., but red also on nape; and F: has red throat.

Red-breasted Sapsucker. *Sphyrapicus ruber.* V6c26.   Chupasavia Pecho Rojo
AK-M. Winter visitor up to 5000', nBC. Very rare; conifers and other woodland.
9" Like Yellow-bellied S., *but darker-backed; head and upper breast nearly all-red.*

Williamson's Sapsucker.*Sphyrapicus thyroideus.* V6c27. Carpintero Garganta Roja
Can-M. Resident, 5000 to 9000', nBC; winter visitor ncH. Rare; pine, pine-oak forest.
9" M: Black, except two white head-stripes, wing-patch, rump and uptacs; red throat; and yellow belly. F: Blackish brown barred; black breast-patch; yellow belly-patch; brownish head and throat; white rump and uptacs; no white on wing.

Ladder-backed Woodpecker. *Picoides scalaris.* V6c76.   Carpintero Listado
US-M,B,H,N. Resident up to 8000', all sub-regions. Common; in desert, semi-desert, or scrub woods, hedgerows, borders, brushy woods-edge, scattered trees, open woods.
Pl.23. 7" Barred black-and-white back; pale gray below with streaked sides; rather narrow black-and-white face-lines heavily spotted wings. M: Crown mostly red. F: Crown black, no red. See Nuttall's Woodpecker.

Nuttall's Woodpecker. *Picoides nuttallii.* V6c77.   Carpintero de Nuttall
US-M. Resident up to 4500', nBC. Common; river-border woods, hedgerows.
Pl.23. 7" Like Ladder-b. W., *but has broader black ear-patch, more black below nape and on sides of neck; and M: red only on hind-crown; F: crown black, no red.*

Hairy Woodpecker. *Picoides villosus.* V6c82.   Carpintero Ocotero
AK-Pan,x.B. Resident, 4000 to 12,000', nBC, H. Common; usually mountain forests or open woods, of pine, pine and oak, or fir, usually on large branches or upper trunk.
Pl.23. 9" to 7" Back, underparts, wing-spots, part of cheek, and superciliary line pale grayish brown (where most U.S. birds are white); wings, scapulars, some head markings, and central tail-feathers, black. M: Small red nape-patch. F: No red.
Birds are progressively smaller, (pale feathers) browner, from n.Mexico to Panama.

Arizona Woodpecker. *Picoides arizonae.* V6c81.   Carpintero de Arizona
US-M. Resident, 3000 to 10,000', nP (Sonora to Nayarit), ncH (Sonora+Chihuahua to Colima+Michoacán). Rare; oak or pine-oak woods, upper trunk or higher branches.
Pl.23. 8" Dark brown above; brown spots below, on white; brown ear-patch and malar streak on white face. M: Red nape-patch. F: No red. See Strickland's W.

Strickland's Woodpecker. *Picoides stricklandi.* V6c80.   Carpintero de Strickland
M. Resident, 8000 to 13,000', cH (Michoacán to Veracruz). Rare; mountain forest.
Pl.22. 8" Like Arizona W., *but back barred, and underparts heavily streaked.*

Brown (Smoky-br.) **Woodpecker.** *Veniliornis fumigatus.* V6c89.   Carpintero Café
M-SAm. Resident up to 5000', P (Nayarit to Chiapas), A, Y. Very rare ncP, Y; rare sP, A; humid areas, dense forest, river-border woods, mixed large trees, hedgerows.
Pl.22. 6" Dark brown; throat and face grayish. M: Nape red, crown streaked red.

Bronzed (Br.-wing.) **Woodpecker.** *Piculus aeruginosus.* V6c104.   Carpintero Verde
M. Resident up to 5000', ncA (Nuevo León to n.Veracruz). Rare; dense humid
lowland forest, cloud forest, woods along river banks. V: one call is a "petulant" *kweer.*
Pl.22. 10" Like Golden-olive W., *but grayer, not so yellowish below or so bronzy
above; red more restricted, and no* red on sides of fore-crown.

Golden-olive Woodpecker. *Piculus rubiginosus.* V6c105.   Carpintero Oliváceo
M-SAm. Resident up to 6000', sP, csA (c.Veracruz to Quintana Roo), Y. Rare;
lowland forest, cloud forest, river-border woods, humid pine-oak, or pine woods. V:
Like N. Flicker's, *clee,* and *cuk-cuk-cuk-cuk.* Also a weak, chattering trill (one pitch).
*Pl.22. 9" M: Red border all around crown; nape and face-streak red; dark olive to
brownish olive above; barred yellowish and dark olive-green below. F: Similar, but
no red face-streak; little or no red on sides of crown in front of red nape-patch.*

Gray-crowned Woodpecker. *Piculus auricularis.* V6c106.   Carpintero Orejiamarillo
M. Resident up to 8000', ncP, ncH. Rare; usually humid pine-oak or pine forest.
Pl.22. 9" Like Golden-olive W. *but more grayish green overall; no* red on nape or
border of crown.

Northern Flicker. *Colaptes auratus.* V6c111.   Carpintero Norteño
Gilded group. *Colaptes auratus chrysoides.*   Carpintero Dorado
   US-M. Resident up to 4000', BC, nP (Sonora to Sinaloa). Common; desert or
   semi-desert with saguaro or other thorny shrubs or cacti suitable for nest cavities.
   *Pl.23. 11" Brown above, barred black; with white rump; buffy brown crown
   and nape; throat and face gray; black chest-band; black-spotted whitish breast
   and belly; yellow under-wings and tail-base. M: Red malar streak. F: No red.*
Red-shafted group. *Colaptes auratus cafer.*   Carpintero Alirrojo
   AK-N,x.B. Resident up to 10,000', nBC, H. Common; open or dense pine or
   oak or pine-oak woods, mountain fir forests, sparse brushy woods, scrub woods.
   Pl.23. 12" Like Gilded Flicker, *but brown of crown, nape, and back, darker,
   more reddish; under-wings and tail-base red, not yellow.*

Chestnut (-colored) **Woodpecker.** *Celeus castaneus.* V6c120.   Carpintero Castaño
M-Pan,x.ES. Resident up to 3000', csA, Y. Rare; dense humid forest, most often on
large low branches or lower portions of trunks. V: a mellow, but slightly metallic *cleek.*
*Pl.22. 10" Appears very dark, with many V-shaped black marks on rich chestnut
above and below; crested head creamy brown; bill greenish ivory. M: Lores, small
part of ear-patch, and broad malar patch, red.*

Lineated Woodpecker. *Dryocopus lineatus.* V6c129.   Carpintero Real
M-SAm. Resident up to 4500', P, A, Y. Rare; humid forest borders, openings, open
scrubby woods, river-border woods; large trees in mixed pastures and hedgerows.
*Pl.22. 12" M: Black; except broadly red forehead, crest, and malar streak;
black-and-whitish barred belly, sides, and untacs; whitish chin; white streak from bill
to and along scapulars. F: Similar, but forehead and malar streak black, not red.*

Flint- (Pale-) **billed Woodpecker.** *Phloeoceastes guatemalensis.* V6c137.   Picotero
M-SAm. Resident up to 4500', P, A, Y. Rare; in dense humid forest, or borders or
openings, river-border woods, open woods, hedgerows; distinctive double-rap pecking.
Pl.22. 14" Like Lineated W., *but sides of face all-red; and M: chin, upper throat and
ear-patch red, not black; and F: chin, upper throat, and front and top of crest, black.*

Imperial Woodpecker. *Campephilus imperialis.* V6c143.   Pitorreal Ocotero
M. Probably extinct; may exist in secluded mountain pine forest, Sonora - Michoacán.
*Pl.47. 21" M: Black; except large white wing-patch; white line along scapulars; and
long, red, up-curled crest. F: Similar, but crest all-black, and curled up and forward.*

OVENBIRDS - FURNARIIDAE - TREPADORES

Seven residents; s.Mexico; small; legs and neck short, tail medium, bill medium;
humid forest and borders; Neotropical. Distinguish by tail, bill, shades of buff. **Pl.24.**

1

PACIFIC LOON
p.1
Win.

WESTERN GREBE
p.2

CLARK'S GREBE
p.2

Im.

BROWN PELICAN
p.5

Sum.

DOUBLE-CRESTED
CORMORANT
p.5

Ad.

Im.

RED-BILLED
TROPICBIRD
p.4

Im.

OLIVACEOUS
CORMORANT
p.5

Im.

BLACK SKIMMER
p.31

BLACK-FOOTED
ALBATROSS
p.2

p.5
ANHINGA

M

F

Im.

PARASITIC
JAEGER
p.28

Win.

HEERMANN'S
GULL
p.29

p.29
LAUGHING GULL

Im.

Dark ph.

XANTUS'S
MURRELET
p.32

Sum.

BC race
Calif. race

Win.

Win.

p.31
BLACK TERN

Im.

Win.
p.30
ROYAL TERN

p.29
RING-BILLED GULL

p.2
LEAST GREBE

2

GREAT TINAMOU
p.1

LITTLE TINAMOU
p.1

BOUCARD'S TINAMOU
p.1

RUFESCENT TINAMOU
p.1

TIGER HERON
p.6

PINNATED
BITTERN
p.6

AGAMI HERON
p. 7

BOAT-BILLED
HERON
p.8

MUSCOVY
DUCK   M
p.9

JABIRU
p.8

SAVANNA
VULTURE
p.12

KING
VULTURE
p.12

DOUBLE-TOOTHED
KITE
p.13

PLUMBEOUS
KITE
p.14

M

p.13
CAYENNE
KITE

F

p.16
HARPY EAGLE

p.13
HOOK-BILLED KITE

p.14
BICOLORED HAWK

Murrell
Butler

GREAT BLUE HERON
p.6

GREEN HERON
p.7

Im.

LITTLE BLUE
HERON
p.7

Molting
Im.

Im.

REDDISH
EGRET
7

Wh. ph.

Wh. ph.

p.7
CATTLE
EGRET

Im.

p.7
GREAT
EGRET

p.7
SNOWY
EGRET

TRICOLORED
HERON
7

Im.

BcNH

Im.

YcNH

Im.

p.7
YELLOW-
CROWNED
NIGHT-HERON

BLACK-
CROWNED
NIGHT-H.
p.7

AMERICAN
BITTERN
6

WHITE
IBIS
p.8

Im.

LEAST BITTERN

p.6

Im.

p.8
ROSEATE SPOONBILL

p.8
WHITE-FACED
IBIS

Im.

p.8
WOOD STORK

AMERICAN FLAMINGO
p.8

p.107
GLOSSY IBIS

Im.

Murrell
Butler

4

MISSISSIPPI KITE p.13

NORTHERN GOSHAWK p.14

COOPER'S HAWK p.14

Im.

Im.

Im.

Im.

BROAD-WINGED HAWK p.15

Black ph.

p.14 SHARP-SHINNED HAWK

Im.

p.16 ROUGH-LEGGED HAWK

Dark ph.

Im.

FERRUGINOUS HAWK p.16

Im.

p.16 RED-TAILED H.

MERLIN p.18

Ir

p.15 RED-SHOULDERED H.

M

p.16 GOLDEN EAGLE Tail of Im.

F

NORTHERN HARRIER p.14

p.17 AMERICAN KESTREL

M

Im.

F

p.13 OSPREY

p.18 PRAIRIE FALCON

p.18 PEREGRINE FALCON

Murrell Butler

RED-THROATED CARACARA
p.17

GREAT BLACK-HAWK
p.15

5

p.14
WHITE HAWK

UTARY EAGLE
p.15

CHESTNUT HAWK
p.15

BLACK-AND-WHITE HAWK-EAGLE
p.17

Im.

ORNATE
HAWK-EAGLE
p.17

BLACK HAWK-EAGLE
p.17

COLLARED MICRASTUR
p.17   Im.

Buff
ph.

CRANE HAWK
p.14

LAUGHING FALCON
p.17

SHARP-SHINNED
(WHITE-BREASTED)
HAWK
p.14

ROADSIDE HAWK
p.15

BARRED MICRASTUR
p.17

Im.

ORANGE-BREASTED FALCON
p.18

MURRELL
BUTLER

p.18
BAT FALCON

6

WHITE-TAILED KITE
p.13

SWALLOW-TAILED KITE
p.13

EVERGLADE KITE
p.13

M

F

p.16
WHITE-TAILED
HAWK

ZONE-TAILED HAWK
p.16

SHORT-TAILED
HAWK
p.15
Black
ph.

GRAY HAWK
p.15

SWAINSON'S HAWK
p.16

HARRIS'S HAWK
p.15

p.18
APLOMADO
FALCON

p.14
COMMON
BLACK-HAWK

p.17 CRESTED
CARACARA

M

M

F

p.21
GAMBEL'S QUAIL

p.21
MOUNTAIN QUAIL

p.20
SCALED QUAIL

M

F

p.21
CALIFORNIA
QUAIL

M

F

p.20
MEARNS'S QUAIL

M

F

p.20
NORTHERN BOBWHITE

N. Bobwhite: Males of
some other Mexican races

Murrell
Butler

GREAT CURASSOW
p.19

M

F

CRESTED GUAN
p.19

WAGLER'S CHACHALACA
p.18

OCELLATED TURKEY
p.19

BLACK CHACHALACA
p.19

M

F

HORNED GUAN
p.19

BEARDED
PARTRIDGE
p.19

M

F

LONG-TAILED
PARTRIDGE
p.19

HIGHLAND
PARTRIDGE
p.20

ELEGANT QUAIL
p.20

SPOTTED WOOD-QUAIL
p.20

GRAY-NECKED RAIL
p.22

RUFOUS-
NECKED
RAIL
p.22

OCELLATED QUAIL
p.20

M

F

M

YUCATAN BOBWHITE
p.20

M

F

SINGING QUAIL
p.20

F

BANDED QUAIL
p.20

YELLOW-
BREASTED
RAIL
p.22

RED RAIL
p.21

SPOTTED RAIL
p.22

UNIFORM RAIL
p.22

Murrell
Butler

8

WHISTLING SWAN
p.9

Im.

CANADA GOOSE
p.9

p.9
BRANT

Im.

p.9
ROSS'S
GOOSE

Im.

Im.

Blue ph.

White ph.

p.9
SNOW GOOSE

Im.

WHITE-FRONTED
GOOSE
p.9

BLACK-BELLIED
TREE-DUCK
p.9

Im.

MALLARD
p.10   F

M

FULVOUS
TREE-DUCK
p.9

F

M

p.10
NORTHERN PINTAIL

F

M

F

p.10
GADWALL

M

F

M

p.10
WOOD DUCK   F

F

p.10
NORTHERN SHOVELER

M

M

p.10
AMERICAN WIGEON

Murrell
Butler

9

GREEN-WINGED TEAL M F
p.10

BLUE-WINGED TEAL F
p.10 M

CINNAMON TEAL
p.10

REDHEAD F M

GREATER SCAUP
p.11 M

CANVASBACK p.11 F M

RING-NECKED DUCK p.11 F M
p.11

LESSER SCAUP

BUFFLEHEAD p.11 F M

RUDDY DUCK p.12

COMMON GOLDENEYE F M F
p.12
MASKED DUCK M

WHITE-WINGED SCOTER Ad. M F M
P.11

Im. M

F.Win.

Ad.M Win. HOODED MERGANSER

Ad.M Sum.

SURF SCOTER
p.11 Im. F

OLDSQUAW p.11

Ad.M Ad. F

BLACK SCOTER p.11 M F

M

F M

RED-BREASTED MERGANSER p.12

COMMON MERGANSER p.12 F

Murrell Butler

10

SORA
p.22

Im.

VIRGINIA RAIL
p.21

Im.

YELLOW RAIL
p.21

BLACK RAIL
p.21

COMMON
GALLINULE
p.22

p.22
PURPLE GALLINULE

AMERICAN COOT   p.22

p.24
BLACK
OYSTERCATCHER

BLACK-NECKED STILT
p.24

Win.

p.24
AMERICAN
AVOCET

p.24
AMERICAN OYSTERCATCHER

Im.

p.21
KING RAIL

p.25
NORTHERN JACANA

p.21
CLAPPER RAIL

LIMPKIN   p.23

WHOOPING CRANE   p.107

Im.

Im.

Im.

SANDHILL CRANE   p.23

Murrell
Butler

11

CK-BELLIED PLOVER
p.23

LESSER GOLDEN
PLOVER
p.23

SEMIPALMATED
PLOVER
p.24

Win.

Win.

M

WILSON'S
PLOVER
p.24

F

DEER
24

M

F

Win.

p.24
SNOWY PLOVER

PIPING PLOVER
p.24

UPLAND
ANDPIPER
p.25

WHIMBREL
p.25

MOUNTAIN
PLOVER

p.24

Win.

M

LONG-BILLED
CURLEW
p.26

F

Win.

HUDSONIAN GODWIT
p.26

SOLITARY
ANDPIPER
25

Win.

MARBLED GODWIT
p.26

p.27
LONG-BILLED DOWITCHER

Win.

p.25
GREATER
YELLOWLEGS

p.25
LESSER
OWLEGS

p.27
SHORT-BILLED
DOWITCHER

p.27
STILT
SANDPIPER

Win.

Murrell
Butler

12

SPOTTED SANDPIPER
p.25

WILLET
p.25

WANDERING TATTL
p.25

Win.

Win.

RUD
TURNSTO
p.2

Win.

Win.

Win.

p.26
BLACK
TURNSTONE

COMMON
SNIPE
p.27

RED KNOT
p.26

p.26
SURF-
BIRD

SEMIPALMAT
SANDPIP
p.26

Win.

Win.

Win.

p.26

LEAST S.
p.27

Win.
p.26
SANDERLING

Sum.

BAIRD'S
SANDPIP
p.27

WESTERN
S.

Win.

Sum.

Win.

WHITE-
RUMPED S.
p.27

p.27
PECTO

p.27
DUNLIN

BUFF-
BREASTED S.
p.27

F

F

WILSON'S
PHALAROPE
p.28

F

M

M

M

p.28
RED PHALAROPE

p.28
NORTHERN
PHALAROPE

Win

Win.

Win.

Murrell
Butler

13

MEXICAN STONE-CURLEW
p.23

p.23
SUNBITTERN

p.22
SUNGREBE

p.32
RUFOUS PIGEON

SCALED PIGEON
p.32

p.33
SHORT-BILLED PIGEON

p.33
MOURNING (SOCORRO) DOVE

p.33
ZENAIDA DOVE

p.33
PLAIN-BREASTED
GROUND-DOVE

M

p.33
RUDDY GROUND-DOVE

F

M

p.33
BLUE GROUND-DOVE

F

F

M

p.34
MONDETOURA DOVE

p.34
CARIBBEAN DOVE

p.34
GRAY-HEADED DOVE

p.34
CASSIN'S DOVE

p.34
LAWRENCE'S QUAIL-DOVE

M

F

p.34
RUDDY QUAIL-DOVE

p.34
WHITE-FACED QUAIL-DOVE

Murrell
Butler

14

SQUIRREL CUCKOO
p.37

STRIPED CUCKOO
p.37

PHEASANT CUCKOO
p.37

LESSER GROUND-CUCKOO
p.37

WESTERN
(VINACEOUS)
SCREECH-OWL
p.38

VERMICULAT
SCREECH-OW
p.38

LESSER ROADRUNNER
p.37

BEARDED
SCREECH-OWL
p.38

p.39
LEAST PYGMY-OWL

p.38
CRESTED OWL

p.39
WOOD-OWL

BARRED (FULVOUS) OWL
p.39

p.39
SPECTACLED OWL

p.39
BLACK-AND-WHITE OWL

p.40
STRIPED OWL

p.40
STYGIAN OWL

p.40
UNSPOTTED
SAW-WHET OWL

F

YUCATAN POOR-WILL

F

F

M

p.41
PIT-SWEET

M

p.42
JAMAICAN POTOO

p.41
EARED POOR-WILL

p.41
CHIP-WILLOW

M

15

CK-BILLED CUCKOO
p.36

YELLOW-BILLED
CUCKOO
p.36

MANGROVE CUCKOO
p.37

GROOVE-BILLED ANI
p.37

p.37

SMOOTH-BILLED ANI

MMULATED

38

EASTERN SCREECH-OWL
Gray ph.   Red ph.
p.38

NORTHERN
PYGMY-OWL
p.39

FERRUGINOUS
PYGMY-OWL
p.39

CoNi Wing

COMMON
NIGHTHAWK
p.40

LeNi Wing

Im.

p.40
NORTHERN
SAW-WHET OWL

WL

p.39
BURROWING OWL

p.40
LESSER NIGHTHAWK

p.37
ATER
OADRUNNER

COMMON
BARN-OWL
p.38

LONG-EARED OWL
p.40

p.39
POTTED OWL

p.39
BARRED OWL

p.40
SHORT-EARED OWL

p.39
GREAT HORNED OWL

Murrell
Butler

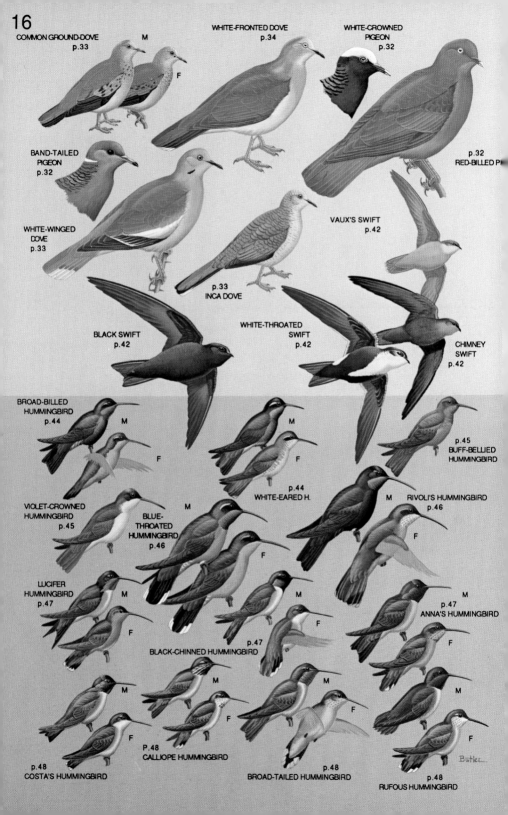

16

COMMON GROUND-DOVE
p.33

M

F

WHITE-FRONTED DOVE
p.34

WHITE-CROWNED
PIGEON
p.32

BAND-TAILED
PIGEON
p.32

p.32
RED-BILLED PI

WHITE-WINGED
DOVE
p.33

VAUX'S SWIFT
p.42

p.33
INCA DOVE

BLACK SWIFT
p.42

WHITE-THROATED
SWIFT
p.42

CHIMNEY
SWIFT
p.42

BROAD-BILLED
HUMMINGBIRD
p.44

M

F

M

F

p.44
WHITE-EARED H.

M

p.45
BUFF-BELLIED
HUMMINGBIRD

VIOLET-CROWNED
HUMMINGBIRD
p.45

BLUE-
THROATED
HUMMINGBIRD
p.46

M

F

M

RIVOLI'S HUMMINGBIRD
p.46

F

LUCIFER
HUMMINGBIRD
p.47

M

F

M

F

M

p.47
ANNA'S HUMMINGBIRD

p.47
BLACK-CHINNED HUMMINGBIRD

F

M

M

F

M

F

M

P.48
CALLIOPE HUMMINGBIRD

F

p.48
COSTA'S HUMMINGBIRD

p.48
BROAD-TAILED HUMMINGBIRD

F

p.48
RUFOUS HUMMINGBIRD

Butler

SOLITARY MACAW
p.35

SCARLET MACAW
p.35

MAROON-FRONTED PARROT
p.35

TbPa

MfPa

p.35
THICK-BILLED PARROT

17

RED-CROWNED
PARROT
p.36

YUCATAN PARROT
p.36
M

F

M - WfPa

M - YuPa

F - WfPa
YuPa

WHITE-FRONTED PARROT
p.35

MEALY PARROT
p.36

p.36
RED-LORED PARROT

P.36
LILAC
CROWNED
PARROT

YELLOW-HEADED
PARROT
p.36

p.35
WHITE-CROWNED PARROT

BROWN-HOODED
PARROT
p.35

ORANGE-FRONTED
PARAKEET
p.35

p.35
TOVI PARAKEET

M

F

GREEN
PARAKEET
p.34

AZTEC
PARAKEET
p.35

MEXICAN   p.35
PARROTLET

p.35
BARRED PARAKEET

18

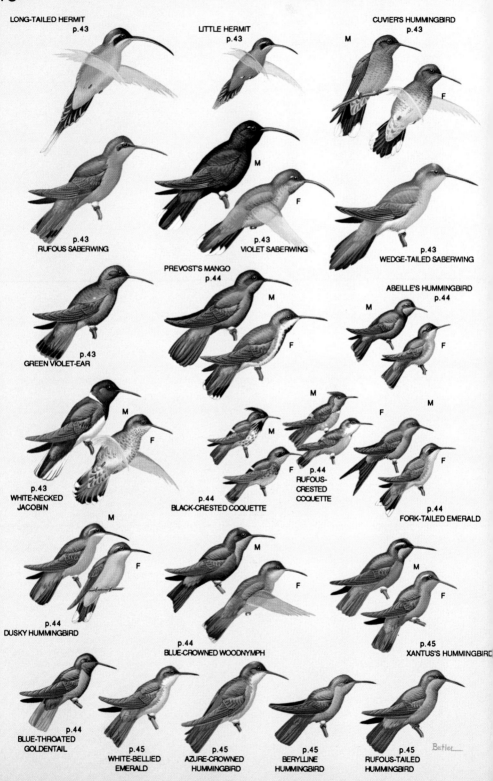

LONG-TAILED HERMIT
p.43

LITTLE HERMIT
p.43

CUVIER'S HUMMINGBIRD
p.43

M

F

p.43
RUFOUS SABERWING

M

F

VIOLET SABERWING
p.43

WEDGE-TAILED SABERWING
p.43

PREVOST'S MANGO
p.44

M

F

ABEILLE'S HUMMINGBIRD
p.44

M

F

GREEN VIOLET-EAR
p.43

M

F

WHITE-NECKED
JACOBIN
p.43

M

F

BLACK-CRESTED COQUETTE
p.44

RUFOUS-
CRESTED
COQUETTE
p.44

M

M

F

FORK-TAILED EMERALD
p.44

M

F

DUSKY HUMMINGBIRD
p.44

M

F

BLUE-CROWNED WOODNYMPH
p.44

M

F

XANTUS'S HUMMINGBIRD
p.45

BLUE-THROATED
GOLDENTAIL
p.44

WHITE-BELLIED
EMERALD
p.45

AZURE-CROWNED
HUMMINGBIRD
p.45

BERYLLINE
HUMMINGBIRD
p.45

RUFOUS-TAILED
HUMMINGBIRD
p.45

Butler

BLUE-TAILED
HUMMINGBIRD
p.45

CINNAMON
HUMMINGBIRD
p.45

STRIPE-TAILED
HUMMINGBIRD
p.45

19

M

F

GUERRERO H.
p.46

p.45
GREEN-FRONTED
HUMMINGBIRD

M

F

p.45
OAXACA
HUMMINGBIRD

p.46
CAZIQUE
HUMMINGBIRD

M

M

F

F

p.46
GREEN-THROATED
MOUNTAIN-GEM

M

F

p.46
GARNET-THROATED
HUMMINGBIRD

p.46
PURPLE-CROWNED FAIRY

M

F

p.46
PLAIN-CAPPED STARTHROAT

M

F

p.46
LONG-BILLED STARTHROAT

M

F

p.47
SLENDER SHEARTAIL

M

F

p.47
MEXICAN SHEARTAIL

M

F

p.47
DUPONT'S HUMMINGBIRD

M

F p.47
BEAUTIFUL HUMMINGBIRD

M

F

p.48
BUMBLEBEE HUMMINGBIRD

Murrell
Butler

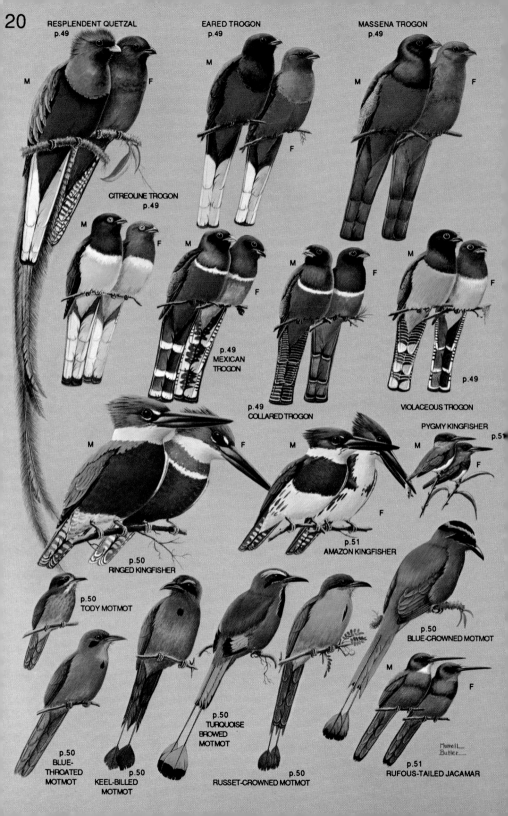

20

RESPLENDENT QUETZAL
p.49

M   F

EARED TROGON
p.49

M

F

MASSENA TROGON
p.49

M   F

CITREOLINE TROGON
p.49

M   F

M   F

M   F

M   F

p.49
MEXICAN
TROGON

p.49
COLLARED TROGON

VIOLACEOUS TROGON
p.49

M   F

M   F

PYGMY KINGFISHER
p.51

M   F

F

p.51
AMAZON KINGFISHER

p.50
RINGED KINGFISHER

p.50
TODY MOTMOT

p.50
BLUE-CROWNED MOTMOT

M   F

p.50
TURQUOISE
BROWED
MOTMOT

Murrell
Butler

p.50
BLUE-
THROATED
MOTMOT

p.50
KEEL-BILLED
MOTMOT

p.50
RUSSET-CROWNED MOTMOT

p.51
RUFOUS-TAILED JACAMAR

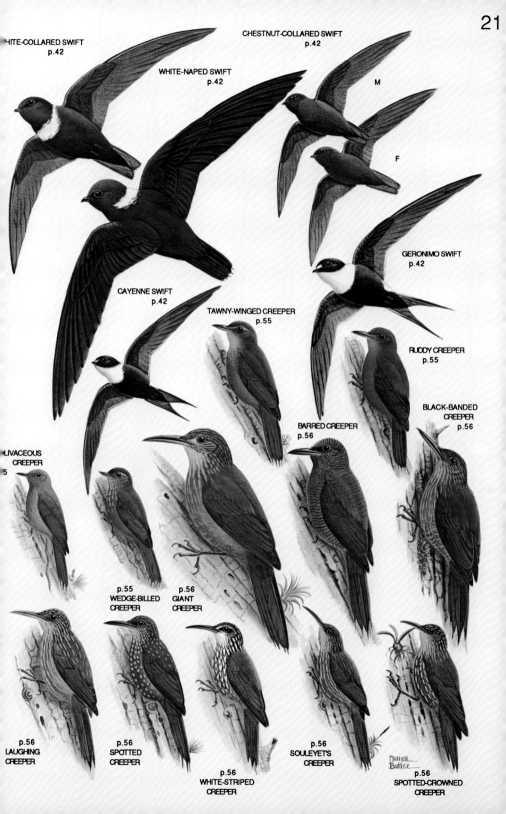

21

WHITE-COLLARED SWIFT
p.42

CHESTNUT-COLLARED SWIFT
p.42

WHITE-NAPED SWIFT
p.42

M

F

GERONIMO SWIFT
p.42

CAYENNE SWIFT
p.42

TAWNY-WINGED CREEPER
p.55

RUDDY CREEPER
p.55

BARRED CREEPER
p.56

BLACK-BANDED
CREEPER
p.56

OLIVACEOUS
CREEPER
5

p.55
WEDGE-BILLED
CREEPER

p.56
GIANT
CREEPER

p.56
LAUGHING
CREEPER

p.56
SPOTTED
CREEPER

p.56
SOULEYET'S
CREEPER

p.56
SPOTTED-CROWNED
CREEPER

p.56
WHITE-STRIPED
CREEPER

Murrell
Butler

22

WHITE-NECKED PUFFBIRD
p.51

F

M

EMERALD TOUCANET
p.51

COLLARED TOUCAN
p.51

p.51
BROWN PUFFBIRD

p.52
KEEL-BILLED TOUCAN

M

F

p.54
GRAY-CROWNED WOODPECKER

M

F

p.54
BRONZED WOODPECKER

M

F

p.54
GOLDEN-OLIVE WOODPECKER

M

F

p.54
CHESTNUT WOODPECKER

M

F

p.54
LINEATED WOODPECKER

M

F

p.52
BALSAS WOODPECKER

M

F

p.52
GOLDEN-CHEEKED WOODPECKER

M

F

p.52
YUCATAN WOODPECKER

M

F

p.54
FLINT-BILLED WOODPECKER

M

F

p.52
BLACK-CHEEKED WOODPECKER

M

F

p.53
BROWN WOODPECKER

M

F

p.53
STRICKLAND'S WOODPECKER

Murrell
Butler

23

M

ELEGANT TROGON
p.49

GREEN KINGFISHER
p.51

F

M

N. (RED-SHAFTED) FLICKER
p.54

M

F

ACORN
WOODPECKER
p.52

M

p.107
(Y.-SHAFTED)
FLICKER

M

F

F

M

M

N. (GILDED)
FLICKER
p.54

M

F

F

GfWo

p.53
HAIRY WOODPECKER

p. 52
GILA W.

F

UTTALL'S
OODPECKER
p.53

M

M

F

M

F

p.53
LADDER-BACKED W.

p.53
ARIZONA W.

p.64
ROSE-THROATED BECARD

HORNED LARK
p.66

PURPLE MARTIN
p.66

M

F

p.67
BARN SWALLOW

CLIFF SWALLOW
p.67

p.66
N. ROUGH-WINGED SWALLOW

p.67
CAVE SWALLOW

p.66
VIOLET-GREEN SWALLOW

GfWo = GOLDEN-FRONTED WOODPECKER - p.52

24

RUFOUS-BREASTED SPINETAIL
p.55

MOUNTAIN LEAFGLEANER
p.55

RUDDY LEAFGLEANER
p.55

BUFF-THROATED
LEAFGLEANER
p.55

p.55
PLAIN XENOPS

p.55
TAWNY-THROATED
LEAFTOSSER

p.55
SCALY-THROATED
LEAFTOSSER

p.56
GREAT ANTSHRIKE

M

F

M

M

F
BARRED ANTSHRIKE
p.57

M

p.57
RUSSET ANTSHRIKE

F

p.57
PLAIN ANTVIREO

F

p.57
SLATY ANTWREN

M

F

p.57
DOTTED-WINGED
ANTWREN

M

F

M

p.57
DUSKY ANTBIRD

F

p.57
BLACK-FACED ANTTHRUSH

p.57
SCALED ANTPITTA

M

p.65
RED-CAPPED
MANAKIN

F

M

F

M

F

p.65
LONG-TAILED MANAKIN

p.65
WHITE-COLLARED MANAKIN

p.65
THRUSH-LIKE MANAKIN

Murrell
Butler

25

LOVELY COTINGA
p.65

M

F

STREAKED ATTILA
p.62

SPECKLED MOURNER
p.62

RUFOUS MOURNER
p.62

RUFOUS PIHA
p.65

CINNAMON BECARD
p.64

MEXICAN BECARD
p.64

M

F

BLACK-CROWNED TITYRA
p.65

...ASKED TITYRA
p.64

M

F

M

F

FORK-TAILED
FLYCATCHER
p.64

STREAKED
FLYCATCHER
p.63

p.63
PIRATIC
FLYCATCHER

...CIAL FLYCATCHER
p.63

NUTTING'S
FLYCATCHER
p.62

p.63

BOAT-BILLED
FLYCATCHER

YUCATAN
FLYCATCHER
p.62

FLAMMULATED
FLYCATCHER
p.63

Murrell
Butler

p.60
TROPICAL PEWEE

p.60
WHITE-THROATED FLYCATCHER

p.61
PINE FLYCATCHER

p.61
YELLOWISH FLYCATCHER

26

TUFTED FLYCATCHER
p.59

BELTED FLYCATCHER
p.59

PILEATED FLYCATCHER
p.59

RUDDY-TAILED
FLYCATCHER
p.59

SULPHUR-RUMPED
FLYCATCHER
p.59

M

F
ROYAL FLYCATCHER
p.59

p.59
MEXICAN SPADEBILL

EYE-RINGED FLATBILL
p.59

p.59
WHITE-EYED FLYCATCHER

p.58
COMMON TODY-BILL

p.58
SLATY-HEADED TODY-BILL

P.58
NORTHERN BENTBILL

p.58
YELLOW-BELLIED ELAENIA

p.58
CARIBBEAN ELAENIA

p.58
GREENISH ELAENIA

p.57
PALTRY TYRANNULET

p.58
YELLOW-BELLIED
TYRANNULET

p.58
SEPIA-CAPPED FLYCATCHER

p.58
OLEAGINOUS FLYCATCHER

Murrell
Butler

BLACK PHOEBE
p.61

SAY'S PHOEBE
p.61

VERMILION FLYCATCHER
p.62

M   F

SCISSOR-TAILED FLYCATCHER
p.64

WESTERN
KINGBIRD
p.64

TROPICAL
KINGBIRD
p.63

p.64
SSIN'S KINGBIRD

SULPHUR-BELLIED
FLYCATCHER
p.63

ICK-BILLED
KINGBIRD
p.64

GREAT KISKADEE
p.63

H-THROATED
YCATCHER
p.62

WESTERN
PEWEE
p.60

p.62
WIED'S
FLYCATCHER

p.62
OLIVACEOUS
FLYCATCHER

p.60
OLIVE-SIDED FLYCATCHER

N. BEARDLESS
FLYCATCHER
p.58

p.60
GREATER PEWEE

p.61
DUSKY FLYCATCHER

p.61
GRAY FLYCATCHER

p.61
BUFF-BREASTED FLYCATCHER

Butler '73

28

WHITE-BELLIED
MARTIN
p.66

M

F

BLACK-CAPPED
SWALLOW
p.66

p.66
MANGRO
SWALLO

GRAY-BREASTED
MARTIN
p.66

WHITE-THROATED MAGPIE-JAY
p.67

TAMAULIPAS CROW
SINALOA CROW
p.69

p.67
COLLIE'S MAGPIE-JAY

TUFTED JAY
p.67

BROWN JAY
p.67

"WHITE-TIPPED"

SAN BLAS JAY
p.68

Im.+Juv.

Juv.

p.68
YUCATAN JAY

AZURE-HOODED
JAY
p.68

OMILTEMI JAY
p.68

BEECHEY'S JAY
p.68

p.68
DWARF JAY

p.68
BLACK-THROATED JAY

p.69
UNICOLORED JAY

Murrell
Butler

CLARK'S NUTCRACKER
p.69

COMMON RAVEN
p.69

CHIHUAHUAN RAVEN
p.69

PINYON JAY
p.69

GREEN JAY
p.68

SCRUB JAY
p.68

MEXICAN JAY
p.68

p.67
STELLER'S JAY

MEXICAN CHICKADEE
p.69

MOUNTAIN CHICKADEE
p.69

p.70
PLAIN TITMOUSE

p.70
TUFTED
(BLACK-CRESTED)
TITMOUSE

BRIDLED TITMOUSE
p.69

M

M

F

p.70
VERDIN

Im.

p.70
BUSHTIT

p.70
PYGMY NUTHATCH

p.70
WHITE-BREASTED
NUTHATCH

30

GRAY WREN
p.71

BARRED WREN
p.71

GIANT WREN
p.7

SPOTTED WREN
p.71

RUFOUS-NAPED WREN
p.71

YUCATAN WREN
p.71

p.71
BOUCARD'S
WREN

PLAIN WREN
p.73

p.72
SINALOA WREN

p.72
BANDED WREN

p.72
RUFOUS-
AND-WHITE
WREN

p.72
WHITE-BROWED
WREN

p.72
HAPPY
WREN

p.72
SPOTTED-
BREASTED WREN

p.73
SOCORRO WREN

p.
CLARIO
WREN

p.73
RUFOUS-BROWED
WREN

p.73
TROPICAL
HOUSE-WREN

p.73
COZUMEL WREN

p.74
HIGHLAND
WOOD-WRE

p.74
LOWLAND
WOOD-WREN

p.74
WHITE-BELLIED
WREN

p.72
SUMICHRAST'S
WREN

p.74
NIGHTIN
WR

Mur
But

WRENTIT
p.78

AMERICAN
DIPPER
p.74

p.73
MARSH WREN

p.70
[C]ROWN CREEPER

p.73
SEDGE WREN

p.73
NORTHERN
HOUSE-WREN

p.71
[CAC]TUS WREN

p.72
CAROLINA WREN

p.73
BEWICK'S WREN

p.78
LONG-BILLED
THRASHER

p.72
ROCK WREN

p.72
CANYON WREN

CURVE-BILLED
THRASHER
p.79

p.79
CALIFORNIA
THRASHER

p.78
[B]ENDIRE'S THRASHER

p.79
[L]ECONTE'S
[T]HRASHER

p.78
NORTHERN
MOCKINGBIRD

TOWNSEND'S
SOLITAIRE
p.75

p.79
CRISSAL THRASHER

p.77
AMERICAN ROBIN

31

32

p.78
COZUMEL
THRASHER

p.79
OCELLATED
THRASHER

p.78
GRAY THRASHER

p.79 BLUE
MOCKINGBIRD

p.79
BLUE-AND-WHITE
MOCKINGBIRD

p.78
BLACK CATBIRD

p.78

SOCORRO
MOCKINGBIRD

p.78 TROPICAL MOCKINGBIRD

p.77
SAN LUCAS ROBIN

M

F

p.77 RUFOUS-COLLARED ROBIN

p.77
RUFOUS-BACKED
ROBIN

p.77
WHITE-THROATED ROBIN

p.77
CLAY-COLORED
ROBIN

p.77
MOUNTAIN
ROBIN

M

F
p.76
BLACK ROBIN

p.76
SLATY SOLITAIRE

M

F

p.77
AZTEC THRUSH

p.76
BROWN-BACKED
SOLITAIRE

p.76
SPOT
THR

p.76
RUSSET
THRUSH

p.76
HIGHLAND
THRUSH

p.76
ORANGE-BILLED
THRUSH

p.76
BLACK-HEADED
THRUSH

Murrell
Butler

ROCK WREN
p.72

CANYON WREN
p.72

p.73
WINTER WREN

p.78
GRAY CATBIRD

p.78
SAGE THRASHER

p.76
WOOD THRUSH

p.76
HERMIT THRUSH

p.76
SWAINSON'S THRUSH

M

p.76
GRAY-CHEEKED THRUSH

Y

M   F

M

p.75
EASTERN BLUEBIRD

P.75
OUNTAIN
UEBIRD

p.79
WATER PIPIT
Win.

F

p.75
WESTERN BLUEBIRD

p.79
AR WAXWING

M

p.79
SPRAGUE'S PIPIT

EUROPEAN STARLING
p.80

p.106
OUSE SPARROW

Im.

Win.

Murrell
Butler

WHITE-LORED GNATCATCHER
p.75

F

M

Win.M

TROPICAL GNATCATCHER
p.75

F

M

BLACK-CAPPED GNATCATCHER
p.75

F

M

Win.M

LONG-BILLED GNATWREN
p.74

M

F

RUFOUS-BROWED PEPPERSHRIKE
p.82

p.80
GRAY SILKY-FLYCATCHER

HIGHLAND SHRIKE-VIREO
p.82

GREEN SHRIKE-VIREO
p.82

p.80
COZUMEL VIREO

p.80
MANGROVE VIREO

p.81
GOLDEN VIREO

p.81
DWARF VIREO

p.82
YUCATAN VIREO

p.80
SLATY VIREO

p.82
TAWNY-CROWNED GREENLET

p.82
LESSER GREENLET

Murrell
Butler

35

M

p.81
BLACK-CAPPED VIREO

p.80
WHITE-EYED VIREO

p.81
HUTTON'S VIREO

p.81
GRAY VIREO

p.81
BELL'S VIREO

p.81
SOLITARY VIREO

p.82
RED-EYED VIREO

p.81
WARBLING VIREO

p.83
ORANGE-CROWNED
WARBLER

p.83
VIRGINIA'S
WARBLER

p.83
COLIMA WARBLER

p.83
LUCY'S WARBLER

M

F

p.89
OLIVE WARBLER

Win.

p.84
YELLOW-RUMPED WARBLER

M

F

p.84
BLACK-THROATED
GRAY WARBLER

p.85
GRACE'S WARBLER

M

F

p.86
MACGILLIVRAY'S WARBLER

M

F

p.87
MEADOW WARBLER

p.87
RED-FACED WARBLER

p.88
PAINTED REDSTART

p.89
BANANAQUIT

Butler

36

BLACK-AND-WHITE WARBLER
p.86
M   F

PROTHONOTARY WARBLER
p.86
M   F

p.86
SWAINSON'S
WARBLER

WORM-EATING W.
p.86

GOLDEN-WINGED W.
p.82
M   F

"BREWSTER'S"

"LAWRENCE'S"

GwWa

p.82
BLUE-WINGED
WARBLER

TENNESSEE W.
p.83
M   F

NASHVILLE W.
p.83
M   F

p.83
NORTHERN
PARULA
M   F

TROPICAL PARULA
p.83
M   F

YELLOW WARBLER
p.83
M   F

MAGNOLIA WARBLER
p.84
M   F

"GOLDEN" W.

PINE WARBLER
p.85
M   F

CAPE MAY WARBLER
p.84
M   F

TOWNSEND'S W.
p.84
M   F

BLACK-THROATED
BLUE WARBLER
p.84
M   F

HERMIT WARBLER
p.84
M   F

BLACK-THROATED GREEN W.
p.84
M   F   Win.

GOLDEN-CHEEKED WARBLER
p.85
M   F

37

M
F
p.85
CERULEAN WARBLER

M
F
p.85
BLACKBURNIAN WARBLER

M
F
p.85
YELLOW-THROATED WARBLER

M
F
p.84
CHESTNUT-SIDED
WARBLER

M
F
p.85
BAY-BREASTED
WARBLER
Win.

M
F
p.85
BLACKPOLL WARBLER

M
F
p.85
PRAIRIE WARBLER

east.
west.
Win.
p.85
PALM WARBLER

p.86
OVENBIRD

p.86
NORTHERN WATERTHRUSH

p.86
LOUISIANA
WATERTHRUSH

p.86
KENTUCKY WARBLER

p.88
YELLOW-BREASTED CHAT

M
F
p.87
HOODED WARBLER

M
F
p.87
WILSON'S WARBLER

M
F
p.87
CANADA WARBLER

M
F
p.86
AMERICAN REDSTART

M
F
p.86
MOURNING WARBLER

Murrell
Butler

38

SPOT-BREASTED WARBLER
p.83

M

F

p.83
SOCORRO PARULA

M

F

p.84
MANGROVE WARBLER

M

F

p.87
BELDING'S
YELLOWTHROAT

M

F

p.87
ALTAMIRA YELLOWTHROAT

M

F

p.87
COMMON (CHAPALA) YELLOWTHROAT

M

F

p.87
BLACK-POLLED YELLOWTHROAT

M

F

p.87
BRUSH YELLOWTHROAT

M

F

p.88
RED-BREASTED CHAT

M

F

p.88
GRAY-THROATED CHAT

p.88
SLATE-THROATED REDSTART

p.88
FAN-TAILED WARBLER

p.87
RED WARBLER

p.88
PINK-HEADED WARBLER

p.88
GOLDEN-CROWNED WARBLER

p.88
BELL'S WARBLER

p.88
RUFOUS-CAPPED WARBLER

p.88
DELATTRE'S WARBLER

Murrell
Butler '71

BLUE-CROWNED TANAGER
p.89

BLUE-HOODED EUPHONIA
p.90

SCRUB EUPHONIA
p.90

YELLOW-THROATED EUPHONIA
p.90

M

M

M

F

F

M

CABANIS'S TANAGER
p.89

GOLDEN-HOODED
TANAGER
F   p.89

OLIVE-BACKED
EUPHONIA
p.90

YELLOW-WINGED
TANAGER
p.90

M

M

F

RED-HEADED TANAGER
p.90

SONG TANAGER
p.92

p.91
CRIMSON-COLLARED TANAGER

M

F

M

F

M

F

ROSE-THROATED
TANAGER   p.91

WHITE-WINGED
TANAGER
p.91

STRIPED TANAGER
p.91

M

M

M

RED-HEADED TANAGER   p.91

F

F

p.90
RED-CROWNED TANAGER

p.91
JUNGLE TANAGER

BLACK-THROATED
SHRIKE-TANAGER
p.90

M

F

M

F

COMMON BUSH-TANAGER
p.92

GRAY-HEADED TANAGER
p.90

ROSY THRUSH-TANAGER
p.92

Murrell
Butler '71

40

PHAINOPEPLA
p.80

LOGGERHEAD SHRIKE
p.80

SUMMER TANAGER
p.91
M

M

F

F

NORTHERN CARDINAL
p.96

HEPATIC TANAGER
p.91
M

M

F

F

M

WESTERN TANAGER
p.91

PYRRHULOXIA
p.96

F

F

M

M

BLACK-HEADED GROSBEAK
p.96

BLUE GROSBEAK
p.97

M

F

F

M

M

LAZULI BUNTING
p.97   M

VARIED BUNTING
p.97

F

F

PAINTED BUNTING
p.97

M

M

EVENING GROSBEAK
p.106
F

HOUSE FINCH
p.105

M

F

M

PURPLE FINCH
p.105

M

F

M

F

F

CASSIN'S FINCH
p.105

M

PINE SISKIN
p.106

COLLARED SEEDEATER
p.100

41

BLACK-HEADED SALTATOR
p.96

BUFF-THROATED SALTATOR
p.96

GRAY SALTATOR
p.95

BLACK-FACED
GROSBEAK
p.96

CRIMSON-COLLARED
GROSBEAK
p.96

M

F

BLUE BUNTING
p.97

M

F

BLUE-BLACK
GROSBEAK
p.97

M

YELLOW GROSBEAK
p.96

M

F

ORANGE-BREASTED BUNTING
p.97

F

YELLOW-FACED
GRASSQUIT
p.100

M

ROSITA BUNTING
p.97

M

F

M

F

F

VARIABLE
SEEDEATER
p.100

M

F

M

F

HOODED
GROSBEAK
p.106

M

F

BLUE-BLACK
GRASSQUIT
p.99

M

F

RUDDY-BREASTED
SEEDEATER
p.100

F

BLUE SEEDEATER
p.100

M

M

M

M

M

F

THICK-BILLED SEED-FINCH
p.100

BLACK-CAPPED SISKIN
p.106

BLACK-HEADED SISKIN
p.106

GRASSLAND YELLOW-FINCH
p.100

Murrell
Butler

42

M

F

p.100
SLATY FINCH

p.98
RUFOUS-CAPPED FINCH

p.98
WHITE-NAPED FINCH

YELLOW-THROATED FINCH
p.98

p.98
CHESTNUT-CAPPED F.

p.98
SAN MARTIN FINCH

p.98
GREEN-STRIPED FINCH

COLLARED TOWHEE

1

2

3

RUFOUS-SIDED (SPOTTED)
TOWHEE
p.99

p.99

4

5

6

Representative types: Collared Towhee x(?) Rufous-sided Towhee

p.99
WHITE-THROATED
TOWHEE

p.98
ORANGE-BILLED SP.

p.98
GREEN-BACKED
SPARROW

p.98
RUSTY-CROWNED SPARROW

p.98
PREVOST'S SPARROW

p.99
WHITE-EARED SPARROW

p.102
STRIPED SPARROW

p.103
SIERRA MADRE
SPARROW

Murrel
Butler

43

E-BREASTED GROSBEAK p.96 M F

M F p.97 INDIGO BUNTING

M F p.97 DICKCISSEL

M F p.106 AMERICAN GOLDFINCH

p.99 GREEN-TAILED TOWHEE

F M p.103 LARK BUNTING

SPER SPARROW p.102

Sum. Win. p.102 CHIPPING SPARROW

Ad. Juv. p.102 FIELD SPARROW

Ad. Im. E-CROWNED SPARROW p.104

Ad. Im. p.104 GOLDEN-CROWNED SPARROW

Bright Dull p.104 WHITE-THROATED SPARROW

p.103 FOX SPARROW

p.104 LINCOLN'S SPARROW

p.104 SWAMP SPARROW

Sum. M F Win. M p.105 McCOWN'S LONGSPUR

Sum. M Win. F Win. M p.105 CHESTNUT-COLLARED LONGSPUR

Murrell Butler

44

BLUE-GRAY GNATCATCHER
p.75
F
M

BLACK-TAILED GNATCATCHER
p.75
F

Sum. M

Win. M

GOLDEN-CROWNED KINGLET
M
p.74
F

RUBY-CROWNED KINGLET
p.74
M
F
M

M

M

GREAT-TAILED
GRACKLE
p.93

F

M

BRONZED COWBIRD
p.93

BROWN-HEADED COWB
p.93
F

M

F

ORCHARD ORIOLE
M
p.93
F

"BULLOCK'S"
M

"BALT."
M

F

ALTAMIRA ORI
p.94

BREWER'S
BLACKBIRD
p.93

SCOTT'S ORIOLE
p.95
M

p.94
NORTHERN
ORIOLE

F

AUDUBON'S ORIOLE
p.94
M

F

M

F

p.92
RED-WINGED BLACKBIRD

HOODED ORIOLE
p.93

M

F

TRICOLORED BLACKBIRD
p.92

M

F

M

YELLOW-HEADED BLACKBIRD
p.92

EASTERN MEADOWLARK
p.92

45

WAGLER'S OROPENDOLA
p.95

MONTEZUMA OROPENDOLA
p.95

YELLOW-BILLED CACIQUE
p.95

MEXICAN CACIQUE
p.95

M

M

F

GIANT COWBIRD
p.93

SINGING BLACKBIRD
p.92

ABEILLE'S ORIOLE
p.95

M

F

p.93
OCHRE ORIOLE

BAR-WINGED ORIOLE
p.93

WAGLER'S ORIOLE
p.93

_ACK-COWLED ORIOLE
p.93

M

F

p.94
YELLOW-TAILED ORIOLE

YELLOW-BACKED ORIOLE
p.94

M

M

ORANGE ORIOLE
p.94

STREAKED-BACKED ORIOLE
p.94

F

M

F

M

F

M

F

M

F

HIGHLAND
HONEYCREEPER
p.89

GREEN HONEYCREEPER
p.89

RED-LEGGED HONEYCREEPER
p.89

SHINING HONEYCREEPER
p.89

Murrell
Butler '71

LESSER GOLDFINCH
p.106
M
F
46

M
F
p.106
LAWRENCE'S GOLDFINCH

RED CROSSBILL
p.105
M

F

"GREEN-BACKED"
G.

OLIVE SPARROW
p.98

BROWN TOWHEE
p.99

ABERT'S TOWHEE
p.99

GRASSHOPPER SPARROW
p.103

SAVANNAH SPARROW
p.103

LARK SPARROW
p.102

RUFOUS-WINGED
SPARROW
p.101

RUFOUS-CROWNED
SPARROW
p.101

CASSIN'S
SPARROW
p.101

BLACK-THROATED
SPARROW
p.102

SAGE SPARROW
p.103

p.101
BOTTERI'S
SPARROW

"SLATE-
COLORED"
J.

"GRAY-HEADED" J.

"OREGON" J.

p.104
DARK-EYED JUNCO

YELLOW-EYED JUNCO
p.105

p.102
CLAY-COLORED SPARROW

M

F

BLACK-CHINNED SPARROW

Im.

p.102
BREWER'S SPARROW

p.102

p.103
SONG SPARROW

47

FIVE-STRIPED SPARROW
p.103

BRIDLED SPARROW
p.101

BLACK-CHESTED SPARROW
p.101

STRIPED-HEADED SPARROW
p.101

CINCHRAST'S
SPARROW
p.101

p.101
OAXACA SPARROW

p.101
RUSTY SPARROW

p.104
ANDEAN
SPARROW

GALAPAGOS
STORM-
PETREL
p.4

COLLARED PLOVER
p.23

BLUE-GRAY
TANAGER
p.90

p.94
SPOTTED ORIOLE

GREAT FRIGATEBIRD
p.6

M

F

WORTHEN'S SPARROW
p.102

p.3
WEDGE-TAILED
SHEARWATER

p.18
WHITE-BELLIED
CHACHALACA

M

F

p.4
RED-FOOTED BOOBY

p.54
IMPERIAL WOODPECKER

48

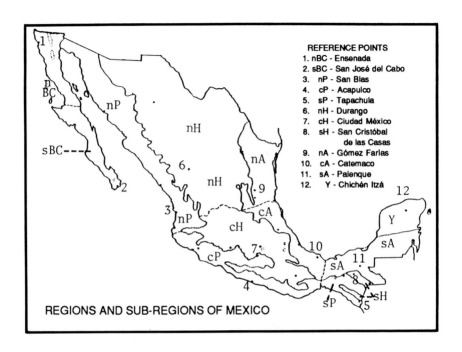

REFERENCE POINTS
1. nBC - Ensenada
2. sBC - San José del Cabo
3. nP - San Blas
4. cP - Acapulco
5. sP - Tapachula
6. nH - Durango
7. cH - Ciudad México
8. sH - San Cristóbal
       de las Casas
9. nA - Gómez Farías
10. cA - Catemaco
11. sA - Palenque
12. Y - Chichén Itzá

REGIONS AND SUB-REGIONS OF MEXICO

STATES OF MEXICO

Rufous-breasted Spinetail. *Synallaxis erythrothorax.* Z4b49.   Chepito
M,G,B,ES,H. Resident up to 2500', sP, csA, Y. Rare; hedgerows, thickets, brushy
borders of humid forest, river-border woods. V: Rasping, *one-two-three-kick.*
Pl.24. 6" *Olive-brown back; gray head; rich reddish brown breast; gray belly; throat
finely streaked; tail rather long, spine-tipped.*

Mountain Leafgleaner (Spec.Fo.-g.).*Philydor variegaticeps.* Z4c20.Trepador Montés
M,G,H,CR-SAm. Resident, 2500 to 8000', sw.edge csH (Guerrero to Chiapas), csA.
Rare; middle branches and twigs, in cloud forest or humid oak or pine-oak woods.
Pl.24. 6" *Brown above, slightly paler below; throat broadly creamy, faintly scaled;
eye-ring and line behind eye buff; with dark line below that. See Buff-throated L'gl.*

Buff-throated Leafgleaner (Fo.g.).*Automolus ochrolaemus.* Z4c44.Trepador Rojizo
M-SAm,x.ES. Resident, sea level to 4000', csA. Rare; undergrowth, humid forest.
Pl.24. 7" *Like* Mountain L'gl.*, but notably larger; most of ear-patch and throat
broadly rich buff; forages closer to the ground, in shrubs or lower branches.*

Ruddy Leafgleaner (Fol.-gleaner). *Automolus rubiginosus.* Z4c50. Trepador Castaño
M-SAm. Resident, 2000 to 8000', csP, sw.edge of csH, csA (San Luis Potosí to
Chiapas). Rare; shrubs and other undergrowth in humid steep-mountain-slope forest.
Pl.24. 8" *Mostly rich brown; throat bright tawny rufous; bill straight, sharp, dark.*

Plain Xenops. *Xenops minutus.* Z4c63.   Barboncito Sencillo
M-SAm,x.ES. Resident up to 2500', csA. Rare; dense humid forest, or borders.
Pl.24. 4 1/2" *Dull brown; reddish wings and tail; buffy eye-stripe, prominent white
sub-malar stripe; faintly streaked chest; short, up-turned bill.*

Tawny-throated Leaftosser. *Scler.mexicanus.* Z4c54. Breñero Gargantianaranjado
M,G,H,CR,P,SAm. Resident, 1500 to 4500', csA (Puebla to Chiapas). Rare; stream
ravines, dense humid forest; on ground or in low shrubs. V: sharp, loud, *chip.*
Pl.24. 6" *Dark brown to reddish brown; throat tawny rufous; bill slender, slightly
decurved, tail short, rounded.*

Scaly-throated Leaftosser. *Sclerurus guatemalensis.* Z4c59.   Tirapalo
M-SAm. Resident up to 3000', sA (e.Veracruz to Quintana Roo). Very rare; walking
on the ground or moving in low shrubs, usually in rocky areas in dense humid forest.
Pl.24. 6" *Like* Tawny-throated Leaftosser, *but darker, duller brown; throat
scalloped brown and buff; bill slightly shorter, and straight.*

NEOTROPICAL CREEPERS - DENDROCOLAPTIDAE - TREPATRONCOS
Twelve residents; more central and southern; medium-small; legs and neck short; tail
medium, strong-tipped; bill short to medium-long, curved or straight; trunks and
branches, humid forest to pine forest. Distinguish by size, streaks or spots. **Plate 21.**

Tawny-winged Creeper. *Dendrocincla anabatina.* Z5a3.   Trepatronco Sepia
M-Pan,x.ES. Resident, near sea level, csA, Y. Rare; dense humid forest, borders.
Pl.21. 7" *Dull olive brown; throat whitish; faint streaks on chest; rufous wing-patch
and tail; buff eye-stripe.*

Ruddy Creeper. *Dendrocincla homochroa.* Z5a5.   Trepatronco Rojizo
M-SAm,x.ES. Resident up to 4500', sP, sA (Oaxaca to Quintana Roo), Y. Rare; low
branches, low tree-trunks or on ground near army ants, in open forest or cloud forest.
Pl.21. 7" *Plain dark dull rufous; throat paler, tawnier; bill straight, grayish brown.*

Olivaceous Creeper. *Sittasomus griseicapillus.* Z5a8.   Trepatronco Cabeza Gris
M-SAm. Resident up to 8000', csP, csH (Jalisco+Chiapas), A, Y. Rare; in dense
humid forest, dense scrubby woods, river-border forest; low to high on tree-trunks.
Pl.21. 6" *Head, upper back, and underparts medium olive-gray; wings, scapulars,
rump, uptacs, and rather long, spine-tipped tail rufous; bill short, slender.*

Wedge-billed Creeper. *Glyphorhynchus spirurus.* Z5a9.   Pico de Cuña
M-SAm,x.ES. Resident, near sea level, csA. Rare; trunks, branches, forest or borders.

Pl.21. *6" Olive-brown, with rufous wings and tail; ear-patch, throat and breast lightly streaked buff; line behind eye buff; bill short, wedge-shaped.*
Giant (S.-b.) Creeper. *Xiphocolaptes promeropirhynchus.* Z5a15.   Trepatronco Gigante
M-SAm. Resident, 5000 to 11,000', csH (San Luis Potosí+Guerrero to Chiapas). Rare; pine woods, pine-oak forest in humid areas, or dense cloud forest, high on trunks.
Pl.21. *12" Olive-brown above; buffy brown below; rufous wings and tail; buffy throat; lightly streaked head and breast; bill long, rather heavy, slightly decurved.*
Barred Creeper. *Dendrocolaptes certhia.* Z5a21.   Trepatronco Barrado
M-SAm. Resident up to 5000', csP (Guerrero to Chiapas), csA, Y. Rare; humid forest, borders, dense river-border woods, usually on lower portions of tree-trunks.
Pl.21. *11" Reddish brown above; paler below; with fine black bars all over, except bright rufous wings and tail; bill heavy, black, or (sw.Oaxaca) pale brown.*
Black-banded Creeper. *Dendrocolaptes picumnus.* Z5a24.   Trepatronco Ocotero
M,G,H,CR-SAm. Resident, 4500 to 7500', sH (Chiapas). Very rare; pine or pine-oak.
Pl.21. *10" Olive-brown above; dull buffy brown below; rufous wings, tail; narrow buffy streaks on head, throat, breast; belly and flanks barred black; bill dark, straight.*
Laughing (Iv.-b.) Creeper. *Xiphorhynchus flavigaster.* Z5a35.   Trepatronco Arañero
M-CR. Resident up to 8000', P, cH (Jalisco), A, Y. Common; mangrove swamps, deciduous woods, forest borders, river-border woods, and tree-dotted pastures. V: mellow descending *tyew-tyew-tyew;* also a mellow, descending, "laughing" whinny.
Pl.21. *8" Dark brown above; buffy brown below; rather heavily streaked; except nearly plain buffy throat; rufous wings, tail; bill long, slender, decurved, pale.*
Spotted Creeper. *Xiphorhynchus erythropygius.* Z5a37.   Trepatronco Manchado
M-SAm. Resident, 4000 to 6500', csP (Guerrero to Chiapas), csA (San Luis Potosí to Chiapas). Rare; cloud forest, or other dense humid forest, middle or higher tree-trunks.
Pl.21. *8" Mostly olive brown with light streaking above, and many buffy spots below; rufous wings and tail; bill mostly dark, rather long.*
White-striped Creeper.*Lepidocolap. leucogaster.* Z5a39. Trepatronco Vientre Blanco
M. Resident, 1800 to 13,000', nP, ncH (Chihuahua to Oaxaca). Rare; somewhat arid but rather dense scrubby woods or river-border woods, or pine, pine-oak, or fir forest.
Pl.21. *9" Plain dull reddish brown back; rufous wings and tail; head and underparts heavily streaked _black_ (or dark olive) _and white_; chin and upper throat white.*
Souleyet's (S.-b.) Creeper.*Lepidocolaptes souleyetii.* Z5a40. Trepatronco de Souleyet
M-SAm. Resident up to 3000', csP (Guerrero to Chiapas), csA. Rare; dense forest, river-border woods, lower-mountain pine woods. V: a descending, rolling chatter.
Pl.21. *8" Dull brown, reddish above, buffy below; rufous wings and tail; lightly streaked above, more heavily below; crown streaked, not spotted; bill long, slender, slightly decurved. See Spotted-crowned Creeper.*
Spotted-crowned Creeper. *Lepidocolaptes affinis.* Z5a42.   Trepatronco Montés
M-SAm,x.B. Resident, 3500 to 11,500', csP (Guerrero to Chiapas), H (San Luis Potosí to Chiapas), csA. Rare+; middle trunks, in cloud forest, pine or pine-oak forest.
Pl.21. *8" Like* Souleyet's Creeper, *but crown finely spotted, not streaked;* (ordinarily occurs at higher elevations than Souleyet's Creeper).

ANTBIRDS - FORMICARIIDAE - PUPEROS, HORMIGUEROS
Nine residents; mostly se.Mexico; legs medium, neck short; bill medium, rather heavy; on or near the ground, thickets, forest; Neotropical; male and female plumages. Distinguish by voice, plumage colors, patterns. **Plate 24.**

Great Antshrike. *Taraba major.* Z6a7.   Bebel Grande
M-SAm,x.ES. Resident up to 2500', csA. Rare; humid thickets, forest borders.
Pl.24. *8" Mainly white below; red eye; thick, black, hook-tipped bill. M: Black above; white wing-bars; black untacs; concealed white back-patch; small crest. F: Similar, but rufous above; no wing-bars.*

Barred Antshrike. *Thamnophilus doliatus.* Z6a17. <u>Gritón de Barras Anchas</u>
M-SAm. <u>Resident up to 5000', sP, A, Y.</u> Common; thickets, scrubby woods, forest
borders, hedgerows. V: an accelerating clucking chatter which ends in an abrupt slurred
note, as if the bird were inhaling on that note. See Citreoline and Black-headed Trogon.
*Pl.24. 6" Iris white. M: Body and wings barred and head streaked, black and
white; floppy crest with partly hidden white patch. F: Rufous above; tawny below;
crown rufous; face streaked blackish on buffy.*

Russet Antshrike. *Thamnistes anabatinus.* Z6a44. <u>Pupero Café</u>
M-SAm,x.ES. <u>Resident, near sea level, sA (Tabasco).</u> Very rare; dense humid forest.
*Pl.24. 6" M: Dull tawny brown above, with rufous wings and tail; tawny buff
below, and on face, shading to more yellowish and grayish on belly and untacs;
cinnamon back-patch may show; bill rather heavy. F: Similar but slightly duller; no
back-patch. Much paler below and on face than* similar birds, Mourners, Pihas, etc.

Plain Antvireo. *Dysithamnus mentalis.* Z6a47. <u>Hormiguero de Matorral</u>
M-SAm,x.N. <u>Resident, near sea level, sA (Chiapas and Campeche).</u> Very rare; forest.
*Pl.24. 4 " Faint wing-bars; short tail. M: Medium to dark gray above and on breast;
throat whitish; belly whitish or pale yellow. F: Browner above, crown rufous.*

Slaty Antwren. *Myrmotherula schisticolor.* Z6a75. <u>Hormiguero Apizarrado</u>
M-SAm,x.B,ES. <u>Resident, 2500 to 4500', sA (Chiapas).</u> Rare; shrubs in humid forest.
*Pl.24. 4" Slender, short bill; short tail. M: Gray with black throat, breast; spotty
wing-bars; white spot under wing. F: Dark brown above; buffy wing-bars; buff or
tawny buff below.*

Dotted-winged Antwren. *Microrhopias quixensis.* Z6a97. <u>Pupero Negro</u>
M-SAm,x.ES. <u>Resident, sea level to 2500', csA.</u> Rare; humid forest, second-growth.
*Pl.24. 4 1/2" M: Black; concealed white back-patch; spotty wing-bars and
tail-corners white. F: Similar but slaty gray above and rufous below.*

Dusky Antbird. *Cercomacra tyrannina.* Z6a118. <u>Hormiguero Tiránico</u>
M-SAm,x.ES. <u>Resident, sea level to 3000', csA.</u> Rare; humid forest borders, thickets.
*Pl.24. 6" M: Slaty gray; faint spotty pale wing-bars, tail-tip; concealed back-patch.
F: Olive-brown above; wings rufous; concealed back-patch below.*

Black-faced Antthrush. *Formicarius analis.* Z6a191. <u>Cabezinegro</u>
M-SAm,x.ES. <u>Resident up to 4000', csA, Y.</u> Rare; walking on ground (tail pointing
straight up) or perched low while singing its long song, in dense humid forest, or
remnants. V: (in M, G, and B) a deliberate whistle, first note higher-pitched - *haa,
ha-ha-ha-ha,* or a mellow rolling *tch-ba-ba-ba-ba-ba-ba-ba-ba,* the last 3 notes higher.
*Pl.24. 7" Dark reddish brown above; dark gray below, paler on belly; pale blue
eye-ring; black throat and part of face, bordered by rufous half-collar; short black tail.*

Scaled Antpitta. *Grallaria guatimalensis.* Z6b8. <u>Cholina</u>
M-SAm,x.B. <u>Resident up to 11,000', csP (Jalisco to Chiapas), cH (Michoacán to
Chiapas), csA.</u> Rare; dense humid forest, hopping on ground or in shrub branches.
*Pl.24. 8" Scalloped blackish on olive back and bluish gray crown; tawny rufous
(cH birds are much paler) below; throat and malar area striped dark brown and buff,
with black necklace; tail very short, rufous; bill rather heavy, blackish.*

FLYCATCHERS - TYRANNIDAE - MOSQUERITOS, MOSQUEROS

Seventy-one species, mostly residents; widespread Mexico; medium-small to very
small; legs and neck short, tail very short to very long, bill mostly medium-short,
flattened; semi-desert to humid forest; widespread New World. Distinguish by voice,
bill shape, tail length, size, behavior, colors, patterns. **Plates 25, 26, and 27.**

Paltry Tyrannulet. *Zimmerius vilissimus.* Z10b11. <u>Mosquerito Centroamericano</u>
M-SAm,x.B. <u>Resident, 1500 to 4000', sP (Chiapas), sA (Chiapas).</u> Rare; humid
forest borders, hedgerows, plantations, and gardens. V: a quiet *peer-deer,* or *pee-wee.*
Pl.26. 4 1/2" Greenish olive above, grayer on crown and nape; pale gray below

with very faint breast-streaks, and yellowish wash on belly and untacs; white forehead and line over eye; bill very short, small.

Yellow-bellied Tyrannulet. *Ornithion semiflavum.* Z10b17. Mosquerito Pequeñito M-CR,x.ES. Resident up to 5000', csA. Rare; humid forest, river-border woods. *Pl.26. 3 1/2" Olive above; crown dark gray; prominent line over eye white; yellow below, faintly streaked; tail and bill very short.*

N.Beardless Flycatcher (Tyr.).*Camptostoma imberbe.* Z10b19.Mosquerito Lampiño US-CR. Resident up to 8000', P, cH (Michoacán to Oaxaca), A, Y. Common; mixed tree-dotted pastures, hedgerows, thickets, scrubby woods, river borders. V: a descending, high-pitched, "mournful" *pee-pee-pee-pee-pee,* or a "sad" squealed *pee-ut. Pl.27. 4" Pale grayish olive; with dark wings (pale brown wing-bars) and tail; pale yellowish belly and untacs; white chin and short line over eye; bill very small.*

Greenish Elaenia. *Myiopagis viridicata.* Z10b34. Papamoscas Verdosa M-SAm. Resident up to 8500', P (Nayarit to Chiapas), H, (México+D.F.), A, Y. Rare; borders, scrub, thickets, pine-oak woods. V: high-pitched *zeet,* or *pee-wee. Pl.26. 5 1/2" Olive-green above; blackish wings and tail; throat and faintly streaked breast pale gray; belly and untacs yellowish; concealed crown-patch.*

Caribbean Elaenia. *Elaenia martinica.* Z10b36. Mosquero Antillano M,B. Resident, near sea level, Y (Is. off Quintana Roo). Common; hedgerows, *ranchos,* scrub woods, borders, thickets. V: a rasping *whee-oo,* and a harsh *pee-ree. Pl.26. 6" Like* Yellow-bellied Elaenia, *but browner above; little or no yellow below.*

Yellow-bellied Elaenia. *Elaenia flavogaster.* Z10b37. Parlotero Grande M-SAm. Resident up to 5000', sP, csA. Common; tree-dotted pastures, old fields, ranchos, hedgerows, forest borders; noisy "agitated" pairs may fly tree-to-tree, catch insects, pick berries. V: a rasping *bee-ee-r,* or harsh *clip-it, clip-beer,* or *clip-clip-peer. Pl.26. 6" Olive above, grayer on head; blackish wings, pale wing-bars; throat whitish; breast pale grayish olive; belly and untacs yellowish; partly hidden white patch in small ragged crest; tail rather long.*

Oleaginous (Ochre-bellied) Flycatcher. *Mionectes oleagineus.* Z10b89. Pipromorfa M-SAm. Resident up to 4000', csA, Y. Rare; in humid forest, borders and openings, coffee plantations, forest remnants; flicks one wing at a time, eats insects and berries. *Pl.26. 5" Dark greenish olive above; throat, chest and sides grayish olive; lower breast, belly and untacs dull rufous tawny; bill slender.*

Sepia-capped Flycatch.*Leptopogon amaurocephalus.*Z10b94.Mosquero Cabezipardo M-SAm,x.ES. Resident up to 3000', csA. Rare; humid forest, edge, river borders. *Pl.26. 5" Greenish olive above; crown and nape dark olive brown; face and breast faintly streaked; throat whitish; breast pale olive; belly yellow; buff wing-bars.*

Northern Bentbill. *Oncostoma cinereigulare.* Z10b133. Sordina M-Pan. Resident up to 4000', sP, csA, Y. Rare; low branches in dense humid forest, often near borders or openings; perches upright. V: a short quiet metallic trill, *bir-r-r-r. Pl.26. 4" Olive-green above, with gray crown and nape; dark wings, two white wing-bars; faintly streaked ear-patch, throat and breast; yellow belly and untacs; bill arched, bent down at tip; iris white; tail short.* See White-eyed Flycatcher.

Slaty-headed Tody-bill (-Flyc.). *Todirostrum sylvia.* Z10b160. Espatulilla Gris M-SAm,x.ES. Resident up to 3000', csA, Y (Quintana Roo). Very rare; inner branches in dense humid forest, scrubby woods, thick brush. V: a quiet mellow *took. Pl.26. 3 1/2" Grayish olive-green above; crown and nape dark gray; wing-bars and wing-feather edgings yellowish; tail short, narrow, graduated; whitish below, with grayish breast; bill somewhat spatulate, dark; iris pale to dark.*

Common Tody-bill (-Flyc.). *Todirostrum cinereum.* Z10b163. Espatulilla Amarilla M-SAm. Resident, near sea level, sP, csA, Y. Rare; hopping among twigs and small branches in brushy pastures, forest borders, scrubby woods, or river borders; holds tail

high, waves it from side to side. V: a musical, whistled trill, and a repeated, "dry" *tick*.
Pl.26. 3 1/2" Blackish olive above, with paler rump, and black crown, nape and ear-patch; underparts bright yellow; wings black with yellowish bars and edges of feathers; black tail narrow at base, white-tipped; bill spatulate, black; iris whitish.
Eye-ringed Flatbill. *Rhynchocyclus brevirostris.* Z10b170. Mosquero Piquicorto
M-SAm. Resident up to 6000', csP (Guerrero to Chiapas), csA, (Puebla to Quintana Roo), Y. Rare; dense humid lowland forest, cloud forest. V: high-pitched *wees*.
Pl.26. 6" Dark olive-green; breast faintly streaked; belly and untacs yellow; prominent white eye-ring; bill very broad, flat; dark above, pale below.
White-eyed Flycatcher.*Tolmomyias sulphurescens.*Z10b173.Mosquerito Ojo Blanco
M-SAm. Resident, sea level to 3000', sP, csA, Y. (Yellow-olive Flycatcher.) Rare; forest borders, scrubby woods, river borders. V: a very high-pitched *weet, weet, weet.*
Pl.26. 5" Like Northern Bentbill, but larger; has broad, flat bill; longer tail; rather prominent "spectacles"; moves around actively, seldom perches quietly upright.
Mexican Spadebill. *Platyrinchus cancrominus.* Z10b178. Picoplano Mexicano
M-CR. Resident up to 3000', csA. Rare; low shrubbery in dense undergrowth of humid forest, thickets along forest borders; usually turns around abruptly on a perch just before flying. V: 2 to 5 notes, a "petulant", abrupt chatter, *ki-di-di-di-dit.*
Pl.26. 4" Brownish above; buffy yellowish below, with white throat, tawny breast; very short flat bill; extremely short tail; white eye-ring; buffy spot on dark ear-patch.
Royal Flycatcher. *Onychorhynchus mexicanus.* Z10c1. Mosquero Real
M-SAm. Resident up to 4000', sP, csA, Y. Very rare; low, in dense humid forest.
Pl.26. 7" Wings and back olive-brown; underparts, rump, uptacs, tail, mostly tawny; bill long, broad, flat; legs, feet yellow; folded crest goes back and down; open crest flares crossways, red in male, tawny-buff in female, bordered and spotted dark.
Ruddy-tailed Flycatcher.*Terenotriccus erythrurus.* Z10c4. Papamoscas Cola Rojiza
M-SAm,x.ES. Resident, near sea level, sA (Tabasco). Very rare; low in humid forest.
Pl.26. 3 1/2" Olive above, with rufous and black wings; bright rufous tail; tawny-rufous below and on rump and uptacs; but throat whitish.
Sulphur-rumped Flycatcher.*Myiobius sulphureipygius.*Z10c6.Papamoscas Saltarín
M-SAm,x.ES. Resident up to 3500', csA, Y (Quintana Roo). Rare; lower branches, dense humid forest; moves often, wings drooping, tail partly spread, bright rump patch usually very conspicuous; short flights. V: a harsh *chip* or *pick*, or a musical *ter-ter-ter.*
Pl.26. 5" Brownish-olive above; blackish brown wings and tail; underparts tawny with white throat and tawnier belly; rump bright creamy yellow.
Belted Flycatcher. *Xenotriccus callizonus.* Z10c20. Papamoscas Chiapaneco
M,G,ES. Resident, 4000 to 6000', sH (Chiapas). Very rare, local; low inner branches, thickets, hedgerows, dense brush along borders; jerks tail up, flicks wings, seldom lowers crest. V: a "petulant" *cheer* or *chip pirr-rr* or a *pert, pert, pick-chi-chew.*
Pl.26. 5" Brownish olive above; crown dark brown; long crest; blackish wings with buffy bars and feather-edgings; yellow below, with tawny-rufous breast-band.
Pileated Flycatcher. *Aechmolophus mexicanus.* Z10c21. Papamoscas Pardo Oscuro
M. Resident, 4000 to 6000', cH (Michoacán to Oaxaca). Very rare, but irregular; in open, arid, scrubby woodland on rocky hillsides or ravines; often flies to ground to pick up insects, flicks tail up, flicks wings, raises and lowers crest. V: a two-phrased song, a whistled *twheeyu;* then a rolling trill and abrupt whistle *tr-r-r-eet-yu* ; also a *chee-up.*
Pl.26. 5 1/2" Grayish to brownish olive above; whitish below, darker on breast; long pointed grayish-brown crest; wing-bars, eye-ring, and lores white; wings dark.
Tufted Flycatcher. *Mitrephanes phaeocercus.* Z10c23. Penachito
M-SAm,x.B. Resident, 4000 to 12,000', H; winter visitor ncP, ncA. Rare; open pine forest, pine-oak, oak, or fir forest; river banks (winter). V: rolling *churree, churree.*
Pl.26. 5" Rufous-olive above; prominent crest; wings and tail blackish, buffy wing-bars; rich tawny-rufous below. See Buff-breasted Flycatcher.

Olive-sided Flycatcher. *Contopus borealis.* Z10c26.　　　　Mosquero Boreal
M-SAm. Summer resident, 4000 to 6000', nBC; transient sBC, ncP, H, ncA; winter
visitor sP, sA. Rare; upper branches of forests, river-border woods, partial clearings.
*Pl.27. 7" Brownish olive above, and on sides and flanks; throat and center of breast
and belly white; semi-hidden white patch each side of rump.* See Greater Pewee.

Greater Pewee. *Contopus pertinax.* Z10c29.　　　　　　Tengofrío Grande
M-N. Resident, 4000 to 11,000', mostly H; transient and winter visitor (some below
4000'), P, ncA. Common; upper branches, open pine woods, pine-oak or fir forest, or
lowland forests, river borders. V: *pert* or *pert-pert*, or a "sad" hesitant *ree-deet, ree-oo
(José Maria* or *Tengofrío)* or *ree-deet, ree-deet, ree-deet, ree-oo;* see Streaked Attila.
Pl.27. 7" Brownish olive, paler below; slight crest. Like Olive-sided Flycatcher,
but no broad white center-streak below; *lower mandible orange; tail slightly longer.*

Western (Wood-) **Pewee.** *Contopus sordidulus.* Z10c33.　　　Tengofrío Común
AK-SAm. Summer resident and transient, 3000 to 9000', BC, P, H; transient sA.
Common; scrubby open woods, borders, open pine woods. V: a rasping *weer* or *peer.*
*Pl.27. 5" Dark olive above and on breast and sides; whitish throat, belly, untacs;
blackish wings, white wing-bars; bill may be yellow-brown below.* See Wood-P.

Wood Pewee (Eastern W.-P.). *Contopus virens.* Z10c34.　　Tengofrío Verdoso
Can-SAm. Transient A, Y. Rare; river-border woods, forest borders, hedgerows, open
woods, second-growth. V: a plaintive *pee-a-wee,* or *pe-wee* (seldom heard in Mexico).
5" Like Western P. (except voice), *but slightly paler below; bill yellowish below.*

Tropical Pewee. *Contopus cinereus.* Z10c32.　　　　　　Tengofrío Tropical
M-SAm. Resident up to 4000', sP, csA, Y. Rare; partial clearings, openings in humid
forest, borders, tree-dotted pastures. V: a liquid, twittering series, or a single *peet.*
Pl.25. 5" Like Western P. (except voice), *but throat to untacs yellowish centrally.*

Yellow-bellied Flycatcher. *Empidonax flaviventris.* Z10c37.　Mosquerito Oliva
Can-Pan. Transient and winter visitor, sP, sH, A. Rare; low in open woods, borders.
*5" Brownish olive above; prominent yellowish eye-ring and wing-bars; throat
pale yellowish; breast yellowish olive; belly and untacs yellow; bill nearly as wide
(at base) as it is long, and yellowish orange below.* V: a quiet, rising *cur-lee.*

Acadian Flycatcher. *Empidonax virescens.* Z10c38.　　Mosquerito Verdoso
Can-SAm,x.ES. Transient A, Y. Rare; wooded stream-valleys, humid forest, borders.
*5 1/2" Mostly olive above, but wings blackish brown with whitish bars; pale
yellowish eye-ring; throat and lower breast whitish; chest and sides grayish olive;
belly and untacs pale yellow; bill nearly as broad (at base) as long, and yellowish
below.* V: a rising, abrupt *wheet;* also a quiet chatter.

Alder Flycatcher. *Empidonax alnorum.* Z10c39.　　Mosquerito de Pantano
AK-SAm.(?) Transient A, Y.(?) (Migration poorly understood.) Rare; thickets, borders;
in summer found in alder swamps, or thickets in bogs or near ponds. V: *fee-bee-o.*
5" Like Acadian F., *but darker and browner above and on chest (contrasts more with
white throat); duller belly and untacs; eye-ring less distinct; bill more orange below.*

Willow Flycatcher. *Empidonax traillii.* Z10c40.　　　Mosquerito Pálido
Can-Pan.(?) Transient BC, P, A, Y.(?) (Migration poorly understood.) Rare; moist
thickets, borders; in summer in wet meadows, drier brushy areas. V: abrupt *fitz-bew.*
5" Like Alder Flycatcher, *but slightly browner above; eye-ring even less prominent.*

White-throated Flycatcher. *Empid. albigularis.* Z10c41. Mosquerito Gargantiblanco
M-Pan,x.ES. Resident csH; summer resident nH (Chihuahua+Tamaulipas to Jalisco+
San Luis Potosí); transient or winter visitor cA. Rare, local; wet meadows, shrub-dotted
moist fields, brushy marshes, borders, dry brush. V: an abrupt, sneeze-like, *er-rick-er.*
Pl.25. 5" Like Alder F., *but slightly browner, white throat more contrasty; breast
may appear vaguely streaked; wing-bars and eye-ring buffier; flanks and untacs may
be buffy; thighs and under-wing coverts cinnamon-buff; bill flesh-color below.*

Least Flycatcher. *Empidonax minimus.* Z10c44.   Mosquerito Mínimo
Can-Pan. Winter visitor P, csH, A, Y; casual nBC. Rare+; open woods, thickets,
borders, wooded parks, or wooded suburban gardens. V: an abrupt, unmusical *chi-bec.*
4 1/2" Like Hammond's F., *but head and upperparts darker; belly and untacs
slightly yellower; throat slightly whiter; bill paler below.*
Hammond's Flycatcher. *Empidonax hammondii.* Z10c45.   Mosquerito Pasajero
AK-N,x.B. Transient or winter visitor nBC, P, H, ncA. Rare+; mountain forests,
mostly conifers in summer; flicks tail up persistently. V: three parts, *si-pit, sup, tre-ip.*
5" Like Dusky F., *but head relatively larger, paler, contrasts more with back; tail
shorter, outer-tail-feathers grayish-margined; bill slightly shorter, and darker below.*
Dusky Flycatcher. *Empidonax oberholseri.* Z10c46.   Mosquerito Oscuro
Can-M,G. Winter visitor BC, nP, H, nA. Rare+; scrubby woods, hedgerows, borders,
open woods; flicks tail up. V: several phrases in sequence, *chippy, chi-wee, tslip.*
Pl.27. 5" Like Gray Flycatcher, *but slightly darker and more olive; with more
contrasty wing-bars and eye-ring; yellower below; bill darker below.*
Gray Flycatcher. *Empidonax wrightii.* Z10c47.   Mosquerito Gris
US-M. Winter visitor sBC, nP, ncH, nA. Rare+; hedgerows, borders, or semi-desert,
or dry pine or pinyon-juniper woods; pushes tail downward. V: an abrupt *chi-bic.*
*Pl.27. 5" Gray above, wings darker; whitish wing-bars and eye-ring; whitish below
(yellower in winter) with pale grayish chest; tail notched, outer feathers white-edged;
bill about twice as long as wide, pale orange at base below, dark-tipped.*
Pine Flycatcher. *Empidonax affinis.* Z10c48.   Mosquerito Pinero
M,G. Resident, 6000 to 13,000', H. Rare+; high branches in dense or open pine,
pine-oak, or fir forest, not restricted to forest borders. V: a mellow, loud *peet* or *pert.*
Pl.25. 5" Like Gray Flycatcher, *but browner; wings darker; wing-bars (tinged
olive) and eye-ring more prominent; yellower below with more olive tinge on chest.*
Western Flycatcher. *Empidonax difficilis.* Z10c49.   Mosquerito Barranqueño
AK-M. Resident, 5000 to 11,000', sBC, H; summer resident nBC; winter visitor csP.
Rare+; shrubby ravines in pine, fir, or other mountain forest. V: an abrupt *hree-deet.*
5" Like Yellow-bellied Flycatcher, *but somewhat browner above and on breast; bill
more orange below; wing-bars buffier, not so prominent; tail somewhat longer.*
Yellowish Flycatcher. *Empidonax flavescens.* Z10c50.   Mosquerito Amarillento
M-Pan,x.B. Resident, 3500 to 10,000', sH, csA (Veracruz+Chiapas); winter visitor sP.
Rare+; cloud forest, pine-oak woods, other humid forest. V: a high-pitched *hree-deet.*
Pl.25. 5" Like Western F. (may be same species), *but yellower above and below.*
Buff-breasted Flycatcher. *Empidonax fulvifrons.* Z10c52.   Mosquerito Canelo
US-ES+H,x.B. Resident, 4000 to 12,000', H; winter visitor nP. Rare+; open pine or
pine-oak, or fir forest, or (winter) river border woods. V: a musical, rolling *pulleet-yew.*
*Pl.27. 4 1/2" Grayish brown above, crown may be darker; pale buff wing-bars and
wing-feather-edgings; eye-ring white; pale tawny below, to whitish belly and untacs.*

Black Phoebe. *Sayornis nigricans.* Z10c56.   Papamoscas Negro
US-SAm. Resident up to 9000', BC, P, H. Rare; near pools, streams, lakes.
Pl.27. 6" Black; but belly, untacs, some feather-edgings, white. V: a harsh *fee-bee.*
Eastern Phoebe. *Sayornis phoebe.* Z10c55.   Papamoscas Fibí
US-M. Winter visitor, sBC, ncP, ncH, A. Rare; hedgerows, borders. V: *fee-bee.*
6" Like Wood Pewee, *but yellower below; head darker; no wing-bars; bill black.*
Say's Phoebe. *Sayornis saya.* Z10c57.   Papamoscas Boyero
AK-M. Resident up to 8000', nBC, nP (Sonora), ncH, nA (Nuevo León+Tamaulipas);
winter visitor sBC, cP, sH, cA. Rare; arid grassy or open semi-desert areas, often in
rocky ravines; on shrubs, tall weeds, fences. V: a "melancholy" *pirr-rr.*
Pl.27. 7" Pale gray above; dark head, wings, and tail; mostly tawny-buff below.

Vermilion Flycatcher. *Pyrocephalus rubinus.* Z10c58.   Cardenalito
M-SAm,x.ES,CR. Resident up to 8500', all sub-regions. Common; arid open areas,
semi-deserts, brushy overgrown fields, parks, gardens; on weeds, fences, wires.
*Pl.27. 5 1/2" M: Black, except scarlet crown and underparts. F+Im: Dull
grayish-brown above; dark ear patch; white throat; white breast streaked gray or
brown; belly and untacs pale yellow, pink, or red.*

Streaked (Bright-rumped) **Attila.** *Attila spadiceus.* Z10d7.   Bigotón
M-SAm. Resident up to 5000', P, csA (Puebla to Quintana Roo), Y. Rare; humid
forest, borders, openings, scrubby woods, river borders, tree-dotted pastures. V: like
Greater Pewee's, but louder, more abrupt, *wheed-ut, wheed-ut, wheed-ut, whee-oo.*
*Pl.25. 8" Variable; usually brown or olive above; rump and uptacs yellow or tawny;
whitish or tawny below; face, throat, breast, streaked; iris whitish, tan, brown or red.*

Speckled Mourner. *Laniocera rufescens.* Z10c131.   Llorona Manchada
M-SAm,x.ES. Resident up to 2500', sA (Oaxaca+Chiapas). Very rare; in dense humid
forest; moves slowly, perches in small trees or shrubs. V: a whistled *peet-a-weet.*
*Pl.25. 9" Like Rufous Mourner and Rufous Piha, but darker brown; has two dull
spotty wing-bars, faint breast-bars, and yellow (m.) or rufous (f.) under-wing-patch.*

Rufous Mourner. *Rhytipterna holerythra.* Z10d11.   Alazán
M-SAm,x.ES. Resident up to 5000', csA, Y. Rare; in dense humid forest or
tree-dotted openings, open humid woods, or borders. V: a "sad" *wheep* or *wheep-wee.*
Pl.25. 8" Dull reddish brown above; tawny-brown below. See Speckled Mourner.

Yucatan Flycatcher. *Myiarchus yucatanensis.* Z10d15.   Copetón Yucateco
M,B. Resident, near sea level, Y. Rare; in open scrubby woods, borders, hedgerows.
*Pl.25. 7" Like Olivaceous F., but wing-bars slightly paler, grayer; inner half of
inner web of tail-feathers rufous; uptacs rufous.* V: a long, rising, whistled note.

Olivaceous (Dusk.-c.) **Flycatcher.***Myiarchus tuberculifer.* Z10d17. Copetón Común
US-SAm. Resident up to 8500', P, H, A, Y; accidental sBC. Common; tree-dotted
pastures, humid to dry forests, openings or borders, hedgerows. V: a "mournful"
whee-oo; or a slow, rolling trill, *peer-r-r,* often with a preceding note, *drew-peer-r-r.*
*Pl.27. 6 1/2" Brownish olive above, with blackish brown to dark brown crown;
rufous-buff wing-bars; pale gray throat, slightly darker gray breast; pale yellow belly;
tail-feathers blackish with only a narrow streak of rufous (or none) on the inner edge.*

Ash-throated Flycatcher. *Myiarchus cinerascens.* Z10d25.   Copetón Cenizo
US-CR,x.B. Resident up to 7000', BC, nP (Sonora), ncH (Chihuahua+Coahuila to
Michoacán), nA (Tamaulipas); winter visitor csP, sH, cA. Common; shrub-dotted dry
grassy fields, open woods, hedgerows, borders. V: a soft *ker-peer,* and a rasping *pert.*
*Pl.27. 7 1/2" Like Olivaceous F., but paler above and on head; paler gray on throat
and breast; paler yellow belly and untacs; whitish wing-bars; and nearly entire inner
web of tail-feathers (except tips) rufous.*

Nutting's Flycatcher. *Myiarchus nuttingi.* Z10d26.   Copetón Acahualero
M-CR,x.B. Resident up to 5500', P, ncH (Chihuahua to Puebla). Rare+; scrubby
woods, borders, rather dry open woods, dry tree-dotted pastures. V: a whistled *pee-r-r.*
*Pl.25. 7" Like Ash-throated Flycatcher, but slightly smaller; tail-tip usually not
darker than rest of tail; voice more like that of the much darker, and nearly uniformly
blackish-brown-tailed Olivaceous Flycatcher.*

Crested (Great-cr.) **Flycatcher.** *Myiarchus crinitus.* Z10d27.   Copetón Viajero
Can-SAm. Transient or winter visitor sP, cH, A, Y. Rare+; borders, open woods,
tree-dotted fields. V: a loud, rolling *ree-eep;* and a rolling, slowing *kree-kree-kree-kree.*
*8 1/2" Like Ash-throated F., but much more rufous on tail; throat and chest darker
gray, contrast sharply with bright yellow belly and untacs; bill orange at base below.*

Wied's (Br.-cr.) **Flycatcher.** *Myiarchus tyrannulus.* Z10d28.   Copetón Portuguesito
US-CR,SAm. Resident up to 7000', P, ncH, A, Y; casual, possibly breeds, BC. Rare+;
open woods, borders, tree-dotted brushy pastures. V: a loud whistled *whee-eep-boo.*

Pl.27. 8 1/2" Like Ash-throated F., *but larger; larger-billed; brighter yellow belly and untacs; somewhat more rufous on tail. Like* Crested F., *but bill all dark, heavier; chest paler gray and not as contrasty with yellow belly; tail much less rufous.*

Flammulated Flycatcher. *Deltarhynchus flammulatus.* Z10d39.   Abejerillo
M. Resident up to 4000', P (Sinaloa to Chiapas). Rare; dense, very low, dry woods, brushy overgrown fields, thickets, low hedgerows; seldom on high or exposed branches. V: a quiet "querulous" *wee-eet,* sliding down then up; a quiet rolling *pr-r-reet.*
Pl.25. 6 1/2" Resembles Ash-throated Flycatcher *somewhat, but more grayish above, with cinnamon-rufous uptacs, wing-bars, and wing-feather edgings; pale gray eye-ring; whitish lores prominent at times; chest pale gray faintly streaked whitish; belly and untacs pale yellow; tail dark brown and rufous; bill rather short, broad, flat.*

Great Kiskadee. *Pitangus sulphuratus.* Z10d41.   Luis Grande
US-SAm. Resident up to 6000', P, ncH (Durango to México), A, Y. Common; in tree-dotted fields, river-border woods, forest borders, open woods, hedgerows; often over water, may catch small fish. V: a very loud nasal *ree,* or *kurree,* or *keep-kurree.*
Pl.27. 9" Reddish brown above, with rufous wings and tail; head broadly striped black-and-white; bright yellow underparts, but white throat; medium-heavy bill.

Boat-billed Flycatcher. *Megarhynchus pitangua.* Z10d42.   Portugués
M-SAm. Resident up to 5000', P (Sinaloa to Chiapas), A, Y. Rare; high in trees of tree-dotted fields, forest borders, river-border woods, luxuriant hedgerows. V: a high-pitched *gú-lick, gú-lick;* a whining *kee-rr-r* or *mew-e-r-r,* or a "dry" *chee-r-r.*
Pl.25. 9" Like Great Kiskadee, *but more olive-brown above; wings and tail more olive-brown than* rufous; *bill broader and thicker; crown duller; voice different.*

Social Flycatcher. *Myiozetetes similis.* Z10d44.   Chatilla Común
M-SAm. Resident up to 5000', P, A, Y. Common; often in groups on branches overhanging rivers or ponds, or in forest borders, or tree-dotted fields; often flutters wings while perched, seems excitable. V: *ki-tee, ki-tee, ki-tee,* or a "petulant" *chee-ee.*
Pl.25. 7" Like Great Kiskadee *but much smaller, smaller-billed; more grayish olive above, no* rufous *on wing; crown duller, grayer, hidden red patch; voice differs.*

Streaked Flycatcher. *Myiodynastes maculatus.* Z10d54.   Ventura Pinta
M-SAm. Summer resident up to 4500', A, Y. Rare; tree-dotted pastures, woods along rivers, humid forest borders or openings. V: a melodious *tyew;* a whining *wa-a-a.*
Pl.25. 8" Like Sulphur-bellied F., *but head-stripes yellower; underparts whiter.*

Sulphur-bellied Flycatcher. *Myiodynastes luteiventris.* Z10d55.   Ventura Meca
US-SAm. Summer resident up to 5500', P, A, Y. Common; tree-dotted fields and pastures, forest borders and openings, river-border woods. V: a high-pitched *peet-chee.*
Pl.27. 8" Streaked dark brown and buff above, but rich rufous rump, uptacs, and tail; streaked white and blackish gray head; yellow below with heavy dark streaks.

Piratic Flycatcher. *Legatus leucophaius.* Z10d56.   Papamoscas Rayado
M-SAm,x.ES. Summer resident up to 3000', csA (San Luis Potosí to Quintana Roo). Rare; in tree-dotted pastures, luxuriant hedgerows, river-border woods, forest borders, usually on outer branches (or utility wires) near hanging nest taken from another species. V: a loud whistled *whee-oo* (pause) then three softer musical notes *te-te-te.*
Pl.25. 6 1/2" Like Streaked (Pl. 25) *and* Sulphur-bellied Flycatchers (Pl.27), *but smaller; is unstreaked olive-brown above and on tail; and has shorter smaller bill.*

Tropical Kingbird. *Tyrannus melancholicus.* Z10d63.   Madrugador Abejero
US-SAm. Resident up to 5000', P, A, Y; rare winter visitor cH, casual BC. Very common; hedgerows, tree-dotted pastures, scrub woods, forest borders. V: chipping, trilling notes, higher-pitched than Couch's Kingbird's; also high-pitched *kittick* notes.
Pl.27. 8" Grayish olive above, with bluish gray crown; blackish wings; white throat; yellow breast, belly and untacs; tail blackish-brown, notched. See Couch's K.

Couch's Kingbird. *Tyrannus couchii.* Z10d64.   Madrugador Mexicano
US,M,G,B. Resident up to 5000', A, Y. Common; tree-dotted pastures, open woods,

ranchos, forest borders. V: a mellow *pert* or *pit;* a rolling *whee-ee-rr-r*, or *ti-peer*. 8" *Like* Tropical K. (Pl.27), but *tail more brownish*. See Cassin's and Western K.

Cassin's Kingbird. *Tyrannus vociferans.* Z10d65.   Madrugador Chilero
US,M,G,H. Resident up to 9000', nBC, nP, ncH; winter visitor sBC, csP, sH. Common; tree-dotted or shrubby pastures, open mesquite-grassland, hedgerows, thickets; perches on wires, posts, shrub-tops. V: a chipping *kiteer, kiteer, kiteer, kiteer*. *Pl.27. 8" Like* Tropical K. *but more contrasty, much darker breast, and tail blacker, square with very narrow pale tip-band.*

Thick-billed Kingbird. *Tyrannus crassirostris.* Z10d66.   Madrugador Piquigrueso
US,M,G. Resident up to 6000', ncP; winter visitor sP. Rare; tree-tops or higher branches in dense scrubby woods, woods borders. V: loud harsh *bur-ree;* or *kit-er-keer*. *Pl.27. 8" Head, back browner; bill thicker; than* in other kingbirds. *Im: Yellower.*

Western Kingbird. *Tyrannus verticalis.* Z10d67.   Madrugador Avispero
Can-CR,x.B. Summer resident, nBC, nP (Sonora), nH (Chihuahua); transient or winter visitor csP, csH, nA. Common; tree-dotted or brushy fields, savannas, borders. *Pl.27. 8" Like* Tropical K., *but bill shorter; sides of square tail whitish-bordered.*

Eastern Kingbird. *Tyrannus tyrannus.* Z10d70.   Madrugador Viajero
AK-SAm. Transient, near sea level, A, Y; accidental sBC, nP, cH. Abundant; flocks in trees in pastures, savannas, borders, hedgerows, or flying 50 to 300 feet above ground. 8" *Upperparts blackish to blackish gray; underparts and tail-tip-band white.*

Scissor-tailed Flycatcher. *Tyrannus forficatus.* Z10d68.   Papamoscas Tijereta
US-Pan. Summer resident, near sea level, nA (Tamaulipas + Nuevo León); transient csP, ncH, A; winter visitor sP, sA, Y; casual BC, nP. Abundant, irregular; tree-dotted pastures, brushy grasslands, hedgerows, utility poles, wires, tree-tops; flocks overhead. *Pl.27. 14" M: Bluish gray above; pale pink and whitish below; red-orange bend-of-wing patch. F+Im: Paler below, tail shorter. See* Fork-tailed F. (Pl.25).

Fork-tailed Flycatcher. *Tyrannus savana.* Z10d69.   Tijerilla
M-SAm. Resident up to 3000', csA; visitor Y. Rare, irregular; in humid to dry tree-dotted pastures, shrubby grassland, hedgerows, atop weeds, shrubs, or small trees. *Pl.25. 16" Tail, wings, and upper part of head black; back pale gray; underparts white; smaller (but tail longer) than* Scissor-tailed Flycatcher. *Im: Tail short, forked.*

Cinnamon Becard. *Pachyramphus cinnamomeus.* Z10a6.   Cabezón Canelo
M-SAm,x.ES. Resident, near sea level, sA. Rare; upper branches, forest or openings. *Pl.25. 5 1/2" Tawny-brown above, with darker brown crown; buffy brown below, breast slightly darker and grayer; much smaller, and paler below than* Rufous and Speckled Mourners, and Rufous Piha.

Mexican (Gray-collar.) Becard. *Pachyramphus major.* Z10a10.   Cabezón Mexicano
M-N. Resident up to 8500', P (Sinaloa to Chiapas), csH (Michoacán to Chiapas), A, Y. Rare; cloud forest, other humid woods, dry scrubby woods, gardens, or *cafetales*. *Pl.25. 5 1/2" M: Mostly blackish above; underparts, collar, rump-patch, tail-tip pale gray to whitish. F: Pattern similar to male's, but mostly rufous above, crown black; and buff below.* This bird bobs its head often. V: a quiet, musical *dewt-tew-tewt*.

Rose-throated Becard. *Pachyramphus aglaiae.* Z10a12.   Degollado
US-Pan. Resident up to 9000', P, H (Durango+Nuevo León to Chiapas), A, Y. Rare; scrubby woods, borders, openings, tree-dotted pastures, wooded river borders; build a 2'-diameter hanging nest. V: a very high-pitched extended note, also a chatter. *Pl.23. 6" M: Bushy head blackish; throat rose-red; races vary in darkness of gray; mostly dark gray above, pale gray below. F: Crown dark gray; collar and rest of plumage vary; mostly reddish brown above; pale buff collar and underparts.*

Masked Tityra. *Tityra semifasciata.* Z10a18.   Puerquito
M-SAm. Resident up to 5000', P, A, Y. Rare; humid tree-dotted pastures, river-border woods, forest borders, openings; usually in pairs, often seen near cavities

(nests or potential nest-sites) in dead trees. V: a rasping, grunt-like *kiddit, kiddit.*
Pl. 25. 8" *M: Mostly very pale gray; but forehead and fore-crown, patch around eye, outer part of wing, and broad tail-band, black; eye-ring and base of bill red. F: Similar, but back, crown, nape, and ear-patch dark grayish brown.*
Black-crowned Tityra. *Tityra inquisitor.* Z10a19. <u>Viuda</u>
M-SAm,x.ES. <u>Resident up to 4000', csA (San Luis Potosí to Quintana Roo), Y</u>. Rare; higher branches of humid forest borders, openings, tree-dotted clearings, river-border woods; often seen in dead trees, in pairs, fly long distances. V: a rasping *sik.*
Pl.25. 8" *Like* Masked T., *but no* red eye-ring or bill-base, *and M: hind-crown black; and F: crown blackish; forehead buff; ear-patch rufous.*

COTINGAS - COTINGIDAE - AZULEJOS, GUARDABOSQUES
Rufous Piha. *Lipaugus unirufus.* Z9a30. <u>Guardabosque</u>
M-SAm,x.ES. <u>Resident up to 2500', csA, Y (Quintana Roo)</u>. Rare; middle branches, dense humid forest, tree-dotted clearings. V: a very loud whistle, *wheet-a-weet.*
Pl.25. 10" *Dark brown above; buffy brown below, with cinnamon throat, darker breast. Larger, larger-billed, more two-toned than* Rufous and Speckled Mourners.
Lovely Cotinga. *Cotinga amabilis.* Z9a35. <u>Azulejo Real</u>
M-CR,x.ES. <u>Resident, near sea level, sA (Veracruz to Chiapas)</u>. Rare, irregular; in middle to upper branches in dense humid forest or tree-dotted openings or clearings.
Pl.25. 8" *M: Cobalt blue; throat and belly-patch purple, may look black; wings and tail black. F: Speckled and scalloped blackish brown above; spotted pale gray below.*

MANAKINS - PIPRIDAE - TURQUITOS
Four residents; southern Mexico; small; large-headed; medium-short legs, short neck, rounded wings, very short to very long tail, short bill; low branches, mostly humid forest borders; Neotropical. Distinguish by tail length, colors, patterns. **Plate 24.**

Thrush-like Manakin. *Schiffornis turdinus.* Z8a2. <u>Turquito Café</u>
M-SAm,x.ES. <u>Resident up to 5000', sA</u>. Rare; undergrowth, dense humid forest.
Pl.24. 7" *Brownish olive above; slightly paler below; wings and tail more reddish brown; legs bluish gray.*
White-collared Manakin. *Manacus candei.* Z8a27. <u>Matraca</u>
M-Pan. <u>Resident, near sea level, csA</u>. Rare; undergrowth or low branches in humid forest or forest borders. V: short notes or trills. Also non-vocal loud snapping sounds.
Pl.24. 4 1/2" *M: Black crown, most of wings, and tail; white throat, breast, and back; yellow belly; greenish rump. F: Mostly grayish green; belly and untacs yellowish, legs orange. Belly yellower, and legs brighter orange than* those of other female manakins; *legs brighter, bill smaller than* those of female euphonias.
Long-tailed Manakin. *Chiroxiphia linearis.* Z8a35. <u>Toledo</u>
M-CR,x.B. <u>Resident up to 2500', sP</u>. Rare, irregular; ravines, thickets, other undergrowth in dry woods, often in flocks. V: a loud, mellow *taw-eet-oo,* or *to-le-do.*
Pl.24. 10", 5" *M: Black; with scarlet crown , pale blue back, two long tail-feathers. F: Greenish olive above; dull buffy greenish below; central tail-feathers noticeably elongated, longer than* those of other female manakins and female euphonias.
Red-capped Manakin. *Pipra mentalis.* Z8a50. <u>Turquito Cabezirojo</u>
M-SAm,x.ES. <u>Resident up to 2500', csA, Y</u>. Rare; undergrowth and low branches in dense humid forest; makes abrupt short flights or jumps, also snapping, whirring, or buzzy noises, during display. V: series of short and long high-pitched notes.
Pl.24. 4" *M: Black; with mostly red head; yellow thighs; white iris. F: Dark grayish green; paler below, and belly slightly yellowish. Not as yellow below as* White-collared M.; *shorter-tailed and has darker legs than* Long-tailed M.; *bill smaller than* in euphonias. *Im.M: May be mostly greenish, but iris white, thighs yellowish.*

LARKS - ALAUDIDAE - ALONDRAS LLANERAS

Horned Lark. *Eremophila alpestris.* Z14a83.   Alondra Cornuda
AK-M,SAm. Resident up to 12,000', BC, ncP (Sonora and Oaxaca), ncH, nA
(Tamaulipas). Common; in short-grass fields, dry pastures, or grassy semi-deserts.
*Pl.23. 7" M: Streaked brownish above; mostly white below; black breast-band;
black patch through and below eye, on white (or yellowish) face; short black "horns";
tail black below, with white margins. F+win.M: Duller. Im: Suggestion of face
pattern and breast-band; tail as in adult; no "horns".*

SWALLOWS - HIRUNDINIDAE - GOLONDRINAS

Thirteen species, mostly residents or summer residents; widespread Mexico; small;
very short legs, short neck, narrow pointed wings; tail short, square, to long, forked;
bill short; feed in flight over open areas, borders; catch flying insects; world- wide.
Distinguish by tail-length and shape; belly, breast, throat colors. **Plates 23 and 28.**

Purple Martin. *Progne subis.* Z15b11.   Martín Azul
Can-SAm. Summer resident up to 10,000', BC, nP (Sonora), ncH (Chihuahua and
Coahuila to Michoacán); transient cP, sA, Y. Very rare; in colonies in tree cacti, or in
large dead trees in grassland or park-like openings; flocks near coast in migration.
*Pl.23. 8" M: Violet-glossed black. F+Im: Dark brown above with slight gloss,
nape may be gray; pale gray-brown below, whitish on belly, untacs, face, and neck.*

White-bellied Martin. *Progne dominicensis.* Z15b12.   Martín Bicolor
M,G. Summer resident, 3000 to 7000', nP, ncH (Sonora+Chihuahua to Michoacán).
Very rare; usually in colonies in oak groves or scattered pines, near suitable nest holes.
Pl.28. 7" M: Blackish purple; belly, untacs white. F+Im: Dark brown, and white.

Gray-breasted Martin. *Progne chalybea.* Z15b13.   Martín Gris
M-SAm. Resident up to 5000', P, Y; summer resident A, (Coahuila to Quintana Roo).
Common (rare winter); usually in colonies around buildings or bridges.
Pl.28. 7" M: Glossy blackish above, whitish below. F+Im: Browner, less glossy.

Tree Swallow. *Tachycineta bicolor.* Z15b1.   Golondrina Invernal
AK-CR. Transient or winter visitor all sub-regions. Rare to common; over open areas
usually near water, rivers, ponds, lakes, coastal lagoons, marshes, dunes and beaches.
*5 1/2" White below; dark greenish blue above; black wings and tail. Im: Brown
above; white below; brown patch on side of breast.* See Mangrove Swallow.

Mangrove Swallow. *Tachycineta albilinea.* Z15b2.   Golondrina Manglera
M-Pan. Resident up to 2500', P, A, Y. Common; often solitary, along lowland rivers,
ponds, lakes, and coastal lagoons, or over shallow pools in marshes and swamps.
*Pl.28. 5" Like Tree S., but rump and uptacs white (whitish or pale gray in
immature).* See Violet-green Swallow.

Violet-green Swallow. *Tachycineta thalassina.* Z15b8.   Golondrina Verde
AK-CR. Resident up to 10,000', sBC, nP (Sonora), cH (Querétaro to Oaxaca);
summer resident nBC, nH; winter visitor csP, sH. Common to rare; gardens, orchards,
parks, other open areas in towns and villages; mixed fields, woods-edge and openings.
*Pl.23. 4 1/2" Like Tree and Mangrove S., but purplish gloss above; sides of face
and sides (only) of rump white. Im: Grayish brown above; sides of rump white.*

Black-capped Swallow. *Notiochelidon pileata.* Z15b20.   Golondrina Cabezinegra
M,G,ES,H. Resident, 5000 to 10,000', sH (Chiapas). Rare; on rocky road-cuts or
cliffs, in openings in pine, pine-oak forest or cloud forest, or very rarely around towns.
*Pl.28. 5" Blackish above, including top and sides of head; also blackish sides,
flanks, and untacs; white throat, breast, and belly; tail rather long, deeply forked.*

N.Rough-winged Swallow.*Stelgido. serripennis.* Z15b25. Golondrina Aliasserrada
AK-Pan. Resident up to 9000', P, H, A; summer resident nBC; transient sBC. Rare to
common; along road cuts, river banks, and arroyos, or open archaeological sites.

Pl.23. 5" Dark grayish brown above; whitish below with brownish wash on throat; tail rather short; slightly forked. See Ridgway's Swallow and Bank Swallow.

Ridgway's Swallow. *Stelgidopteryx ridgwayi.* Z15b25.   Golondrina Cuevera
M,G, B. Resident up to 1500', csA, Y. Common; dirt banks, road cuts, ruins.
5" Like Rough-winged S., *but darker above, whiter below; untacs black-tipped.*

Bank Swallow. *Riparia riparia.* Z15b31.   Golondrina Ribereña
AK-SAm. Summer resident up to 1000', na (Tamaulipas and Nuevo León; transient all sub-regions (except BC?); winter visitor nP, cH. Abundant to rare; often in large loose flocks, over tree-dotted pastures, or lakes, swamps, marshes and coastal lagoons.
5" Much like Rough-winged S., *but throat white; dark band across breast.*

Cliff Swallow. *Hirundo pyrrhonota.* Z15b64.   Golondrina Risquera
AK-SAm. Summer resident up to 8000', nBC, nP (Sonora and Sinaloa), ncH, na, Y (Quintana Roo), transient sBC, sH, csA. Common; near bridges, dams; in towns.
Pl.23. 5 1/2" Forehead whitish (or rufous in some birds); face rufous; throat broadly blackish; rump buffy; tail square. Im: Mostly darker, duller, especially head.

Cave Swallow. *Hirundo fulva.* Z15b65.   Golondrina Pueblera
US,M,CR. Resident up to 7000', sP (Chiapas), sH (Chiapas), Y; summer resident, nH, na. Irregular; in colonies in towns, old buildings, ruins, caves, sink-holes.
Pl.23. 5 1/2" Like rufous-foreheaded form of Cliff S. *but throat cinnamon-brown.*

Barn Swallow. *Hirundo rustica.* Z15b39.   Golondrina Tijerilla
AK-SAm. Summer resident up to 10,000', nBC, nP (Sonora), ncH; transient sBC, nA, Y; winter visitor P, csH, csA. Common; in towns, villages, parks, fields, *ranchos.*
Pl.23. 6" Blackish blue above; mostly rufous below, with incomplete breast-band; tail long, deeply forked with some white spots. Im: Duller.

CROWS and JAYS - CORVIDAE - QUEIXQUES, URRACAS, CUERVOS
Twenty-three residents; widespread Mexico; medium legs, short neck, rounded wing, medium to very long tail, medium bill; dry woods to humid forest; worldwide. Distinguish by size, bill and plumage colors and patterns, tail-shape. **Plates 28, 29.**

Steller's Jay. *Cyanocitta stelleri.* Z51a74.   Cháchara Copetona
AK-N,x.B. Resident, 5000 to 13,000', H; casual BC. Common; alone or in small flocks in pine, pine-oak or fir forests, or openings, from ground to upper branches. V: slow, harsh *chaa, chaa, chaa, chaa.* (Chiapas birds often do not raise crest.)
Pl.29. 12" Head, long crest, breast and upper back, blackish; lower back, rump, belly, untacs, rich medium blue; wings and tail barred black and blue; some have white or pale blue spots or streaks on head or throat.

Collie's (Black-throated) **Magpie-Jay.** *Calocitta colliei.* Z51a105. Urraca Copetona
M. Resident up to 5000', nP. Common; open woods, hedgerows, river borders.
Pl.28. 27" Purplish blue above; white below; curling crest, throat and cheeks black; very long slender tail, which is blue above, white and black below.

White-throated Magpie-Jay. *Calocitta formosa.* Z51a104. Urraca Garganta Blanca
M-CR,x.B. Resident up to 5000', csP. Common; open woods, river borders.
Pl.28. 21" Like Collie's M.-J., *but paler blue above; tail shorter; throat and face white; breast-band black.*

Brown Jay. *Psilorhinus morio.* Z51a103.   Papán Oscuro
US-Pan,x.ES. Resident up to 4000', A, Y. Common; in small noisy flocks, in dense forest, river-border woods, forest borders or openings, scrubby woods, thickets.
Pl.28. 17" Dark brown above, with blackish head, throat, and chest; whitish belly; tail rather long, rounded, all-dark-brown, or brown at base and broadly white-tipped. The southern form (white-tipped tail) is much more contrasty blackish and white.

Tufted Jay. *Cyanocorax dickeyi.* Z51a87.   Urraca Pinta
M. Resident, near 6000', nH (s.Sinaloa, sw.Durango, n.Nayarit). Rare; and restricted

range; usually in humid pine-oak, oak, or oak-fir forests in barrancas or on steep slopes.
Pl.28. 15" Blackish blue back, wings, rump, uptacs, basal part of tail (above), throat, and prominent, rounded crest; white hind-neck, breast, belly, tail-tip.
Green Jay. *Cyanocorax yncas.* Z51a98.   Queixque Verde
US,M,G,B,H,SAm. Resident up to 5000', P (Nayarit to Chiapas), A, Y. Common (rare ncP); scrubby open woods, thickets, river-border woods, to cloud forest.
Pl.29. 10" Greenish above; violet-blue crown and part of cheek; black rest of cheek and throat; outer tail feathers broadly yellow. Northern birds have yellowish green underparts and brown iris; southern birds are yellow below, and have a yellow iris.
San Blas Jay. *Cyanocorax sanblasiana.* Z51a100.   Queixque San Blasiano
M. Resident up to 4000', ncP (Nayarit to Guerrero). Common; small flocks in mangrove swamps and nearby broad hedgerows, dense scrubby woods, and thickets.
Pl.28. 13" Black, except blue back, rump, wings, and tail; small forehead-crest; black bill, white iris, blackish legs. Im+Juv: Like adult, but forehead-crest much larger, bill yellow, iris dark brown.
Yucatan Jay. *Cyanocorax yucatanica.* Z51a101.   Cháchara
M,G,B. Resident, near sea level, sA (Tabasco+Chiapas to Quintana Roo), Y. Common (Y), rare (sA); small flocks in dense scrubby woodland, thickets, or borders.
Pl.28. 13" Like San Blas Jay, but not crested; has yellow legs, and Im: has whitish tail-corners; and Juv: has white *head and underparts.*
Beechey's (Purpl.-back.) **Jay.** *Cyanocorax beechei.* Z51a99.   Queixque de Beechey
M. Resident up to 2000', nP (Sonora to Nayarit). Rare; scrubby woods, thickets.
Pl.28. 16" Black; with violet-blue back, wings, rump, and tail; not crested; black bill; orange-yellow legs; white iris. F: Iris yellowish. Im: Bill yellowish, iris dark.
Azure-hooded Jay. *Cyanolyca cucullata.* Z51a82.   Azul de Toca
M,G,H,CR,P. Resident, 3000 to 5000', csA (San Luis Potosí to Chiapas). Rare; in dense undergrowth of dense humid forest, especially cloud forest, often in small flocks.
Pl.28. 12" Mostly black head, back, and breast; but very pale blue patch from mid-crown to lower hind-neck; rest of plumage violet-blue.
Black-throated Jay. *Cyanolyca pumilo.* Z51a74.   Queixque Oscuro
M,G,ES,H. Resident, 5000 to 9000', sH. Rare; in secluded portions of cloud forests.
Pl.28. 10" Dark blue; but throat and face black, bordered with white line above.
Dwarf Jay. *Cyanolyca nana.* Z51a78.   Queixque Chico
M. Resident, 5000 to 10,000', cH (Veracruz and Oaxaca). Rare; in secluded portions of cloud forest, humid pine-oak or fir forest, middle or upper branches, often in groups.
Pl.28. 9" Mostly dark grayish blue, with black sides of face, and pale blue throat.
Omiltemi (White-throated) **Jay.** *Cyanolyca mirabilis.* Z51a80. Queixque Omiltemeño
M. Resident, 7000 to 11,000', cH (s.mts.Guerrero+Oaxaca). Rare; humid forest.
Pl.28. 10" Mostly dark grayish blue, with white throat and face-border; and black face, crown, hind-neck, and breast-band.

Scrub Jay. *Aphelocoma coerulescens.* Z51a75.   Queixque de Ceja Blanca
US-M. Resident up to 11,000', BC, ncH. Rare; in small flocks, in lower branches, of open woods, hedgerows, and borders. V: a harsh *chreek*, or *chak-chak-chak-chak*.
Pl.28. 12" Like Mexican Jay, but somewhat browner above; has a white throat, white line over eye, and dark breast-band.
Mexican (Gray-breasted) **Jay.** *Aphelocoma ultramarina.* Z51a76.   Grajo Azul
US-M. Resident, 4000 to 11,000', ncH (Sonora and Nuevo León to Colima and Veracruz). Common; in small flocks in pine, pine-oak, or oak woodland, or woods borders, or nearby thickets. V: a loud, "questioning", somewhat musical *quenk, quenk*.
Pl.29. 12" Grayish blue above, darker ear-patch and line through eye; whitish below with grayish breast; may be vaguely streaked; little contrast. See Scrub Jay.

Unicolored Jay. *Aphelocoma unicolor.* Z51a77.   Grajo Azulejo
M,G,ES,H. Resident, 5000 to 10,000', csH (Hidalgo to Guerrero and Chiapas). Rare;
in secluded parts of humid pine, pine-oak or cloud forest. V: a single musical *chwenk.*
*Pl.28 13" Dark, slightly purplish, blue; ear-patch darker; throat may be faintly
streaked. Im: Similar, but lower mandible yellowish.*

Pinyon Jay. *Gymnorhinus cyanocephalus.* Z51a106.   Queixque Piñonero
US-M. Resident, 4000 to 8000', nBC; winter visitor nh (Sonora+Chihuahua). Very
common nBC, very rare nh; open pine or juniper woods, in flocks, often on ground.
Pl.29 11" Grayish blue; throat streaked whitish; tail short; bill pointed, slender.

Clark's Nutcracker. *Nucifraga columbiana.* Z51a44.   Cascanueces
Can-M. Resident, 6000 to 10,000', nBC, nh (Nuevo León); winter visitor sBC, nH
(Sonora). Rare, isolated; coniferous forest, forest borders, openings, often on ground.
*Pl.29. 12" Pale gray; except white face and untacs; black wings with some white;
and white tail with black central feathers; bill pointed.*

American Crow. *Corvus brachyrhynchos.* Z51a4.   Cuervo Norteamericano
AK-M. Resident, near sea level, nBC; winter visitor nP (Sonora). Common; often in
large flocks, grassy fields or farmland, often near woodland borders or hedgerows.
17" Black; tail square-tipped. Larger than Tamaulipas and Sinaloa C. *V: a harsh kah.*

Sinaloa Crow. *Corvus sinaloae.* Z51a7.   Cacalote Sinaloense
M. Resident up to 3000', nP (s.Sonora to Nayarit). Common; usually in flocks, in
open woods or brushy grassland, or farmland, especially in river valleys or near water.
V: high-pitched cawing notes, more like Brown Jay's than like Tamaulipas Crow's.
Pl.28. 15" Black; tail square-tipped. See Tamaulipas Crow and American Crow.

Tamaulipas Crow. *Corvus imparatus.* Z51a8.   Cacalote Tamaulipeco
US-M. Resident up to 2000', ncA (Nuevo León to n.Veracruz). Common; often in
large flocks, in open brushy grassland, farm fields, semi-desert, or river-border woods.
Pl.28. 15" Black; tail square-tipped. V: a guttural *boys* or *carrk.* See Sinaloa C.

Chihuahuan Raven. *Corvus cryptoleucus.* Z51a36.   Cuervo de Cuello Blanco
US-M. Resident up to 7000', nP (Sonora+Sinaloa), nh (Chihuahua+Coahuila to
México), nA. Common; in open, dry, brushy grassland, or semi-desert; more often in
desert or semi-desert than Common R., less often on tree-dotted rocky mountainsides.
Pl.29. 21" Like Common R., *but neck feathers white at (usually concealed) base.*

Common Raven. *Corvus corax.* Z51a37.   Cuervo Grande
AK-N,x.B. Resident, sea level to 18,000', BC, P, H. Rare to common; usually
solitary or in pairs, rocky, tree-dotted or wooded mountainsides, or open rough terrain.
Pl.29. 25" Black; throat shaggy; head and bill rather large; tail wedge-shaped.

TITMICE, CHICKADEES - PARIDAE - COPETONCITOS, MASCARITAS

Seven residents; mostly highlands; small; medium legs, short neck, rounded wings,
medium tail, very short bill; arboreal, semi-desert to pine-oak woods; north temperate,
arctic, some tropical. Distinguish by shades of gray, pattern, crest or not. **Plate 29.**

Mexican Chickadee. *Parus sclateri.* Z37a6.   Mascarita Mexicana
US-M. Resident, 6000 to 13,500', ncH. Common; in mountain pine, pine-oak, or fir.
*Pl.29. 5" Grayish above; but crown (broadly), throat, and upper breast, black; belly
white; sides, flanks, untacs gray.*

Mountain Chickadee. *Parus gambeli.* Z37a7.   Mascarita Montañesa
AK-M. Resident, 4000 to 8000', nBC. Common; usually in mountain pine forest.
Pl.29. 5" Like Mexican C., *but white line over eye; smaller bib; paler sides, flanks.*

Bridled Titmouse. *Parus wollweberi.* Z37a13.   Copetoncito con Freno
US-M. Resident, 4000 to 9000', ncH. Common; mixed open oak woods in mountains.
*Pl.29. 5" Gray above; very pale gray below; black "bib", line through eye, and
ear-patch border; crest black and gray.* V: *wheeta-wheeta-wheeta.*

Plain Titmouse. *Parus inornatus.* Z37a45.   <u>Copetoncito Sencillo</u>
US-M. <u>Resident, 1500 to 7000', BC, nH (Sonora)</u>. Common; in chaparral, stream
valleys, piñon-juniper, oak or pine-oak woodlands. V: clear *wheeta-wheeta-wheeta.*
Pl.29. 5 1/2" Nearly uniform gray; paler below; crest shorter than that of Tufted T.
Tufted Titmouse. *Parus bicolor.* Z37a46.   <u>Copetoncito Norteño</u>
Can-M. <u>Resident up to 7500', ncH (e.Chihuahua+Coahuila to e.Guanajuato+ Hidalgo),</u>
<u>ncA (Nuevo León to c.Veracruz)</u>. Common; in scrubby woods, hedgerows, borders.
Pl.29. 5 1/2" (Black-crested group). *Gray, paler below; crest black; flanks rufous.*
Verdin. *Auriparus flaviceps.* Z37e9.   <u>Valoncito</u>
US-M. <u>Resident up to 7000', BC, nP (Sonora to Sinaloa), ncH (Chihuahua+ Coahuila</u>
<u>to Guanajuato+Hidalgo), nA</u>. Common; shrub-tops, semi-desert or desert scrub.
Pl.29. 3 1/2" Mostly medium gray above, pale gray below, but all or part of head
yellow; rufous wrist-patch usually hidden. Im: Head and wrist-patch gray.
Bushtit. *Psaltriparus minimus.* Z37d8.   <u>Sastrecito</u>
Can-M,G. <u>Resident up to 12,000', BC, H</u>. Common, irregular; usually in flocks,
lower branches in open oak or pine-oak woods, borders, piñon-juniper, or chapparral.
Pl.29. 4" Grayish above; whitish below; with long tail; crown and flanks may be
grayish or brownish; ear-patches may be grayish, brownish, or black. M: Iris dark.
F: Iris white. Birds from southern Sonora south are mostly black-eared; from
northern Sonora north some juveniles may be black-eared; BC birds not black-eared.

NUTHATCHES - SITTIDAE - SALTAPALOS
Three residents; northwest and central highlands; small; legs, neck and tail short; bill
medium-short, straight, pointed; climb up and down trunks and branches, forests; world
temperate. Distinguish by colors, patterns, and calls. **Plate 29.**
Red-breasted Nuthatch. *Sitta canadensis.* Z36e11.   <u>Saltapalo Canadense</u>
AK-M. <u>Resident, near sea level, BC (Guadalupe I.); casual winter visitor nH (Sonora),</u>
<u>nA (Nuevo León)</u>. Very rare; nesting (Guadalupe I.) and wintering mainly in conifers.
4" Like White-breasted N., *but smaller; rufous below; long black line through eye,*
white line over eye. F+Im: Similar, but paler and duller.
White-breasted Nuthatch. *Sitta carolinensis.* Z36e16.   <u>Saltapalo Blanco</u>
Can-M. <u>Resident, 4000 to 11,000', BC, ncH</u>. Rare; in pine, pine-oak, or fir forest.
Pl.29. 5 1/2" M: Gray above; crown and hind-neck black; white below; some
rufous on thighs, belly, or untacs; white patches on black tail. F: Duller; crown gray.
Pygmy Nuthatch. *Sitta pygmaea.* Z36e7.   <u>Saltapalo Enano</u>
Can-M. <u>Resident, 6000 to 13,000', nBC, ncH (Sonora+Nuevo León to Morelos+</u>
<u>Veracruz)</u>. Rare to abundant; in small very active groups in pine, pine-oak and fir
forest, low branches to tree-tops; voicing tinkling, chippering notes almost constantly.
Pl.29. 4" Gray above; white below; crown brown; nape-spot whitish; tiny tail.

NORTHERN CREEPERS - CERTHIIDAE - CORTECERITOS
Brown Creeper. *Certhia americana.* Z35a1.   <u>Cortecerito</u>
AK-M,G,H,N. <u>Resident, 6500 to 13,000', H; winter visitor nP; casual nBC</u>. Rare;
finds food in bark as it climbs trunks or large branches in pine, pine-oak, or fir forest.
Pl.31. 5" Climbs up like Tropical Creepers, *and is streaked black and brown above,*
and has brown tail with pointed-tipped feathers; but is <u>un</u>streaked white below, and
has blackish brown and whitish wings, <u>not</u> rich rufous wings.

WRENS - TROGLODYTIDAE - SALTAPAREDES
Thirty-three species, almost all residents; widespread Mexico; tail very short to
medium; bill slightly decurved or straight, slender, medium-short to medium-long;
ground to upper branches, semi-desert to humid forest; mostly new world tropical,
temperate. Distinguish by voice, patterns, bill and tail length. **Plates 30, 31, 33.**

Barred (Band-backed) **Wren.** *Campylorhynchus zonatum.* Z24a8.   <u>Carrasquita</u>
M-SAm. <u>Resident up to 10,000', sH (Chiapas), csA (Hidalgo to Campeche)</u>.
Common; small flocks, middle or upper branches, dense humid forest, moist pine forest
or tree-dotted fields near forest. V: rasping notes, *ji-ji-ji-jit, jit, ji-jit,* or harsh *crack*.
   *Pl.30. 7" Barred black and pale buff above, spotted black on white below, except
   cinnamon belly, flanks, and untacs, with few dark spots or bars, mostly on flanks.*

Gray (Gray-barred) **Wren.** *Campylorhynchus megalopterum.* Z24a10.   <u>Sonaja Parda</u>
M. <u>Resident, 6500 to 12,000', cH (Jalisco+Puebla to Oaxaca)</u>. Common; small flocks
in middle or upper branches, humid pine-oak or fir forest. V: very harsh rasping notes.
   *Pl.30. 7" Appears gray; actually blackish-and-white; barred above, but streaked on
   head and neck; spotty streaks and spotty bars below, on whitish.*

Giant Wren. *Campylorhynchus chiapense.* Z24a6.   <u>Chupahuevo</u>
M. <u>Resident, near sea level, sP (Chiapas)</u>. Common; hedgerows, tree-dotted brushy
fields, river-edge woods. V: a rollicking *chort-chort-chort-chort;* also *wock-o, wock-o.*
   *Pl.30. 8" Mostly plain dark chestnut above; primaries blacker, <u>unbarred or faintly
   barred</u>; crown and hind-neck black; line through eye black; underparts and face white,
   with faint salmon or buff wash on flanks and untacs.* See Rufous-naped Wren.

Rufous-naped Wren. *Campylorhynchus rufinucha.* Z24a5.   <u>Sonaja Nuca Rojiza</u>
M-CR,x.B. <u>Resident up to 2000', csP (Colima+México to Chiapas), cA (c.Veracruz)</u>.
Abundant; usually in pairs, in hedgerows, small-tree-dotted brushy fields, or scrubby
open woods, or woods borders.   V: loud, rollicking *joricky-joricky-joricky.*
   *Pl.30. 6" Crown mostly black; nape rufous; whitish line over eye; black line
   through eye; back and rump streaked or spotted or plain rufous; wings <u>barred</u>;
   underparts whitish or dull grayish buff, may be partly spotted or barred.*

Spotted Wren. *Campylorhynchus gularis.* Z24a2.   <u>Matraca Manchada</u>
M. <u>Resident, 3000 to 8500', nP (Sonora and Sinaloa), ncH (Chihuahua to Michoacán
+México; also Tamaulipas to Hidalgo)</u>. Rare, irregular; in hedgerows and scrubby
vegetation of rather arid terrain, also in lower levels of open oak or pine-oak woodland.
   Pl.30. 7" Like Boucard's W., *but has short bars, not spots, on flanks; few or no
   spots on belly and untacs; much darker brown, less buffy rufous, above. Im:
   Similar, but unspotted and unbarred whitish below; crown blackish.*

Boucard's Wren. *Campylorhynchus jocosum.* Z24a1.   <u>Matraca Alacranera</u>
M. <u>Resident, 3000 to 8000', cP (Guerrero+Oaxaca), cH (Morelos+Guerrero to
Oaxaca)</u>. Rare; dense scrubby arid areas, or brushy parts of pine or pine-oak woods.
   *Pl.30. 7" Rufous above, heavily streaked black and buff; brown crown and line
   through eye; whitish line over eye; <u>malar streak black</u>; entire underparts
   boldly spotted, except throat. Im: Spotted below, but not boldly.* See Cactus Wren
   and Spotted Wren.

Yucatan Wren. *Campylorhynchus yucatanicus.* Z24a3.   <u>Matraca Yucateca</u>
M. <u>Resident, near sea level, Y (Yucatán)</u>. Rare to common; scrubby woodlands,
hedgerows, overgrown fields, thickets, mainly near coast, sometimes inland (Uxmal).
   *Pl.30. 7" Dark brown or blackish above, barred on wings, tail, and rump, and
   streaked on neck and back, with whitish; line over eye whitish; <u>malar streak black</u>;
   underparts whitish, spotty streaks on throat and breast, and bars on belly and flanks.*

Cactus Wren. *Campylorhynchus brunneicapillum.* Z24a4.   <u>Matraca Grande</u>
US-M. <u>Resident up to 7000', BC, nP (Sonora and Sinaloa), ncH (Chihuahua+ Nuevo
León to Jalisco+Hidalgo), nA (Tamaulipas)</u>.   Common; scrubby semi-desert,
overgrown brushy fields, hedgerows, thickets. V: a rasping *cha-cha-cha-cha-cha-cha.*
   *Pl.31. 7 1/2" Blackish forehead; blackish or chocolate-brown crown; white line
   over eye; dull reddish brown above, streaked with black and white; tail and wings
   barred; heavy spotting on breast; little or no spotting on buffy belly, flanks, and
   untacs.* See Boucard's Wren and Yucatan Wren.

Rock Wren. *Salpinctes obsoletus.* Z24a16.   Saltaladera
Can-CR,x.B.   Resident, near sea level to 13,000', BC, nP (Sonora+Sinaloa), H.
Common; open dry country especially hills, on ruins, or on ground, rocks, boulders.
*Pls.31,33. 5 1/2" Grayish above, with narrow spotty whitish streaks; rufous rump;
white line over eye; whitish below, with narrow streaks on breast and sides; pale
buffy belly, and barred untacs; may be very worn and faded.*

Canyon Wren. *Catherpes mexicanus.* Z24a17.   Saltapared Risquero
Can-M.   Resident up to 11,000', BC, P, ncH, nA (Nuevo León+Tamaulipas).
Common; rocky cliffs, archaeological sites, abandoned buildings, steep rocky hillsides,
rock walls.   V: a descending series of loud *chu-wee* notes, ending in a buzzy note.
*Pls.31,33. 5 1/2" Mostly reddish brown above and below, with fine spotty streaks
(barred wings and tail); gray crown and ear-patch; broadly white throat and breast.*

Sumichrast's(Sl-b)Wren. *Hylorchilus sumichrasti.* Z24a18. Saltapared de Sumichrast
M. Resident, 1000 to 3500', csA (Veracruz, Oaxaca?, Chiapas).   Very rare; only in a
few areas of large rocks and boulders covered by dense humid forest. V: an abrupt *tink.*
*Pl.30. 5 1/2" Very dark brown above; mostly dark brown below, obscurely
barred and speckled; breast paler; face, throat, dull tawny; short tail; rather long bill.*

Spotted-breasted Wren. *Thryothorus maculipectus.* Z24a36.   Saltapared Cluequita
M-CR. Resident up to 4500', sP (Chiapas), A, Y.   Common; thickets, hedgerows,
forest borders, openings, river-border woods. V: a loud, rythmic *wee-sée, wee-lée-ree.*
*Pl.30. 5" Unbarred reddish brown above; white line over eye; face streaked; throat
and breast heavily spotted; belly plain rufous; untacs barred. Im: Few small spots.*

Rufous-and-white Wren. *Thryothorus rufalbus.* Z24a45.   Saltapared Rojizo
M-Pan,x.B.   Resident, 1000 to 5000', sP (s.Chiapas).   Rare; brushy woodland
borders, undergrowth in forest, *cafetales*, tall weeds in overgrown fields. V: a varied
series of mellow low-pitched phrases, like hoots or trills of small owl; also *cho-cho-cho.*
*Pl.30. 5 1/2" Bright plain rufous above; wings and tail barred; plain white below;
except barred untacs; face streaked; white line over eye, dark line through eye.*

Sinaloa Wren. *Thryothorus sinaloa.* Z24a48.   Saltapared Sinaloense
M. Resident up to 7000', ncP (Sonora to w.Oaxaca) Common; tree-dotted shrubby
grassland, brushy gulleys, scrubby woods and borders. V: Like Banded Wren's, varied
patchwork of loud, clear notes, some trills, hoots, *chew-chew*, and chipping notes.
Pl.30. 5 1/2" Like Plain Wren,but duller brown above and on flanks, untacs barred.

Banded Wren. *Thryothorus pleurostictus.* Z24a47.   Saltapared Arañero
M-CR,x.B.   Resident up to 5000', csP (Michoacán+México to Chiapas).   Common;
thickets, especially in stream valleys, hedgerows, scrubby woods, borders. V: varied
phrases, musical trills, hooting notes, chipping notes; like canary song, lower-pitched.
*Pl.30. 5 1/2" Rich rufous above; white line over eye; clear white below, except
heavy neck-streaks which extend to heavy bars on sides, flanks, belly, and untacs.*

Carolina Wren. *Thryothorus ludovicianus.* Z24a43.   Saltapared Carolinense
Can-M.   Resident up to 7000', nH (Coahuila, Nuevo León, Tamaulipas), nA.   Rare;
hedgerows, brushy grasslands, open woods, and borders. V: *toreetle-toreetle-toreetle.*
*Pl.31. 5 1/2" Rufous above; wings and tail barred; white line over eye; rich tawny
below, except pale buffy throat and barred untacs.*

White-browed Wren. *Thryothorus albinucha.* Z24a44.   Saltapared Yucateco
M,G,B,N.   Resident, near sea level, sA (Tabasco), Y.   Rare; thickets, hedgerows,
borders, undergrowth of scrubby woods. V: loud, *chortle-dee-chortle-dee-chortle-dee.*
*Pl.30. 5" Brown above; white line over eye; face streaked; tail and uptacs grayish;
heavily barred tail-sides; white below; flanks washed pale rufous; untacs barred.*

Happy Wren. *Thryothorus felix.* Z24a35.   Saltapared Reyezuelo
M. Resident up to 7000', ncP.   Common; thickets, hedgerows, woods borders, scrub
woods, forest undergrowth. V: Like Spotted-breasted W.'s, *see-sée, wee-lée-vee.*
Pl.30. 5" Rufous above; white line over eye; face streaked; breast buffy, to nearly

whitish on throat, more rufous on belly and flanks; untacs barred.

Plain Wren. *Thryothorus modestus.* Z24a49. <u>Saltapared Sencillo</u>
M-Pan. <u>Resident up to 5500', sP</u>. Common; tall grass or weeds, weedy brushy woods borders, weedy road shoulders, overgrown fields. V: a very high-pitched note or two notes, then usually two loud and mellow, low-pitched notes, *see-deet, clu-lu.*
Pl.30. 5 1/2" Grayish brown above; rump and tail more reddish; white line over eye; very few and faint face-streaks; whitish throat, breast, and belly; reddish brown or buffy brown flanks and unbarred untacs. Im: Darker and duller below.

Bewick's Wren. *Thryomanes bewickii.* Z24a25. <u>Saltapared Tepetatero</u>
Can-M. <u>Resident up to 9500', BC, nP (Sonora), ncH, nA (Nuevo León+Tamaulipas).</u>
Rare+; parks, vacant lots, gardens, thickets, woods, borders. V: One note, then a trill.
Pl.31. 5" Grayish or brownish above, whitish below; untacs barred; tail-sides broadly barred, white-tipped. Im: Breast scalloped; untacs brownish, faintly barred.

Socorro Wren. *Thryomanes sissonii.* Z24a26. <u>Saltapared de Isla Socorro</u>
M. <u>Resident, near sea level, cP (Socorro I.).</u> Rare+; brush-dotted fields, thickets.
Pl.30. 5" Like Bewick's W., but buffier below; no white tail-tips; untacs spotted.

Northern House-Wren. *Troglodytes aedon.* Z24a57. <u>Saltapared Cucarachero</u>
Can-M. <u>Resident, 3000 to 13,000', nBC, ncH; winter visitor, sBC, ncP, ncA.</u> Rare+ ; hedgerows, woods borders, undergrowth in open woods, river-borders, forest.
Pl.31. 5" Races vary. Dull brown to dull reddish-brown above; grayish to buffy brown below; with paler belly; wings, tail, flanks, and untacs barred; tail short. Im: "Scaly" lower throat and breast.

Tropical House-Wren. *Troglodytes musculus.* Z24a58. <u>Matraquita Común</u>
M-SAm. <u>Resident, sea level to 10,000', sP, sH, csA (se.Veracruz to Quintana Roo), Y.</u> Common; thickets, brushy fields, hedgerows, woods borders, gardens, vacant lots.
Pl.30. 4 1/2" Like buffier race of N.House-Wren, but flanks unbarred, or in some birds faintly barred; somewhat paler below, with whiter throat.

Cozumel Wren. *Troglodytes beani.* Z24a59. <u>Matraquita de Cozumel</u>
M. <u>Resident, near sea level, Y (Cozumel I.).</u> Common; thickets, yards, vacant lots.
Pl.30. 4 1/2" Like Tropical H.-W.,but nearly white below; bars on untacs broader.

Clarion Wren. *Troglodytes tanneri.* Z24a56. <u>Saltapared de Isla Clarión</u>
M. <u>Resident, near sea level, cP (Clarión I.).</u> Rare+; thickets, scrubby woods.
Pl.30. 5" Like N.House-W., but grayer above; whitish below; flanks unbarred.

Rufous-browed Wren. *Troglodytes rufociliatus.* Z24a60. <u>Saltapared Cejirojo</u>
M,G,ES,H. <u>Resident, 7000 to 10,000', sH (Chiapas).</u> Rare; usually among epiphytes on trunks, middle branches, in humid dense pine or pine-oak woods, or cloud forest.
Pl.30. 4 1/2" Like Tropical House-W., but face, breast, and line over eye rich reddish tawny; belly and untacs buffy; flanks heavily barred.

Winter Wren. *Troglodytes troglodytes.* Z24a55. <u>Saltapared Invernal</u>
AK-M. <u>Winter visitor nH (Nuevo León+Coahuila).</u> Very rare; brushy stream-valleys.
Pl.33. 4" Dark reddish brown above; pale grayish brown below; buffier on breast; heavily barred belly, flanks, and untacs; very short tail; short bill.

Sedge Wren. *Cistothorus platensis.* Z24a21. <u>Saltapared de Cienaga</u>
Can-SAm. <u>Resident up to 10,000', csH (Nayarit to Veracruz; Chiapas), csA (s.Veracruz to Tabasco); winter visitor nA.</u> Very rare, local; in open marsh, marshy meadows, dense tall grass. V: metallic, chattering, warbling notes; also a metallic *chep.*
Pl.31. 4 1/2" Back streaked black and white; crown finely streaked brown and buff; underparts whitish, tinged pale rufous on sides, flanks, and untacs; tail and bill short.

Marsh Wren. *Cistothorus palustris.* Z24a24. <u>Saltapared Pantanero</u>
Can-M. <u>Resident, around 8000', cH (D.F., Hidalgo, México, and Puebla); summer resident, near sea level, nBC; winter visitor sBC, nP, ncH, ncA.</u> Rare, local; marshes, marshy borders of ponds, canals, lakes. V: metallic, rattling song; and a metallic *chuck.*

Pl.31. 5" Like Sedge W., *but crown and rump not* streaked; *back more heavily streaked; bill and tail longer; more prominent white line over eye.*

White-bellied Wren. *Uropsila leucogastra.* Z24a65.   <u>Saltapared Cantarina</u>
M,G,B,H. <u>Resident up to 1800', cP (Jalisco to Guerrero), A, Y.</u> Common A+Y, rare cP; scrubby thorny woods, brushy fields, thickets. V: a rapid, rythmic *chip-it-ti-pee.*
    Pl.30. 4" Grayish-brown above; white below, with dull buff flanks and untacs; line over eye white; tail short.

Lowland (W-br.) **Wood-Wren.** *Henicorhina leucosticta.* Z24a66. <u>Saltapared Gallinita</u>
M-SAm. <u>Resident up to 3500', sP, csA (San Luis Potosí to Quintana Roo).</u> Rare+; humid forest undergrowth, forest borders. V: rythmic *hur-dée-hur-dée-ho,* or *pur-dee.*
    Pl.30. 4" Dark reddish brown above; streaked face; white line over eye; white throat and breast; rusty belly and untacs; tail very short. Im: Similar, but breast gray.

Highland (Gray-br.) **Wood-Wren.** *Henicorhina leucophrys.* Z24a67.   <u>Saltabreña</u>
M-SAm, x.B,N. <u>Resident, 3000 to 10,000', csP, csH (Jalisco+México to Oaxaca),</u> <u>csA (San Luis Potosí to Chiapas).</u> Rare+; often in pairs, undergrowth of dense humid forest or cloud forest, thickets in forest openings or along borders. V: in cA (and sA) a <u>rapidly</u> repeated rythmic *chur-rée-chur-rée,* up then down, but on Pacific slopes of Oaxaca (other csP?) and western Panama (rest of Middle America?) it is more complex, like Spotted-breasted Wren's, *wee-dée, tee-whéedle-dee,* often sung antiphonally.
    Pl.30. 4" Like Lowland Wood-W., *but breast and upper belly dark gray, not* white.

Nightingale Wren. *Microcerculus philomela.* Z24a69.   <u>Cholincillo</u>
M-CR,x.ES. <u>Resident up to 3500', sA (Chiapas).</u> Rare, local; dense humid forest undergrowth. V: intriguing, long deliberate series of random(?)-pitch musical notes.
    Pl.30. 4" Dark brown above; blackish wings and tail; whitish throat and part of face; medium gray breast and belly; reddish brown flanks and untacs. Birds vary, may have scaly throat and barred flanks. Im: Darker and scalier throat and breast.

DIPPERS - CINCLIDAE - TORDOS ACUATICOS

American Dipper. *Cinclus mexicanus.* Z22a3.   <u>Tordo Acuático</u>
AK-Pan,x.B,ES. <u>Resident, 3500 to 8000', H.</u> Rare; along fast-flowing streams in mountain forest, walking on banks, rocks, or in shallow water, or diving under water.
    Pl.31. 7" Plump body; dark gray, except white eyelids, yellowish legs; short tail.

GNATCATCHERS, KINGLETS - SYLVIIDAE - REYEZUELOS, PERLITAS

Eight residents; widespread Mexico; very small; legs, neck, and wings proportional; tail short to medium; bill short to very long; semi-desert brush to humid forest; north temperate, world. Distinguish by bill length, tail and head-pattern. **Plates 34, 44.**

Golden-crowned Kinglet. *Regulus satrapa.* Z25c5.   <u>Reyezuelo de Oro</u>
AK-M,G. <u>Resident, 7500 to 12,000', csH (Michoacán+Hidalgo to Chiapas); winter</u> <u>visitor nBC, nA (Tamaulipas).</u> Rare+; high up in dense humid pine-oak or fir forests.
    Pl.44. 3 3/4" M: Grayish olive above, paler below; two white wing-bars; head striped black and white, with crown patch orange (male), yellow (female); tiny bill.

Ruby-crowned Kinglet. *Regulus calendula.* Z25c6.   <u>Reyezuelo de Rojo</u>
AK-M,G. <u>Resident, near sea level, nBC (Guadalupe I.); winter visitor BC, ncP, ncH,</u> <u>ncA.</u> Common; forest, open woods, tree-dotted fields, thickets, borders; flicks wings.
    Pl.44. 3 3/4" Grayish olive above; whitish below, with darker breast; white wing-bars on blackish wings; white eye-ring; tiny bill. M: Hidden red crown-patch.

Long-billed Gnatwren. *Ramphocaenus rufiventris.* Z25b3.   <u>Saltón Picudo</u>
M-SAm. <u>Resident up to 3000', sP (Chiapas), csA, Y.</u> Rare; undergrowth of dense forest or forest borders, or thickets. V: a musical, extended trill, usually rising in pitch.
    Pl.34. 5" Bill long, slender, straight, orange; back grayish olive; crown brown; buff below, with more cinnamon breast (and sides of neck and face), and white throat, usually speckled; tail short, graduated, white-tipped.

Blue-gray Gnatcatcher. *Polioptila caerulea.* Z25b5.   <u>Perlita Común</u>
Can-M,G,B,H. <u>Resident up to 8000', all sub-regions</u>. Rare, summer; common,
winter; shrub-dotted fields, thickets, open woods, borders, scrubby woods; tail held up.
*Pl.44. 4 1/2 M: Pale bluish gray above; white feather-edgings on blackish wings;
forehead and sides of crown narrowly black; eye-ring white; long tail mostly black
above, white below. F: Paler, duller, no black on head.*

Black-tailed Gnatcatcher. *Polioptila melanura.* Z25b4.   <u>Perlita Colinegra</u>
US-M. <u>Resident up to 7000', BC, nP (Sonora), ncH (Chihuahua+Nuevo León to
Jalisco+Guanajuato)</u>. Rare+; scrubby woods, borders, hedgerows, overgrown fields.
Pl.44. 4" Like Blue-gray Gn., *but tail black with narrow white sides, above and
below; and Sum.M: entire crown black; and Win.M: crown gray, but may have some
black on sides of crown (like* Blue-gray Gn.*), or on forehead and fore-crown.*

Black-capped Gnatcatcher. *Polioptila nigriceps.* Z25b8.   <u>Perlita Cabeza Negra</u>
US-M. <u>Resident up to 3500', ncP (Sonora+Chihuahua to Colima)</u>. Rare+; scrubby
woods and borders, river valleys, thickets, hedgerows, tree-dotted brushy fields.
Pl.34. 4 1/2" Like Blue-gray Gn., *but Sum.M: entire crown black (like* Sum.M.
White-lored Gn., *but range is more northern); and F.+Win.M: like* female Blue-gray
Gnatcatcher, *but eye-ring less prominent, tail slightly longer; cheeks may be whiter.*

White-lored Gnatcatcher. *Polioptila albiloris.* Z25b9.   <u>Pispirria</u>
M-CR,x.B. <u>Resident up to 4000', csP (Michoacán to Chiapas), Y</u>. Rare+; in
tree-dotted grassy, brushy, open fields, vacant lots, hedgerows, dense brush, thickets.
Pl.34. 4 1/2" Like Blue-gray Gn., *but Sum.M: entire crown black to eyes; and
Win.M: crown black; lores and line over eye white; and F: lores and line over eye
white.* See Tropical Gn., which has broader white line over eye, <u>all year</u>, M. and F.

Tropical Gnatcatcher. *Polioptila plumbea.* Z25b10.   <u>Perlita Plomiza</u>
M-SAm,x.ES. <u>Resident, near sea level, sA (Campeche+Quintana Roo)</u>. Rare+; dense
forest, forest borders, or humid tree-dotted brushy fields, usually middle-level branches.
Pl.34. 4 1/2" Like winter White-lored Gnatcatcher, *all year, but has broader white
line over eye* (note also different geographic distribution and preferred habitat).

THRUSHES - TURDIDAE - PRIMAVERAS, CHEPITOS
About twenty residents, seven transients or winter visitors; widespread Mexico; small
to medium-small; legs, neck, wings, tail, and bill mostly medium; mostly medium to
humid habitat, suburban to forest; world temperate, tropical. Distinguish by leg,
eye-ring, and bill colors; voice, plumage colors and patterns. **Plates 31, 32, 33.**

Eastern Bluebird. *Sialia sialis.* Z21a107.   <u>Ventura Azulillo</u>
Can-N. <u>Resident, 3000 to 9000', ncP, H, ncA (Tamaulipas to n.Veracruz)</u>. Rare+, H;
rare, ncP+ncA; gardens, parks, villages, tree-dotted fields, forest borders and openings.
*Pl.33. 6 1/2" M: Medium blue above; bright rufous below and on sides of neck,
with white belly and untacs. F: Paler, duller. Worn birds may appear very drab.*

Western Bluebird. *Sialia mexicana.* Z21a108.   <u>Ventura Azul</u>
Can-M. <u>Resident, 5000 to 13,000', nBC, ncH (Sonora+Nuevo León to Michoacán+
Veracruz); winter visitor nP</u>. Rare+; tree-dotted grasslands, open woods, borders.
*Pl.33. 6 1/2" M: Entire head and throat, and most of upperparts, purplish blue;
but usually some rufous on back; rufous breast and sides; white belly and untacs. F:
Like* Eastern B. female, *but throat and sides of neck gray; usually brownish-backed.*

Mountain Bluebird. *Sialia currucoides.* Z21a109.   <u>Ventura de Llano</u>
AK-M. <u>Winter visitor nBC, nP, ncH, nA</u>. Rare; in tree-dotted open areas, junipers.
Pl.33. 6 1/2" Like Eastern and Western B., *but M: grayish blue above; pale blue
and white below; and F: throat, breast, flanks, and sides of neck usually pale
grayish; never more than faintly tinged rufous below.*

Townsend's Solitaire. *Myadestes townsendi.* Z21a113.   <u>Jilguero Norteño</u>
AK-M. <u>Resident, 5000 to 10,000', nH (Sonora and Coahuila to Jalisco); winter visitor</u>

nBC, nP. Rare+; middle or upper branches, large trees in pine or open pine-oak forests.
Pl.31. 8" Gray; perches upright; eye-ring and sides of tail white; wing-patch buffy.

Brown-backed Solitaire. *Myadestes obscurus.* Z21a114. Jilguero Común
M,G,B,ES,H. Resident, 2000 to 10,500', ncP (Sonora to Colima), H, A (Tamaulipas to Chiapas). Rare+; upper branches, in rather dense humid forest, river-border woods, scrubby woods, pine, pine-oak, or fir forest. V: a cascade of sibilant yet musical notes.
Pl.32. 8" Head and upper back gray; brownish rump and scapulars; wings rufous; underparts pale grayish, throat (and eye-ring) white; black sub-malar line.

Slaty (Sl.-col.) **Solitaire.** *Myadestes unicolor.* Z21a120. Clarín
M-N. Resident, 2500 to 5000', sP, csA (Hidalgo to Chiapas). Rare+; humid forest.
Pl.32. 8" Dark gray, but white eye-ring; whitish tail-sides and tail-tip; bill short.

Orange-billed Thrush. *Catharus aurantiirostris.* Z21a245. Chepito Pico Anaranjado
M-SAm,x.B. Resident, 2500 to 7500', ncP (Sinaloa to Guerrero), H, A. Common; in hedgerows, gardens, parks, woodland borders, undergrowth of humid forest, thickets.
Pl.32. 6 1/2" Tawny-brown above, whitish below; bill, eye-ring, and legs orange.

Russet (Nightingale-) **Thrush.** *Catharus occidentalis.* Z21a247. Chepito Serrano
M. Resident, 5000 to 12,000', ncH. Rare+; in pine, pine-oak, or fir forest, or borders.
Pl.32. 6 1/2" Like Highland T., *but tawnier above, has buffy wing-patch (visible only on extended wing); bill mostly black; breast has obscure streaks or scallops.*

Highland (Ruddy-c.Ni.-) **Thrush.** *Catharus frantzii.* Z21a248. Chepito de Montaña
M-Pan,x.B. Resident, 5000 to 10,000', csH (Jalisco+San Luis Potosí to Chiapas). Rare+; undergrowth of dense humid mountain forest, forest borders, nearby thickets.
Pl.32. 6 1/2" Grayish rufous above; unstreaked whitish below, darker and grayer on breast; no buffy wing-patch; *bill orange below.* See Russet Thrush.

Black-headed (N.-) **Thrush.** *Catharus mexicanus.* Z21a249. Chepito Solitario
M-Pan,x.B,ES. Resident, 2000 to 6000', A. Rare+; cloud forest, nearby lush gardens.
Pl.32. 6 1/2" Dark olive above; top and sides of head black; throat whitish, faintly streaked; breast grayish; belly and untacs white; bill and eye-ring orange.

Spotted (N.-) **Thrush.** *Catharus dryas.* Z21a250. Chepito Pinto
M,G,H,SAm. Resident, 4000 to 10,000', sH. Very rare; cloud forest undergrowth.
Pl.32. 7" Dark bluish gray above; head all-black, except white throat, belly, untacs; salmon to orange breast, with dark spots; bill, eye-ring, and long legs, orange.

Veery. *Catharus fuscescens.* Z21a251. Mirlillo Rojizo
Can-SAm,x.ES,N. Transient csA, Y. Very rare; thickets, scrubby woods or borders.
Pl.33. 7" Tawny-brown above; white below; breast lightly spotted brown on buff.

Gray-cheeked Thrush. *Catharus minimus.* Z21a252. Mirlillo de Cara Gris
AK-SAm,x.ES,N. Transient sA, Y. Rare+; borders, or scrubby to tall forest.
Pl.33. 7" Like Swainson's T., *but has gray cheeks, and less noticeable eye-ring.*

Swainson's Thrush. *Catharus ustulatus.* Z21a253. Mirlillo de Swainson
AK-SAm. Transient or winter visitor all sub-regions. Rare+; dense forest and borders.
Pl.33. 7" Uniform grayish- to brownish-olive above; prominent buffy eye-ring, buffy cheeks; whitish below, except breast buffy, heavily spotted blackish brown.

Hermit Thrush. *Catharus guttatus.* Z21a254. Mirlillo Solitario
AK-M,G,ES. Winter visitor, BC, P, H, ncA. Rare+; in woods, gardens, dense forest.
Pl.33. 6 1/2" Like Gray-cheeked T., *but browner cheeks, back; rufous rump, tail.*

Wood Thrush. *Hylocichla mustelina.* Z21a255. Mirlillo de la Selva
Can-SAm. Winter visitor, csP, A, Y. Rare+; humid forest, open or scrubby woods.
Pl.33. 7 1/2" Rufous above, brighter on head and upper back, with duller rump and tail; underparts boldly spotted, black on white.

Black Robin. *Turdus infuscatus.* Z21a299. Primavera Negra
M,G,ES,H. Resident, mostly 5000 to 12,000', H (Guerrero+Tamaulipas to Chiapas). Rare (very rare visitor below 5000'); middle and upper branches in dense humid forest.

ROBINS 77

Pl.32. 9" M: Black; narrow eye-ring red; bill, legs yellow. F: Dark brown; throat buffy, streaked. Female is darker than female Rufous-collared R. See Mountain R.

Mountain Robin. *Turdus plebejus.* Z21a309.   Primavera Piquinegra
M-Pan,x.B. Resident, around 8000', sH (Chiapas). Rare; humid forest edge, openings.
Pl.32. 10" Blackish olive-brown above; paler, buffier below, with faintly streaked throat; bill and legs black. V: a loud *kwang.*

Clay-colored Robin. *Turdus grayi.* Z21a316.   Primavera Merulín
US-SAm. Resident up to 5500', csP (Oaxaca+Chiapas), A, Y. Abundant; in gardens, parks, hedgerows, river-border woods, dense humid forest and borders, farms.
Pl.32. 9" Races vary. Grayish olive to olive-buff above; mostly tawny olive to rich buff below; throat pale buff, faintly streaked; bill brownish yellow.

White-throated Robin. *Turdus albicollis.* Z21a319.   Primavera Bosquera
M-SAm. Resident up to 12,000', P, H, A. Common up to 5000' in A, sP; rarer ncP, H; in dense humid forest, forest borders, plantations, lush gardens, river borders.
Pl.32. 9" Races vary. Buffy olive to dark olive-gray above; pale grayish brown to olive gray below; with white throat patch partly and heavily streaked black; narrow eye-ring orange; bill and legs yellowish.

Rufous-backed Robin. *Turdus rufopalliatus.* Z21a321.   Primavera Chivillo
US-M. Resident up to 8000', ncP, cH (D.F.+México to Oaxaca). Rare+, local, in cH; in gardens, hedgerows, parks, plantations, open to dense woods, and borders.
Pl.32. 9" Head and neck (except brown-streaked white throat) gray; back, scapulars, and wing-coverts dull buffy rufous; rump, uptacs, tail and flight-feathers gray; breast and sides tawny-rufous; belly and untacs white. F: Paler and duller.

Grayson's Robin. *Turdus graysoni.* Z21a322.   Primavera de las Islas
M. Resident up to 2000', cP (Tres Marias Is.+Nayarit). Common, islands, very rare, mainland; plantations, open to rather dense forest, hedgerows, borders, scrubby woods.
9" May be a race of the Rufous-backed R., but is much duller and grayer than average male Rufous-backed R., has very little rufous or brown, and is larger-billed.

Rufous-collared Robin. *Turdus rufitorques.* Z21a324.   Primavera Collarejo
M,G,ES,H. Resident, 5000 to 10,000', sH (Chiapas). Common; in open to dense pine or pine-oak forest, or woodland borders, or tree-dotted grassy fields and roadsides.
Pl.32. 10" Bill and legs yellowish. M: Black, except rich rufous breast and broad full collar; striped throat. F: Much paler and duller; pale grayish brown or medium brown instead of black; pale tawny instead of rufous; shows trace of pale collar.

American Robin. *Turdus migratorius.* Z21a325.   Primavera Real
AK-M,G. Resident, 5000 to 11,000', ncH; winter visitor, BC, nP, ncA, Y. Common; gardens, parks, hedgerows, woodland borders, pine woods, dense pine-oak woods.
Pl.31. 10" M: Blackish and dark gray above; white eye-ring; mostly orange-brown below; black-striped white throat; white belly and untacs. F: Duller.

San Lucas Robin. *Turdus confinis.* Z21a326.   Primavera del Cabo
M. Resident, about 4000 to 6000', sBC. Rare+; mountain woods, borders, openings.
Pl.32. 10" Pale brownish gray above; mostly buff below; throat faintly streaked.

Varied Thrush. *Ixoreus naevius.* Z21a232.   Mirlo Pinto
AK-M. Winter visitor BC. Very rare, or casual; tree-dotted areas, woods, borders.
9" M: Dark slaty gray above; black breast-band and ear-patch; buffy rufous wing-bars and wing-feather-edgings; rufous-orange eye-line, malar area, throat, and breast, and whitish belly and untacs. F: Similar, but much duller and paler.

Aztec Thrush. *Ridgwayia pinicola.* Z21a233.   Primavera Pinta
US-M. Resident, 6000 to 10,000', ncH. Very rare; borders, or pine-oak or fir forest.
Pl.32. 8" M: Breast, entire head, and upperparts blackish brown, "scaly" or streaked above; white belly, untacs, uptacs, wing-patches and tail-tip. F: Somewhat paler, duller, and more prominently streaked.

WRENTITS - CHAMAEIDAE - CAMEAS
Wrentit. *Chamaea fasciata.* Z26a1.   Camea
US-M. Resident up to 7500', nBC. Common; in dry, dense, scrubby vegetation. V: a
soft *chirr;* also a loud accelerating series of bouncing, chattering, musical notes.
Pl.31. 6" *Dark grayish brown; paler and faintly streaked below; iris white; tail long.*

THRASHERS - MIMIDAE - CUITLACOCHES
Fifteen residents, three winter visitors; mostly northern; medium-small; legs and neck
medium-short, rounded wings, medium-long tail, medium-short to medium-long bill,
straight or decurved; mostly on ground; semi-desert to moist forest ; new world
temperate, tropical. Distinguish by bill-shape, colors, patterns. **Plates 31, 32, 33.**

Gray Catbird. *Dumetella carolinensis.* Z23a1.   Maullador
Can-Pan,x.ES. Winter visitor csP, A, Y. Common; forest undergrowth and borders.
Pl.33. 8" *Slate gray, except black cap and dark reddish brown untacs.*

Black Catbird. *Melanoptila glabrirostris.* Z23a2.   Pájaro Gato
M,G,B,H. Resident near sea level, Y. Common on Cozumel Island, rare elsewhere;
in scrubby woods or borders, gardens, hedgerows, thickets, humid forest openings.
Pl.32. 8" *Glossy black, with violet and blue-green gloss; slender bill, catbird shape.*
V: many different phrases, often repeated persistently; also clucks, chirps, chucks.

Northern Mockingbird. *Mimus polyglottos.* Z23a5.   Cenzontle Norteño
Can-M. Resident up to 10,000', BC. ncP, ncH, ncA. Rare+; thickets, hedgerows,
tree-dotted pastures, farms, gardens, parks, plantations, forest borders.
Pl.31. 9" *Gray above; whitish below, with grayish breast; blackish wings and tail,*
with white outer tail-feathers; wing-bars and wing-patch white; iris pale yellow.

Tropical Mockingbird. *Mimus gilvus.* Z23a6.   Cenzontle Tropical
M-SAm,x.N,CR. Resident up to 7500', sP, sH, sA, Y. Common; among scattered
trees, thickets, hedgerows, farmyards, gardens - parks, scrubby woods, borders.
Pl.32. 10" *Like* Northern M., *but much less white on wing, more on tail-tip.*

Sage Thrasher. *Oreoscoptes montanus.* Z23a18.   Mirlo de las Chias
Can-M. Winter visitor BC, nP, nH, nA. Rare; open arid areas, shrub-dotted fields.
Pl.33. 8" *Brownish gray above; heavy streaks of black on whitish below;*
faint line over eye; white wing-bars; tail-corners white; bill short.

Socorro Mockingbird. *Mimodes graysoni.* Z23a17.   Mirlo de Isla Soccoro
M. Resident, near sea level, cP (Socorro I.). Very rare; thickets, scrubby woods.
Pl.32. 11" *Grayish brown above; whitish below; flanks and untacs brown-streaked.*

Brown Thrasher. *Toxostoma rufum.* Z23a19.   Cuitlacoche Rojizo
Can-M. Winter visitor nP, nA. Very rare; hedgerows, borders, scrubby woods,
11" *Like* Long-billed T., *but more reddish above; rufous head; browner streaks*
below; somewhat shorter, straighter bill; yellow iris (yellowish gray in immature).

Long-billed Thrasher. *Toxostoma longirostre.* Z23a20.   Cuitlacoche Alacranero
US-M. Resident up to 5000', ncA. Rare+; scrubby woods, thickets, borders.
Pl.31. 11" *Grayish rufous above; sides of head pale gray; whitish below with*
heavy black streaks; white wing-bars; iris orange or orange-yellow; bill decurved.

Cozumel Thrasher. *Toxostoma guttatum.* Z23a21.   Cuitlacoche de Cozumel
M. Resident, near sea level, Y (Cozumel I.) Common; scrub woods, edges, thickets.
Pl.32. 10" *Rich rufous above; heavy black streaks below; iris red (ad.); wing-bars.*

Gray Thrasher. *Toxostoma cinereum.* Z23a22.   Cuitlacoche Ceniciento
M. Resident, near sea level, BC. Common; scrubby brushy areas, semi-desert.
Pl.32. 10" *Brownish gray above; heavy black streaks (of triangular spots) on white*
to pale buff below; iris orange-yellow.

Bendire's Thrasher. *Toxostoma bendirei.* Z23a23.   Cuitlacoche Sonorense
US-M. Resident, near sea level, nP (Sonora; winters to Sinaloa); (winter visitor BC?).

Common; in open arid country, semi-desert, scrubby woods, thickets, brushy fields. *Pl.31. 10" Like* Curve-billed T., *but slightly browner above; bill shorter, straighter; finer streaks; paler yellow iris.*

Ocellated Thrasher. *Toxostoma ocellatum.* Z23a24.   Cuitlacoche Pinto
M. Resident, 4500 to 10,500', cH (Guanajuato+Hidalgo to Oaxaca). Very rare; dense scrubby woods, or humid forests of oak, pine and oak, or fir, or borders or openings. *Pl.32. 10" Brownish olive above; faint line over eye; blackish wings, with faint wing-bars; white below, boldly black-spotted on breast and sides; iris yellow.*

Curve-billed Thrasher. *Toxostoma curvirostre.* Z23a25.   Cuitlacoche Común
US-M. Resident up to 11,000', nP, ncH, nA (Nuevo León+Tamaulipas). Common; shrubby gardens, parks, thickets, scrub woods, borders. V: loud *whit-whit.* *Pl.31. 11" Medium gray above; buffy gray below, darker breast, with obscure or prominent spots; tail-corners pale buff or whitish; bill decurved; iris orange-yellow.*

California Thrasher. *Toxostoma redivivum.* Z23a27.   Cuitlacoche Californiano
US-M. Resident, near sea level, nBC (w. side). Common; scrubby woods, chaparral. *Pl. 31. 11" Dark brownish gray above; whitish line over eye; unspotted gray breast; belly and untacs cinnamon-buff; bill long, strongly decurved; iris dark brown.*

Crissal Thrasher. *Toxostoma crissale.* Z23a28.   Cuitlacoche Crisal
US-M. Resident up to 8000', nBC, nP (Sonora), nH (Chihuahua+Coahuila to Zacatecas+Hidalgo). Rare, local; in arid areas with dense scrubby or thorny vegetation. *Pl.31. 11" Like* California T., *but untacs (crissum) rich reddish brown; more prominent sub-malar streak; no pale line over eye; iris pale brown to yellowish.*

Leconte's Thrasher. *Toxostoma lecontei.* Z23a26.   Cuitlacoche del Desierto
US-M. Resident, near sea level, BC, nP (Sonora). Rare+; semi-desert, thickets, scrub. *Pl.31. 11" Like* California T., *but mostly pale gray; tail darker; untacs pale tawny.*

Blue Mockingbird. *Melanotis caerulescens.* Z23a3.   Mulato Común
M. Resident up to 10,000', ncP, ncH, ncA (Tamaulipas to Veracruz). Common, irregular; cloud forest, other humid forest, borders, thickets, scrub woods. *Pl.32. 10" Dark blue with some pale blue streaks; black face; red iris. Im: Blackish.*

Blue-and-white Mockingbird. *Melanotis hypoleucus.* Z23a4. Mulato Pecho Blanco
M,G,ES,H. Resident, 3500 to 9000', sH (Chiapas), sA (Chiapas). Rare+; in scrubby woods, forest borders, scattered thickets and hedgerows, undergrowth in open woods. *Pl.32. 10" Like* Blue M., *but throat, breast, and upper belly white. Im: Blackish.*

WAGTAILS, PIPITS - MOTACILLIDAE - ALONDRAS de AGUA

Water Pipit. *Anthus spinoletta.* Z17a45.   Alondra Acuática
AK-M,G,ES. Winter visitor, BC, nP, ncH, ncA, Y. Common, irregular; short grass or bare open fields, or lake shores or pastures; often in flocks, bobs tail as it walks. *Pl.33. 6" Grayish-olive above, faintly streaked; buffy to whitish below, with narrow streaks (sum.) or heavy streaks (win.); legs dark; outer tail-feathers white.*

Sprague's Pipit. *Anthus spragueii.* Z17a48.   Alondra de la Majada
Can-M. Winter visitor, ncP, ncA. Rare; in grass taller than that preferred by Water P. *Pl.33. 6" Like* Water P., *but prominent "scaly" streaks above; legs yellow to pink.*

SILKY FLYCATCHERS - BOMBYCILLIDAE - CAPULINEROS

Two residents, mostly highlands; one winter visitor, widespread; medium-small; legs, neck, and bill short; tail short to medium; semi-desert to mountain forest; world temperate, few tropical. Distinguish by colors, tail-length, crest. **Plates 33, 34, 40.**

Cedar Waxwing. *Bombycilla cedrorum.* Z33b3.   Chinito
AK-Pan. Transient and winter visitor up to 10,000', all sub-regions. Common, irregular; usually in flocks in gardens, parks, open woodland, forest borders, orchards. *Pl.33. 6" Crested; cinnamon brown head, back, and chest; black throat and mask;*

yellowish belly; gray rump; yellow-tipped gray and black tail. Juv: Dull; streaked.
Gray Silky-Flycatcher. *Ptilogonys cinereus.* Z33c1.   Capulinero Gris
M,G. Resident, 4000 to 11,000', H. Common; in pine-oak or fir forests, or borders, or pure pine or oak woods, often in small flocks eating mistletoe berries, or flycatching. *Pl.34. 8" Crested; short black bill. M: Mostly pale brownish gray; belly white; flanks tawny; untacs yellow; tail blackish with broad white cross-bar below. F: Similar, but more cinnamon-gray above and below.*
Phainopepla. *Phainopepla nitens.* Z33c3.   Capulinero Negro
US-M. Resident or winter visitor up to 8000', BC, nP (Sonora), ncH (Chihuahua+ Coahuila to nw.Oaxaca+Veracruz). Common, north; rare and irregular, south; usually in tree-dotted dry shrubby areas, or semi-desert; perches upright on wires, tree-tops. *Pl.40. 7" Crested; iris red. M: Glossy black except large white patch in extended wing. F: Brownish gray, with darker crest and tail; dull wing-patch; scalloped untacs.*

SHRIKES - LANIIDAE - VERDUGOS

Loggerhead Shrike. *Lanius ludovicianus.* Z31b17.   Verdugo Americano
Can-M. Resident up to 10,000', BC, nP (Sonora to n.Nayarit), ncH; winter visitor cP, sH, A. Rare; tree-dotted pastures, open dry old fields, hedgerows, and borders. *Pl.40. 8" Gray above; whitish below; black mask; black wings with white patch; rounded black tail white-tipped; bill short, stout, hooked at tip, black.*

STARLINGS - STURNIDAE - ESTORNINOS

European Starling. *Sturnus vulgaris.* Z53a82.   Estornino
AK-M. Resident up to 7000', nBC, nP(Sonora), ncH (Chihuahua to D.F.), nA (Tamaulipas),Y; extending its range. Common; parks, gardens, cities, pastures, farms. *Pl.33. 8" Glossy black; short tail; pointed bill. Winter: Many small buff spots; black bill. Summer: Obscurely speckled; bill yellow. Juv: Dark brownish gray.*

VIREOS - VIREONIDAE - VIREOS

Twenty-three species, mostly residents; widespread Mexico; small; medium-short legs, neck, wing, tail; short bill; arboreal, scrubby woods to humid forest; new world temperate, tropical. Distinguish by wing bars, colors, patterns. **Plates 34 and 35.**

Slaty Vireo. *Neochloe brevipennis.* Z56c1.   Vireo Gusanero
M. Resident, 4000 to 6000', cH (Jalisco+Veracruz to Oaxaca). Very rare, local; in rather open pine-oak woods, mixed scrubby woods, low brush and scattered taller trees. *Pl.34. 4 1/2" Mostly dark gray; but crown and wings, and tail (partly), bright olive-green; and chin, belly, and untacs white; iris white.*

White-eyed Vireo. *Vireo griseus.* Z56c4.   Vireo Ojiblanco
Can-Pan,x.ES. Resident up to 4000', ncA (Coahuila to Veracruz); transient or winter visitant cP, sA, Y. Rare+; thickets, hedgerows, borders, brushy stream valleys. *Pl.35. 4 1/2" Grayish green above; pale yellowish wing-bars; yellow eye-ring and lores; whitish below with yellow wash; iris white. V: staccato chík-per-whéeoo-chík.*
Mangrove Vireo. *Vireo pallens.* Z56c5.   Vireo Pálido
M-CR. Resident, near sea level, nsP (Sonora to Nayarit; Chiapas), Y. Common Y; rare, local nsP; mangrove swamps or (Y) inland thickets, scrubby woods, hedgerows. *Pl.34. 4 1/2" Like White-eyed V., but much more yellowish below; and iris brown.*
V: a rolling, rasping *weer, weer, weer,* or *jury, jury, jury;* unlike that of Wh.-eyed V.
Cozumel Vireo. *Vireo bairdi.* Z56c9.   Vireo de Cozumel
M. Resident, near sea level, Y (Cozumel I.). Common; thickets, scrub woods, edge. *Pl.34. 4 1/2" Grayish-brown above; pale yellow wing-bars and feather-edgings on black wings; sides of face cinnamon; white below with cinnamon flanks and sides.*

Bell's Vireo. *Vireo bellii.* Z56c10.   <u>Vireo Aceitunado</u>
US-N. <u>Resident, sea level to 6000', nP (Sonora), nH (Chihuahua+Coahuila to Zacatecas), nA (Tamaulipas+Nuevo León); summer resident nBC; transient or winter visitor sBC, csP, cH, cA.</u> Rare; river-border willows, brushy arroyos, thickets.
Pl.35. 4 1/2" Grayish above; faint wing-bars; whitish below; white eye-ring, lores.

Black-capped Vireo. *Vireo atricapillus.* Z56c3.   <u>Vireo de Gorra Negra</u>
US-M. <u>Resident, around 4000', nH (Coahuila); transient or winter visitor ncP, cH, nA.</u>
Rare; large shrubs or small trees in dry scrubby woods, thickets, hedgerows, borders.
Pl.35. 4" M: Olive-green above; head and face black with white eye-ring and lores; pale yellow wing-bars; white below with yellowish wash on flanks. F: Similar, but paler and duller; has dark gray, not black, head and face (darker than Solitary V.'s).

Dwarf Vireo. *Vireo nelsoni.* Z56c12.   <u>Vireo Enano</u>
M. <u>Resident, 5000 to 8000', cH (Jalisco+Guanajuato to Oaxaca); winter visitor (?) nP.</u>
Very rare; thickets and scrubby hedgerows, brushy hillsides, stream-side cypresses.
Pl.34. 4" Olive-gray above; two narrow white wing-bars; partial white eye-ring; white below with olive wash on sides and flanks; breast may be tinged buffy.

Gray Vireo. *Vireo vicinior.* Z56c11.   <u>Vireo Gris</u>
US-M. <u>Summer resident, 3000 to 5000', nBC, nH (Coahuila); winter visitor sBC, nP, nH.</u> Rare; brushy areas, pinyon-juniper, thickets, chaparral; bobs tail up and down.
Pl.35. 4 1/2" Gray above; one faint wing-bar; narrow white eye-ring, gray lores.

Solitary Vireo. *Vireo solitarius.* Z56c19.   <u>Vireo Solitario</u>
Can-CR. <u>Resident, 1000 to 9500', sBC, H; transient or winter visitor, nBC, P, A.</u>
Rare, breeding; common, winter; low, dry, brushy woods, to pine and pine-oak forest.
Pl.35. 5" Gray above; bluish gray head; prominent white spectacles; white wing-bars on blackish wings; white below, with grayish sides and yellowish flanks.

Yellow-throated Vireo. *Vireo flavifrons.* Z56c20.   <u>Vireo Garganta Amarilla</u>
Can-SAm. <u>Transient nsP, ncA; winter visitor sA, Y.</u> Rare; open woods, river borders.
5 1/2" Yellow-green above, with pale gray rump; two white wing-bars; yellow "spectacles"; yellow throat and breast; white belly and untacs.

Hutton's Vireo. *Vireo huttoni.* Z56c2.   <u>Vireo Pardillo</u>
Can-M,G. <u>Resident, 3000 to 12,000', BC, nP (Sonora), H.</u> Common; in pine, pine-oak, or fir forest, or in scrubby oak woodland, in the middle or upper branches.
Pl.35. 4" Dull greenish gray above; two white wing-bars; <u>white lores</u> and <u>partial eye-ring</u>; pale grayish to whitish below with yellowish wash. Like Ruby-crowned Kinglet, *but has heavier bill;* doesn't flick wings ; repeated one- or two-note song.

Golden Vireo. *Vireo hypochryseus.* Z56c13.   <u>Vireo de Oro</u>
M. <u>Resident, 2000 to 5500', ncP.</u> Common, especially around 4000'; dry shrubby open woods , brushy arroyos, scrubby woods, borders. V: *weer, weer, weer, peek.*
Pl.34. 5" Olive yellow above; superciliary line and underparts bright yellow.

Warbling Vireo. *Vireo gilvus.* Z56c25.   <u>Vireo Gorjeador</u>
AK-N,x.B. <u>Resident, 3000 to 8500', sBC, ncH; transient or winter visitor nBC, P, A.</u>
Rare, summer; common, winter; pine-oak forest, river-edge forest, openings, borders.
Pl.35. 5" Gray or olive-gray above, including crown; whitish below, with sides tinged greenish olive; gray line through eye; white line over eye; no wing-bars.

Brown-capped Vireo. *Vireo leucophrys.* (Z56c25).   <u>Vireo Gorricafé</u>
M,G,H,CR-SAm. <u>Resident, 3500 to 7000', H (mostly Atlantic slopes,Tamaulipas to Chiapas).</u> Rare, local; cloud forest, remnants, small openings, tall trees in lush gardens.
5" Like Warbling Vireo, *but crown much browner; upperparts mostly brownish gray.*

Philadelphia Vireo. *Vireo philadelphicus.* Z56c21.   <u>Vireo Filadelfia</u>
Can-SAm. <u>Transient or rarely winter visitant csH, csA, Y.</u> Rare; open woods, borders.
5" Mostly greenish gray above; white line over eye; blackish line through eye; no wing-bars; *mostly <u>pale yellow</u> below, with whitish belly and untacs; short bill.*

Red-eyed Vireo. *Vireo olivaceus.* Z56c22. Vireo Ojirojo
AK-SAm. Transient up to 5000', sP, A, Y. Common; in dense or open forest,
river-border woods, gardens and parks with numerous trees, forest borders.
*Pl.35. 6" Olive-green above, crown medium-gray, narrowly black-bordered; white
line over eye; dark line through eye; white below; iris red (adult) or brownish (imm.).*

Yellow-green Vireo. *Vireo flavoviridis.* (Z56c22). Vireo Común
US-Pan. Summer resident up to 5000', P, A, Y. Abundant; middle and upper
branches, river borders, humid forest borders, openings, parks, lush gardens, swamps.
6" Like Red-eyed V., but faint crown-border; greenish yellow sides, flanks, untacs.

Yucatan Vireo. *Vireo magister.* Z56c23. Vireo Yucateco
M,B,H. Resident, near sea level, Y (Quintana Roo). Common; middle or upper
branches, scrubby woods or forest borders, mangrove swamps, coastal tall-tree forests.
*Pl.34. 6" Greenish gray above; buffy line over eye; dark line through eye; dull
yellowish below with gray wash on sides and flanks; bill large.*

Tawny-crowned Greenlet. *Hylophilus ochraceiceps.* Z56c38. Vireo Leonado
M-SAm,x.ES. Resident, near sea level, csA (s.Veracruz to Quintana Roo). Rare;
usually 15 to 20' above the ground in dense humid forest, forest borders, and openings.
*Pl.34. 4 1/2 " Olive-brown above, with tawny crown; gray throat and sides of
face; brownish yellow breast and sides; greenish yellow belly and untacs; white iris.*

Lesser Greenlet. *Hylophilus decurtatus.* Z56c39. Vireo Verde
M-SAm. Resident, near sea level, sP (Chiapas), csA (San Luis Potosí+Puebla to
Quintana Roo), Y. Common; moving actively in middle branches in humid forest.
*Pl.34. 4" Olive-green above; crown and sides of face gray; white eye-ring and lores;
white below with yellowish green sides, flanks, and untacs.*

Highland (Chₜs.) Shrike-Vireo.*Vireolanius melitophrys.* Z56b1. Follajero Oliváceo
M,G. Resident, 4000 to 11,000', H (Jalisco+San Luis Potosí to Chiapas). Very rare,
local; high branches, pine, pine-oak, or fir forest. V: loud, low-pitched *whip, whee-ur.*
*Pl.34. 6 1/2" M: Grayish olive above, with gray crown and hind-neck collar; white
below; rufous breast-band; face mostly white, with yellow line over eye, black line
through eye, and black malar streak; iris white. F: Paler, duller.*

Green Shrike-Vireo. *Smaragdolanius pulchellus.* Z56b2. Follajero Verde
M-Pan,x.ES. Resident up to 3000', csA. Rare; forest crown in dense humid forest,
rarely lower at forest border. V: loud, persistent, *wheet-ur, wheet-ur, wheet-ur.*
Pl.34. 6" Green above (blue crown); yellow-green below but yellow throat, untacs.

Rufous-browed Peppershrike. *Cyclarhis gujanensis.* Z56a1. Alegrín
M-SAm. Resident, sea level to 8000', sP, sH, A, Y. Rare+; river-border woods,
forest, borders, tree-dotted fields. V: five or six notes, repeated often, then changed.
*Pl.34. 6 1/2" Olive-green above, with gray crown and side of face; rufous forehead
and line over eye; heavy bill. Races vary below, bright yellow to pale dull yellow.*

WOOD-WARBLERS - PARULIDAE - VERDINES

Sixty-eight species, transients or winter visitors, residents or summer residents;
widespread Mexico; medium legs and tail, short neck, rounded wings; short, slender
bill; mostly arboreal, dry woods and borders, to marshes or humid forest; new world
tropical, temperate. Distinguish by colors, patterns, voice. **Plates 35, 36, 37, 38.**

Blue-winged Warbler. *Vermivora pinus.* Z57a4. Gusanero Aliazul
Can-Pan. Transient or winter visitor sP, A, Y. Rare; dense humid forest, open woods.
*Pl.36. 4 1/2" M: Hind-neck and upperparts brownish gray; head and underparts
mostly bright yellow; black line through eye; white bars on bluish wings F: Duller*

Golden-winged Warbler. *Vermivora chrysoptera.* Z57a3. Gusanero Alidorado
Can-SAm. Transient csA, Y. Very rare; open or scrubby woods, shrubby fields, edge.
*Pl.36. 4 1/2" M: Bluish gray above, with yellow crown; white malar streak and line
over eye; black throat and ear-patch; white below; yellow on wing. F: Duller; paler.*

Golden-winged Warbler x Blue-winged Warbler hybrids. (Z57a3 x Z57a4).
Pl.36. "Brewster's W." Like Blue-winged, *but white mostly replaces yellow.*
Pl.36. "Lawrence's W." Like Golden-winged, *but yellow replaces white.*
Tennessee Warbler. *Vermivora peregrina.* Z57a5.   Verdín Semillero
AK-SAm. Transient or winter visitor BC, P, sH, A, Y. Rare, except sP; middle or
upper branches in humid forest, open woods, tree-dotted pastures, borders, hedgerows.
Pl.36. 4 1/2" M: Grayish green above; white below; head pale gray; white line over
eye. F.+Win.M+Im: More yellowish overall; faint wing-bar.
Orange-crowned Warbler. *Vermivora celata.* Z57a6.   Gusanero Cabezigris
AK-M,G,B. Resident, near sea level, nBC; winter visitor sBC, P, H, A, Y. Abundant,
north; rarer, southeast; open pine, pine-oak, fir forest, thickets, gardens, parks, borders.
Pl.35. 4 1/2" Races vary. Greenish gray to grayish olive above; yellowish gray to
grayish yellow below, with faint streaks; faint line over eye; hidden crown-patch.
Nashville Warbler. *Vermivora ruficapilla.* Z57a7.   Verdín de Mono
Can-M,G,B,ES,H. Transient or winter visitor BC, P, H, A. Common; undergrowth
or low branches in open or dense woods, hedgerows, thickets, gardens, parks, borders.
Pl.36. 4 1/2" Greenish olive above; wings darker; white eye-ring; gray head; bright
yellow below, from throat to untacs. F+Im: Duller.
Virginia's Warbler. *Vermivora virginiae.* Z57a8.   Gusanero de Anteojos Blancos
US-M. Winter visitor ncH. Rare; tree-dotted brushy areas, scrubby woods, arroyos.
Pl.35. 4 1/2" Gray above; crown-patch rufous; white eye-ring; breast, rump, and
untacs bright yellow; throat and belly whitish.   Im: Crown gray; breast, belly buff.
Colima Warbler. *Vermivora crissalis.* Z57a9.   Gusanero Colimense
US-M. Summer resident, 5000 to 8000', nH (Coahuila, Nuevo León, Tamaulipas);
winter visitor cH. Rare; undergrowth of open or scrubby pine, or oak or fir forests.
Pl.35. 5" Like Virginia's W., *but browner; untacs and rump buffier; breast whitish.*
Lucy's Warbler. *Vermivora luciae.* Z57a10.   Gusanero de Lucy
US-M. Resident, near sea level, nP (Sonora); summer resident nBC; transient BC;
winter visitor ncP. Common; arroyos, river valleys, open or dense woods, borders.
Pl.35. 4" Like Colima Warbler, *but entirely white below; has rufous rump-patch.*
Spot-breasted (Cr-ch.) **Warbler.***Vermivora superciliosa.* Z57a12. Gusanero Brillante
M-N,x.B. Resident, 3500 to 12,000', H. Common; in pine, pine-oak, or fir forests.
Pl.38. 4 1/2" Greenish olive back; gray head, with white line over eye; yellow
throat and breast, with yellow breast-patch; belly and untacs white.
Northern Parula. *Parula americana.* Z57a13.   Verdín Silvestre
Can-CR. Transient or winter visitor cH, A, Y. Rare; river-edge, dense or open woods.
Pl.36. 4 1/2" M: Grayish blue above; yellowish olive back-patch; yellow throat and
breast, black and red breast-patch; belly, untacs, partial eye-ring, wing-bars, white.
F: Paler and greener above; only a trace of breast-patch, or none.
Tropical Parula. *Parula pitiayumi.* Z57a14.   Verdín Espalda Verde
US-SAm. Resident up to 4000', P, A. Rare+, local; humid forest, river borders.
Pl.36. 4 1/2" Like Northern Parula, *but throat and upper breast tawnier; no*
eye-ring; *no well-defined breast-patch; and M: ear-patch black.*
Socorro Parula. *Parula graysoni.* (Z57a14).   Verdín de Socorro
M. Resident, near sea level, cP (Socorro I.); wanders sBC. Rare+; scrubby woods.
Pl.38. 4 1/2" Like Tropical Parula, *but less tawny below, and no* black ear-patch.
Yellow Warbler. *Dendroica petechia.* Z57a15.   Verdín Amarillo
AK-SAm. Summer resident, near sea level, and 5000 to 9000', nBC, nP (Sonora),
ncH, Y (Cozumel Island); transient or winter visitor all sub-regions. Common; in
gardens, parks, scrubby woods, river-border woods, scattered trees, thickets, borders.
Pl.36. 4 1/2" M: Greenish yellow above (crown rufous in "Golden" W. - Coz. I.);
yellow below, streaked rufous; tail mostly yellow below. F: Unstreaked, yellowish.

Mangrove Warbler. *Dendroica erithachorides.* Z57a16.   <u>Verdín Manglero</u>
M-SAm. <u>Resident, near sea level, sBC, P, A, Y</u>. Rare+, local; in or near mangroves.
Pl.38. 4 1/2" Like Yellow Warbler, *but entire head rufous in male.*

Chestnut-sided Warbler. *Dendroica pensylvanica.* Z57a17.   <u>Verdín Pardoblanco</u>
Can-SAm. <u>Transient or winter visitor P, A, Y</u>. Common transient, rare in winter; in
dense humid forest, river-border woods, open scrubby woods, borders, hedgerows.
*Pl.37. 4 1/2" Sum.Ad: Back and rump heavily streaked black on yellowish green;
two white wing-bars; white below with broad chestnut streak on side; black line
through eye. Im.+Win.Ad: Bright yellow-green above; white below; wing bars;
no* black on face; *may be faintly streaked above; may show trace of rufous on sides.*

Magnolia Warbler. *Dendroica magnolia.* Z57a37.   <u>Verdín Pechirayado</u>
AK-Pan. <u>Transient or winter visitor P, csH, A, Y</u>. Common; open woods, woodland
edge, river-border woods, lush gardens, orchards, tree-dotted pastures, tall hedgerows.
Pl.36. 4 1/2" Much like Yellow-rumped W., *but yellow, not* white, *background
below; broad mid-tail-bar (most of tail below)* white.

Cape May Warbler. *Dendroica tigrina.* Z57a35.   <u>Verdín Atigrado</u>
Can-Pan,x.G,ES. <u>Transient or winter visitor sH, Y; casual nP, nH</u>. Very rare; usually
restricted to islands; middle or upper branches, dense scrubby woods, borders.
*Pl.36. 4 1/2" Sum.M: Black-streaked olive above, with yellow rump; side of head
yellow, with chestnut ear-patch; yellow below with heavy black streaks. F+Win.M:
Paler and duller; sides of head mostly gray; yellow on side of neck. Im: Still paler
and duller; no yellow except on rump; trace of pale color on side of neck.*

Black-throated Blue Warbler. *Dendroica caerulescens.* Z57a19.   <u>Verdín Azuloso</u>
Can-M,G,B,CR,SAm. <u>Winter visitor sH, Y; casual BC, nP</u>. Very rare; woods-edge.
Pl.36. 5" M: Bluish gray above; black face, throat, sides; below (and spot on wing)
white. *F: Greenish- to brownish-gray; whitish spot on wing and line over eye.*

Yellow-rumped Warbler. *Dendroica coronata.* Z57a38.   <u>Verdín de Toca</u>
   Myrtle group. *D. c. coronata.*   <u>Verdín de Toca</u>
     AK-Pan. <u>Transient or winter visitor, all sub-regions</u>. Common; variety of habitats.
     *5" Sum.M: Streaked bluish gray above; rump, crown, and side-patch
     yellow; face black and white; breast black; throat, belly and untacs white.
     Sum.F: Duller; brownish; streaked below. Im+Win.Ad: Like summer female,
     but no* crown-patch, *faint side-patch.*
   Audubon's group. *D. c. auduboni.*   <u>Verdín de Audubón</u>
     AK-M,G,B,H. <u>Resident, 4000 to 9000', nBC, nsH (Chihuahua, Durango,
     Chiapas); winter visitor sBC, ncP, csH, ncA</u>. Common; wide variety of habitats.
     Pl.35. 5" Like Myrtle group, *but throat usually yellow(ish); no line over eye.*

Black-throated Gray Warbler. *Dendroica nigrescens.* Z57a28. <u>Verdín Gargantinegro</u>
Can-M. <u>Resident, 4000 to 6000', nBC, nP (Sonora); winter visitor sBC, cP, ncH,
ncA</u>. Rare+; open pine or pine-oak woods, borders, scrubby woods, tall hedgerows.
Pl.35. 4 1/2" Like Blackpoll and Black-and-white W., *but faint, not* bold, *streaks
above; blackish ear-patch; and yellow spot in front of eye may be visible.*

Townsend's Warbler. *Dendroica townsendi.* Z57a29.   <u>Verdín Negriamarillo</u>
AK-CR,x.B. <u>Winter visitor BC, nP, H</u>. Common; pine, pine-oak, or fir forest, edges.
Pl.36. 4 1/2" Like Black-throated Green and Hermit W., *but streaked black on
greenish above; much darker ear-patch, and considerable yellow on breast.*

Hermit Warbler. *Dendroica occidentalis.* Z57a30.   <u>Verdín Coronado</u>
Can-N,x.B. <u>Transient or winter visitor BC, nP, H</u>. Rare+; pine or pine-oak woods.
*Pl.36. 4 1/2" Face and crown mostly yellow, with dark markings up back of head;
streaked above; only faint streaks below; no* yellow below. See Townsend's W.

Black-throated Green Warbler. *Dendroica virens.* Z57a32.   <u>Verdín Pecho Negro</u>
Can-Pan. <u>Transient or winter visitor, nBC, P, csH, A, Y</u>. Rare+; forest, edge, parks.

Pl.36. 4 1/2" *Sum.M: Unstreaked olive-green back and crown; white wing-bars; yellow face, with faint ear-patch; throat (broadly) and sides (streaked) black; breast, belly, and untacs white. Sum.F+Im+Win.M: Similar but chin and upper throat yellow or whitish; lower throat streaked or blotched with black or gray.*

Golden-cheeked Warbler. *Dendroica chrysoparia.* Z57a31.   Verdín Ocotero
US-M,G,H,N. Transient e.H, nA. Rare; open pine woods, borders, or mixed woods.
Pl.36. 4 1/2" *M: Plain black back, crown, and throat; white wing-bars; face yellow, black line through eye; white breast and belly; streaked sides. F+ Im: Similar, but olive above; throat mostly white.* See Hermit and Black-throated Green Warbler.

Blackburnian Warbler. *Dendroica fusca.* Z57a36.   Verdín Pasajero
Can-SAm. Transient nsP, cH, A, Y. Rare; river-bank woods, forest, tree-dotted fields.
Pl.37. 5" *M: Black and white streaked above; orange face, throat, and chest, with black ear-patch; white wing-patch, belly, and untacs. F+Im: Similar, but duller; orange tinged face, throat, upper breast; dark ear-patch; whitish streaks above.*

Yellow-throated Warbler. *Dendroica dominica.* Z57a27.   Verdín Cejiblanco
US-Pan. Transient or winter visitor P, sH, A, Y. Rare+; pine woods, palm forests.
Pl.37. 5" *Like Grace's W., but blacker face-patch; white neck-patch and line over eye; plain gray back.*

Grace's Warbler. *Dendroica graciae.* Z57a24.   Verdín Pinero
US-N. Resident, 3500 to 9000', H (and nearby upper slopes of P and A). Rare+; open pine woods, or pine mixed with some oak, or borders; middle or upper branches.
Pl.35. 4 1/2" *Bluish gray above; streaked back; gray cheek and sides of neck; yellow throat, chest and line over eye; white belly, untacs,wing-bars; streaked sides.*

Pine Warbler. *Dendroica pinus.* Z57a23.   Verdín de los Pinos
Can-M. Winter visitor nA (Tamaulipas). Very rare; pine, or very rarely deciduous trees.
Pl.36. 5" *Olive above, unstreaked; two white wing-bars; faint line over eye; yellow throat and breast faintly streaked; white belly, untacs. Im: Whitish throat and breast.*

Prairie Warbler. *Dendroica discolor.* Z57a33.   Verdín de las Praderas
Can-M,B,H. Transient or winter visitor Y. Rare+; scrubby woods, borders, on islands.
Pl.37. 4 1/2" *Rufous streaks on greenish above; black-bordered yellow ear-patch; all-yellow below with heavy black side-streaks. F: Duller. Im: Much duller.*

Palm Warbler. *Dendroica palmarum.* Z57a39.   Verdín Playero
Can-M,B,H,N. Winter visitor, BC, cP, Y. Rare+; on ground or low shrubs, in openings, grassy areas, open shores or stream-banks or clearings ; bobs tail persistently.
Pl.37. 5" *Rump greenish yellow, untacs yellow; faint wing-bars. Races vary from rufous streaks on yellow below, rufous cap, and yellow line over eye, to mostly gray streaks on whitish below, gray cap, and white line over eye.*

Bay-breasted Warbler. *Dendroica castanea.* Z57a42.   Verdín Castaño
Can-SAm. Transient nsA, Y; casual BC, cP. Rare; humid forest, borders, hedgerows.
Pl.37. 5" *White wing-bars; black legs; streaked black, on brownish or greenish above; whitish belly. Sum.M: Black mask; buff neck-patch; chestnut crown and throat. F+Win.M: Similar, but whitish throat; only faint rufous on sides. Im: Faint streaks above, fainter below; untacs whitish or buff.* See immature Blackpoll W.

Blackpoll Warbler. *Dendroica striata.* Z57a41.   Verdín de Cabeza Negra
AK-SAm,x.ES,H,N. Casual transient nH, sP; sight report BC. Very rare; open woods.
Pl.37. 5" *White wing-bars; pale legs. Sum. M: Streaked black on pale olive above; white below with sides streaked black; black crown; white cheeks and throat. F+Win.M: Streaked above and below on whitish or pale yellow. Im: Heavier streaks, whiter untacs than* immature Bay-breasted W. See Blk-thr.Gray and Blk-and-wh.W.

Cerulean Warbler. *Dendroica cerulea.* Z57a18.   Verdín Azulado
Can-SAm,x.ES. Transient cA, Y; accidental BC. Very rare; open woods, borders.
Pl.37. 4 1/2" *White wing-bars. M: Blue crown; black streaks on blusish above and on white below; black lower-throat-band. F+Im: Blue- or olive-gray above; may be*

bluer on crown; pale line over eye; faint streaks on buffy yellowish below.

Black-and-white Warbler. *Mniotilta varia.* Z57a1.   Mezclilla
Can-SAm. Transient or winter visitor all sub-regions. Rare+; woods, hedgerows, edge.
Pl.36. 5" M: Striped black and white; plain white belly; white stripe down center of crown; black throat. F: Fainter streaks below; white throat. See Blackpoll Warbler.

American Redstart. *Setophaga ruticilla.* Z57a44.   Calandrita
AK-SAm. Transient or winter visitor all sub-regions. Rare+; woods, mangroves, edge.
Pl.37. 5" Ad.M: Black, with white belly and untacs; orange side-, wing-, and tail-patches. F: Grayish above; yellow patches. 1st yr.M: Like F. but darker, patches more orange.

Prothonotary Warbler. *Protonotaria citrea.* Z57a50.   Verdín Protonotario
Can-SAm,x.ES. Transient or winter visitor cP, sH, csA, Y; accidental nBC. Very rare;
scrubby woods, forest borders, moist hedgerows, other wet, low-lying wooded areas.
Pl.36. 5 1/2" Bill black. M: Entire head, breast and sides orange; belly and untacs white; wings blue-gray; tail black, blue-gray, and white. F: Like male but duller.

Worm-eating Warbler. *Helmitheros vermivorus.* Z57a49.   Pulgonero
Can-Pan. Transient or winter visitor nsP, A, Y. Rare; dense forest, river-border woods.
Pl.36. 5" Brownish gray above; whitish with buff wash below; head striped black and tawny-buff; legs, and sharp bill, pale yellowish.

Swainson's Warbler. *Limnothlypis swainsonii.* Z57a48.   Verdín de Swainson
US-M,B. Transient or winter visitor A, Y. Very rare; dense scrubby woods, thickets.
Pl.36. 5" Olive-brown above; grayish below; reddish brown crown; line over eye.

Ovenbird. *Seiurus aurocapillus.* Z57a45.   Verdín Suelero
Can-SAm. Transient or winter visitor P, cH, A, Y; accidental BC. Rare; undergrowth
of dense forest, scrubby woods, river-border woods; walks on ground, head bobbing.
Pl.37. 6" Greenish brown above; broad, black-bordered, orange crown-streak; white below with heavy black streaks; legs pink; tail short.

Northern Waterthrush. *Seiurus noveboracensis.* Z57a46.   Verdín Charquero
AK-SAm. Transient or winter visitor sBC, P, cH, A, Y. Rare+; mangrove swamps,
edges of ponds or lakes, streams, pools, nearby thickets; bobs tail and body as it walks.
Pl.37. 6" Underparts, and line over eye, basically yellowish; but may be nearly white in western races; heavily streaked below; throat speckled. See La.Waterthrush.

Louisiana Waterthrush. *Seiurus motacilla.* Z57a47.   Verdín Arroyero
Can-SAm. Transient or winter visitor P, H, A, Y; casual BC. Rare+; mostly walking
along shores or banks of fresh-water lagoons, ponds, streams, swamps; bobs tail.
Pl.37. 6" Like Northern W., but underparts and line over eye basically white; flanks and untacs buffy; throat plain white, without speckles.

Kentucky Warbler. *Oporornis formosus.* Z57a61.   Verderón Cachetinegro
Can-SAm. Transient or winter visitor, nsP, A, Y. Rare; forest undergrowth, thickets.
Pl.37. 5" Yellowish green above; yellow spectacles; long black vertical line below eye; bright yellow below. Im: Duller; line below eye shorter.

Mourning Warbler. *Oporornis philadelphia.* Z57a63.   Verderón Llorón
Can-SAm,x.ES. Transient csP, cH, A; accidental BC. Rare; undergrowth, thickets.
Pl.37. 5 1/2" Ad: Yellowish olive above; yellow below; head and throat gray; and M: lower throat blackish. Im: Throat tinged yellowish; faint eye-ring. See McG.'s W.

Macgillivray's Warbler. *Oporornis tolmiei.* Z57a64.   Verdín de Tolmie
AK-Pan, x.B. Resident, 7000 to 8000', nH (Nuevo León); winter visitor BC, P, H, A.
Very rare resident; rare+,transient; gardens, parks, humid forest, borders, scrub woods.
Pl.35. 5" Like Mourning W., but partial eye-ring prominent above and below eye.

Common Yellowthroat. *Geothlypis trichas.* Z57a51. Tapaojito Común
   Common group. *G. t. trichas.* Tapaojito Común
   AK-Pan. Resident up to 8500', nBC, ncP (Sonora to Colima), ncH, nA (Tamaulipas); winter visitor sBC, sP, sH, csA, Y. Common; marshes, wet areas.
   4 1/2" M: Grayish-bordered black mask; yellow throat, breast, and untacs; brownish sides; white belly; yellowish brown above. F: Like M., but no mask; and top and sides of head yellowish green.
   Chapala group. *G. t. chapalensis.* Tapaojito de Chapala
   M. Resident, around 5500', cH (marshes around Lake Chapala, Jalisco). Rare+.
   Pl.38. 4 1/2" Like Common group, *but M: has very broad yellow area bordering mask; and M+F: underparts almost entirely yellow.*

Belding's Yellowthroat. *Geothlypis beldingi.* Z57a52. Verdín de Antifaz
   M. Resident, near sea level, sBC. Common; coastal or river-valley marshes, wet areas.
   Pl.38. 5" M: Mask has yellow (G. b. beldingi) or broad gray (G. b. goldmani) border; mostly bright yellow below; whitish belly in some. F: Has no mask.

Altamira Yellowthroat. *Geothlypis flavovelata.* Z57a53. Verdín de Altamira
   M. Resident coastal ncA. Rare+; in or near brackish or near-coast fresh-water marshes.
   Pl.38. 5" M: Very broad yellow border behind mask; yellow below. F: No mask.

Black-polled Yellowthroat. *Geothlypis speciosa.* Z57a56. Verdín Pantanero
   M. Resident, around 8000', cH (Michoacán, Guanajuato, D.F., México.). Common, local; large fresh-water marshes or marshy areas near lakes, ponds, slow-moving water.
   Pl.38. 5" Like Common Y., *but M: mask larger, merging into blackish crown; mostly golden yellow below; and F: little or no white on belly.*

Brush (Hooded) Yellowthroat. *Geothlypis nelsoni.* Z57a57. Verdín Enmascarado
   M. Resident, 4000 to 10,000', ncH (Coahuila+Nuevo León to Oaxaca). Rare, local; weedy, brushy, rather dry slopes, brushy undergrowth of open pine or pine-oak woods.
   Pl.38. 5" Like Common Y. *(M: mask has gray border), but M+F: darker and greener above; all-yellow below, tinged grayish or brownish on sides and flanks.*

Meadow Warbler (Gr.-cr.Y.). *Chamaethlypis poliocephala.* Z57a60. Verdín Carbonero
   US(now?)-Pan. Resident up to 5500', P (Sinaloa to Chiapas), A, Y. Rare+, local; tall-grass fields, or other dense tall herbaceous growth, thickets, weedy hedgerows.
   Pl.35. 5 1/2" M: Dull yellowish green above, but forehead and lores black; crown and nape gray; bright yellow below; partial eye-ring; bill thick, yellowish. F: Duller.

Hooded Warbler. *Wilsonia citrina.* Z57a69. Verdín de Capucha
   Can-Pan. Transient or winter visitor A, Y. Rare: humid forest undergrowth, borders.
   Pl.37. 5 1/2" White tail-patches. M: Yellow face; black hood, including throat; yellowish brown above; yellow below. F: No hood; greenish crown, yellow throat.

Wilson's Warbler. *Wilsonia pusilla.* Z57a70. Pelucilla
   AK-Pan. Transient or winter visitor all sub-regions. Common; most wooded situations.
   Pl.37. 4 1/2" Yellowish olive above; no white or bright yellow on tail; most of head and underparts bright yellow. M: Circular black cap. F.+Im: Crown olive.

Canada Warbler. *Wilsonia canadensis.* Z57a71. Verdín Collarejo
   Can-SAm. Transient sP, csH, A, Y. Rare; dense forest undergrowth, thickets, borders.
   Pl.37. 5" M: Dark bluish gray above; yellow spectacles; yellow below, with white untacs; black streaky necklace. F.+Im: Duller; necklace faint or absent.

Red-faced Warbler. *Cardellina rubrifrons.* Z57a72. Coloradito
   US-M,G,ES,H. Summer resident, 5000 to 10,000', nH (Sonora+Chihuahua to Sinaloa+Durango); winter visitor csH. Rare; pine, pine-oak, or fir forest, scrubby oaks.
   Pl.35. 5" White nape, rump, and underparts (except red throat and chest, and forehead and fore-crown); black of hind-crown extends to cheek.

Red Warbler. *Ergaticus ruber.* Z57a73. Orejas de Plata
   M. Resident, 6000 to 12,000', ncH (Chihuahua+Hidalgo to Oaxaca). Rare+; mostly lower to middle branches in fir forest, but also dense humid pine-oak or pine woodland.

Pl.38. 5" Red, but pale gray (blackish, nw.) ear-patch. Im: Dull red; dark ear-patch.

Pink-headed Warbler. *Ergaticus versicolor.* Z57a74.　　　　　Platinado
M,G. Resident, 7000 to 10,000', sH (Chiapas). Rare+; open pine woods, or pine-oak.
Pl.38. 5" Dark red to brownish red, but entire head, throat, and chest silvery pink.

Painted Redstart. *Myioborus pictus.* Z57a75.　　　　　　Pavito Ocotero
US-N,x.B. Resident, 4000 to 9000', H. Rare+; pine or pine-oak woods, borders.
*Pl.35. 5" Black; with white wing-patch, outer tail-feathers, part of belly and untacs;
red lower breast and upper belly; black sides and flanks.*

Slate-throated Redstart. *Myioborus miniatus.* Z57a76.　　　Pavito Selvático
M-SAm. Resident, 1500 to 12,000', nP, H (Chihuahua+San Luis Potosí to Chiapas),
csA (San Luis Potosí to Chiapas). Common; cloud forest, lowland forest, pine-oak.
*Pl.38. 5" Dark blue-gray above; chestnut crown; mostly red below, with blackish
throat and white untacs; tail long, white-cornered, often fanned; no white on wing.*

Fan-tailed Warbler. *Euthlypis lachrymosa.* Z57a86.　　　　Pavito Amarillo
M-N,x.B. Resident up to 6000', P, ncA. Rare; humid forest undergrowth, river-bank
woods, scrubby woods, and rocky hillsides, often on ground; fans and droops tail.
*Pl.38. 6" Bluish gray above; black-bordered yellow crown; white tail-corners;
yellow below with white untacs, dark tawny wash on breast; white spot before eye.*

Golden-crowned Warbler. *Basileuterus culicivorus.* Z57a99. Verdín Coronidorado
M-SAm. Resident up to 5000', nP (Nayarit+Jalisco), A. Common; humid forest.
*Pl.38. 5" Greenish olive above, yellow below; broad, black-bordered, orange
crown-stripe; pale yellow eye-ring. V: a loud, deliberate, weety, weety, wítchu.*

Rufous-capped Warbler. *Basileuterus rufifrons.* Z57a100.　　　　Larvitero
M,G,B. Resident up to 8000', ncP, H, A. Rare+; borders, open woods, scrub.
*Pl.38. 5" Ad: Crown and white-bordered (all around) ear-patch rufous; throat and
breast yellow; belly and untacs white (or yellow, s.cA+sA). Im: Much duller,
browner; buffy wing-bars; head pattern grayish green and whitish; underparts buffy.*

Delattre's Warbler. *Basileuterus delattrii.* Z57a101.　　　Verdín de Delattre
M-SAm,x.B. Resident up to 5000', sP (Chiapas). Rare+; humid forest, borders.
Pl.38. 5" Like Ruf.-cap. W., but all-yellow below; no white line below ear-patch.

Bell's (Golden-browed) Warbler. *Basileuterus belli.* Z57a102.　　Verdín de Bell
M,G,ES,H. Resident, 4000 to 12,000', H (Sinaloa+Tamaulipas to Chiapas). Rare+;
pine-oak or fir forest, cloud forest, or other humid deciduous forest, usually in shrubby
undergrowth or lower tree-branches. V: a rasping zi-zi-zi, like Katydid call; also a song.
*Pl.38. 5" Like Delattre's W., but crown black-bordered; line over eye yellow. Im:
Brown above; two buff wing-bars; mostly grayish green below; yellow belly, untacs.*

Yellow-breasted Chat. *Icteria virens.* Z57a117.　　　　　　　　Arriero
Can-Pan. Resident up to 8000', nP, ncH (Chihuahua+Coahuila to México), ncA
(Tamaulipas to San Luis Potosí); summer resident BC; winter visitor csP, sH, sA, Y.
Rare+; in borders, hedgerows, dense thickets in brushy fields, low shrubby vegetation.
*Pl.37. 7" Yellowish brown above; white spectacles and line below dark lores;
bright yellow throat and breast; white belly and untacs; rather thick black bill.*

Red-breasted Chat. *Granatellus venustus.* Z57a114.　　　Rosillo Occidental
M. Resident up to 4000', P (Sinaloa to Chiapas). Rare; scrubby woods, thickets.
*Pl.38. 5 1/2" M: Blue-gray above;with red breast, center of belly and untacs; white
throat and patch behind eye, on black face and breast-band (no breast-band in Tres
Marías Is. birds); white sides and flanks; black tail with white sides and corners. F:
No red; no breast-band; head and upperparts buff and gray; underparts mostly buff.*

Gray-throated Chat. *Granatellus sallaei.* Z57a115.　　　　　Rosillo Oriental
M. Resident up to 4000', csA, Y. Rare; scrubby woods, thickets, undergrowth.
*Pl.38. 5" M: Head, throat, and upperparts bluish gray, with white patch behind eye;
breast, belly, untacs red, but sides and flanks white. F: No red; duller gray above;*

mostly whitish below, with buffier throat and breast; buff streak behind eye.

Olive Warbler. *Peucedramus taeniatus.* Z57a112. Verdín Oliváceo
US-N,x.B. Resident, 5000 to 12,000', H. Rare+; tree-tops, usually in open pine
woods, also pine-oak or other mountain forests. V: musical *wheeta, wheeta, wheeta.*
Pl.35. 5" Grayish above; mostly white below. M: *Entire head and upper breast
orange-brown except black mask; white wing-bars and tail-patches. F+Im: head and
upper breast yellowish; mask gray; faint wing-bars.*

Bananaquit. *Coereba flaveola.* Z57c1. Platanero
M-SAm,x.ES. Resident up to 3500', csA, Y (Quintana Roo). Rare+ to abundant;
dense humid forest, clearings, borders, scrubby woods, parks, gardens, hedgerows.
*Pl.35. 4 1/2" Mostly black above with yellowish rump-patch; white line over eye;
white wing-spot; whitish below, except yellow breast. Im: Much duller, paler.*

TANAGERS - THRAUPIDAE - TANGARAS, PIRANGAS

Thirty-one species, almost all residents; mostly lowlands; small to medium-small;
medium-short legs and neck; short to medium-short tail; short to medium-short bill,
somewhat heavy; mostly pine or pine-oak forest, or humid forest and borders; shrub
layer to highest branches; new world temperate and tropical. Distinguish by colors,
patterns, leg- and bill-color and size, tail-length, and voice. **Plates 39, 40, 45, 47**

Cabanis's (Azure-rumped) **Tanager.** *Tangara cabanisi.* Z59a72. Gusanero Alinegra
M,G. Resident, 3000 to 6000', sP (Chiapas). Very rare; cloud forest, openings, edges.
*Pl.39. 6" Pale blue back and rump; purplish-blue crown; black wings and tail, with
blue feather-edges; whitish blue below; scalloped black collar above and below.*

Golden-hooded (-mask) **Tanager.** *Tangara larvata.* Z59a108. Gusanero Enmascarado
M-SAm,x.ES. Resident, near sea level, csA (Oaxaca to Quintana Roo). Rare; dense
rain forest, river-border woods, or other humid forest, openings, borders, lush gardens.
*Pl.39. 5 1/2" Mostly black; with blue rump, wrist-patch, and flanks; golden tawny
hood; black and blue mask; pale blue wrist-patch and flanks; white belly.*

Green Honeycreeper. *Chlorophanes spiza.* Z59a22. Mielero Verde
M-SAm,x.ES. Resident, near sea level, sA. Rare; humid forest, borders, lush gardens.
Pl.45. 5 1/2" Bill decurved. M: *Bright bluish green, with black crown and mask;
mostly yellowish bill; red iris.* F: *Medium green above; pale yellowish green below.*

Shining Honeycreeper. *Cyanerpes lucidus.* Z59a19. Pavito Azul
M-SAm,x.ES. Resident, 1000 to 4000', sA (Chiapas). Rare, local; dense humid forest.
Pl.45. 4 1/2" Like Red-legged H., *but* M: *throat black; crown and back violet-blue;
legs bright yellow; and* F: *more heavily streaked below; throat buff; legs dull yellow.*

Red-legged Honeycreeper. *Cyanerpes cyaneus.* Z59a21. Reinita
M-SAm. Resident up to 4000', sP, csA (San Luis Potosí+Puebla to Quintana Roo), Y.
Common; dense humid forest, borders, lush tall hedgerows, gardens, parks.
*Pl.45. 4 1/2" M: Mostly violet-blue, with black back, wings, and tail; crown pale
blue; legs bright red. F+Win.M: Dull yellowish green above; pale greenish yellow
below, faintly streaked; legs dull reddish. (Molting birds are dappled, red-legged.)*

Highland Honeycreeper (Cin.-b. Fl'piercer). *Diglossa baritula.* Z59a1. Pico Chueco
M,G,ES,H. Resident, 6000 to 11,000'. Rare; pine-oak or fir forests, borders, gardens.
Pl.45. 4 1/2" Upper mandible hooked at tip over up-curved lower mandible. M:
Blackish- to bluish-gray above and on throat; mostly rufous below. F: *Olive-gray
above, mostly buffy brown below. Im.M: Like ad.m., but duller.*

Blue-crowned Tanager (Chlorophonia). *Chlorophonia occipitalis.* Z59a38. Cilindro
M-N,x.B. Resident, 3000 to 10,000', csA (Veracruz to Chiapas), sH. Rare; middle or
upper branches of humid forest, openings, borders, often in flocks in or near mistletoe.
*Pl.39. 5 1/2" M: Rich yellowish green, with bright yellow breast, center of belly,
and untacs; crown pale blue; narrow breast-band brown.* F: *Duller; no* breast-band.

Scrub Euphonia. *Euphonia affinis.* Z59a42.   Monjita Gargantinegra
Scrub group. *E. a. affinis.*   Monjita Gargantinegra
M-CR. Resident up to 4500', sP, A, Y. Rare+; scrubby woods, tree-dotted
fields, hedgerows, humid forest, borders, gardens, orchards, often in mistletoe.
*Pl.39. 3 3/4" M: Forehead broadly yellow; breast, belly, and untacs rich
yellow; throat and upperparts blackish blue. F: Grayish green above;
yellowish forehead, rump; blackish wings and tail; dull yellowish green below.*
Godman's group. *E. a. godmani.*   Monjita de Godman
M. Resident up to 4500', ncP (Sonora to Guerrero). Rare; borders, scrub woods.
Like Scrub group, *but M: more lemon yellow, less orange; lower belly and
untacs white, and F: has gray hind-crown and nape.*

Yellow-throated Euphonia.*Euphonia hirundinacea.*Z59a51.Monjita Gargantiamarilla
M-Pan. Resident up to 4500', A, Y. Common; humid forest, borders, gardens.
Pl.39. 4" Like Scrub E., *but M: throat yellow; and F: whitish below; yellow sides.*

Blue-hooded Euphonia. *Euphonia elegantissima.* Z59a53.   Monjita Elegante
M-Pan. Resident, 2000 to 9500', nP, H, A. Rare+; middle or upper branches, cloud
forest, other humid forest, pine-oak or fir forest, lush gardens; often flocks in mistletoe.
*Pl.39. 4 1/2" Crown broadly bright light blue. M: Blackish violet above (+throat
and face); rich orange-brown below. F: Dull yellowish green; throat brownish.*

Olive-backed Euphonia. *Euphonia gouldi.* Z59a58.   Monjita Selvática
M-Pan,x.ES. Resident, near sea level, csA. Rare; dense humid forest, small openings.
*Pl.39. 3 3/4" M: Bronze-green to grayish green; forehead yellow; belly and untacs
tawny; sides speckled yellow. F: Duller; forehead dark rufous; belly yellowish.*

White-vented Euphonia. *Euphonia minuta.* Z59a61.   Monjita Chiquita
M-G,B,N-SAm. Resident up to 2000', sA (Chiapas). Very rare; in dense humid forest.
3 1/2" Like Godman's group of Scrub E. *(white belly, untacs), but M:
orange-yellow, not* lemon-yellow; *and F: crown not* gray; *yellowish
breast forms a broad band between pale gray throat and whitish belly; rump greenish.*

Blue-gray Tanager. *Thraupis episcopus.* Z59a225.   Obispillo
M-SAm. Resident up to 4500', sP, csA; now regular Y, introduced (?). Common,
csA; rare to rare+, sP, Y; often in pairs; tree-dotted fields, borders, gardens, orchards,
parks, river-border woods. V: high-pitched chippering song; a very high-pitched *wees.*
Pl.47. 6 1/2" Pale grayish blue, darker above; bright medium blue wrist-patch.

Yellow-winged Tanager. *Thraupis abbas.* Z59a229.   Buscahigo
M-N. Resident up to 5000', A, sP, Y. Rare+: humid forest, borders, orchards.
*Pl.39. 7" Head grayish violet; to dark-scalloped bluish back; grayish olive
underparts and rump; bluish tinge on breast; wings black, with yellowish olive
coverts, and yellow spot (a stripe when wing is extended).*

Striped-headed Tanager. *Spindalis zena.* Z59a224.   Cuadrillero Pintado
M(+ W.I.) Resident, near sea level, Y (Cozumel I.). Common; scrub woods, borders.
*Pl.39. 6 1/2" M: Yellowish olive above, brownish rump; head, wings, tail, black
and white (yellow throat patch); breast and collar dark tawny, bordered yellow
behind; grayish belly. F: Greenish gray above, paler below; white wing-spot.*

Gray-headed Tanager. *Eucometis penicillata.* Z59a182.   Tangara Cabezigris
M-SAm,x.ES. Resident up to 3000', csA, Y. Rare; mostly dense humid forest.
Pl.39. 6 1/2" Yellowish green above; bright yellow below; but entire head gray.

Black-throated Shrike-Tan.*Lanio aurantius.*Z59a185. Acalandriado Garganta Negra
M,G,B,H. Resident up to 3500', csA. Rare; high branches, dense humid forest.
*Pl.39. 8" Bill heavy, flattened, hooked-tipped. M: Mostly yellow, but tail, wings,
and entire head, black; small white patch near wrist. F: Rich olive brown above;
rump tawnier; head more grayish olive; belly yellow; untacs tawny.*

Red-crowned (Ant-) **Tanager.** *Habia rubica.* Z59a201.   Tangara Hormiguera
M-SAm. Resident up to 4000', P (Nayarit to Chiapas), A, Y. Rare+; in thickets, dense

undergrowth of humid forest, river-border woods; often follows ant swarms. *Pl.39. 7" Bill dark above, pale brownish below. M: Plumage brownish red, paler below, with somewhat paler red throat; red crown-patch black-bordered. F: Dull brownish olive, paler below; throat slightly more yellowish; crown patch tawny.*

Jungle (Red-thr. Ant-) **Tanager.** *Habia fuscicauda.* Z59a202.   Tangara Selvática
M-SAm. Resident up to 4000', sP, A, Y. Rare+; humid forest, thickets, borders. *Pl.39. 7" Like Red-crowned T., but bill blackish; throat-patch much more contrasty, buffy (F.), pinkish red (M.); crown-patch less obvious (M.), absent (F.).*

Rose-throated Tanager. *Piranga roseogularis.* Z59a209.   Aguacatero
M,G,B. Resident, near sea level, Y. Rare; scrubby woods, humid forest, borders. *Pl.39. 6" M: Gray, paler below; with red crown, wings, tail; and pinkish untacs, and throat to center-chest. F+Im: Grayish, with pale buff-yellow throat and untacs.*

Hepatic Tanager. *Piranga flava.* Z59a207.   Piranga Encinera
US-SAm. Resident, 4000 to 9000', H. Common; open pine or pine-oak woods, edge. *Pl.40. 7 1/2" Bill blackish gray; no crest. M: Dull red, with grayish cheek-patch. F.+Im: Grayish to yellowish green above, yellow below; grayish cheek-patch.*

Summer Tanager. *Piranga rubra.* Z59a208.   Piranga Avispera
US-SAm. Summer resident up to 6000', nBC, nP (Sonora), nH (Chihuahua+ Coahuila to Durango; transient or winter visitor all sub-regions. Rare+; open woods, river-border woods, tree-dotted fields, borders, gardens, and orchards; in upper branches. *Pl.40. 7" Like Hepatic T., but bill brownish yellow, no gray cheek-patch; and M: brighter red; and F.+Im: brighter yellow below, paler yellowish green above.*

Scarlet Tanager. *Piranga olivacea.* Z59a210.   Piranga Olivácea
US-SAm. Transient cA (Veracruz), cP (Jalisco), Y. Very rare; dense forest, borders. *7" Bill brownish yellow. M: Wings, tail, black; otherwise scarlet (Sum.), or greenish above, yellowish below (Win.). F+Im: Like winter male, but wings and tail duller (but still darker than those of female and immature Summer T.).*

Western Tanager. *Piranga ludoviciana.* Z59a211.   Piranga Cabeziroja
AK-SAm. Summer resident (?), around 4000', nBC; transient or winter visitor BC, P, H, ncA. Rare+; pine, pine-oak, or fir forest, river-border woods, gardens, orchards. *Pl.40. 7" Sum.M: Yellow; with red head; black back, tail, and wings; one broad yellow wing-bar, one narrower, whitish. Win.M: Like sum.m., but the yellow is duller and greener; head yellowish, with faint red wash around base of bill. F.+Im: Like win.m., but grayish green above, white wing-bars.*

Striped (Flame-colored) **Tanager.** *Piranga bidentata.* Z59a206.   Tangara Rayada
M-Pan,x.B. Resident, 3000 to 6000', P, A. Rare+; cloud forest, partial clearings, edge. *Pl.39. 7" M: Red or orange-red; back heavily streaked black; two white bars on black wings; white corners on black tail. F: Like m. but basically yellowish, not red.*

White-winged Tanager. *Piranga leucoptera.* Z59a212.   Mixto Colorado
M-SAm. Resident, 2500 to 5000', A, sP. Rare+; cloud forest, other humid forest, borders, tree-dotted clearings, shady *cafetales.* Call-notes: a quiet, buzzy *wheet-wheet. Pl.39. 5 1/2" M: Scarlet, with black mask, tail, wings, and bill; and two white wing-bars. F: Yellowish, not red; dark wings and tail; white wing-bars.*

Red-headed Tanager. *Piranga erythrocephala.* Z59a213.   Aguacatero Real
M. Resident, 3000 to 8500', ncP, ncH (Sonora+Chihuahua to Oaxaca). Rare; in open grassy pine-oak woods, pure oak woods or mixed scrubby woodland, or river borders. *Pl.39. 6" M: Dull yellowish green above, yellow below, with red crown, face, and throat. F: Duller yellowish, with gray cheeks, and no red.*

Crimson-collared Tanager. *Ramphocelus sanguinolentus.* Z59a216. Tongonito Real
M-Pan,x.ES. Resident up to 4000', csA. Rare; humid forest openings, borders. *Pl.39. 7 1/2" M+F: Black; with red rump, untacs, hind-crown, nape, broad collar.*

Song (Sc.-rump.) **Tanager.** *Ramphocelus passerinii.* Z59a222.   Rabadilla Escarlata
M-Pan,x.ES. Resident, near sea level, sA. Rare+; humid borders, tree-dotted clearings.
Pl.39. 7" *M: Velvety black, with scarlet rump-patch. F: Mostly dull orange-green,
browner and brighter below and on rump; wings and tail blackish; head grayer.*
Rosy Thrush-Tanager. *Rhodinocichla rosea.* Z59a175.   Tangara Canora
M,CR-SAm. Resident up to 3000', ncP (Sinaloa to Guerrero). Rare+; on or near
ground, scrub woods, borders, thickets. V: loud *chor-ee-cho,* or *chu-wee-oo-bar.*
Pl.39. 8" *M: Slate-gray above, with darker wings, crown and cheeks; underparts,
and line over eye, rosy-red; flanks gray. F: Brownish gray above; tawny below.*
Common Bush-Tanager. *Chlorospingus ophthalmicus.* Z59a134.   Chinchinero
M-SAm. Resident, 2500 to 11,500', csP, cH (México to Oaxaca), csA (San Luis
Potosí to Chiapas). Common; undergrowth in humid forest, lush hedgerows, gardens.
Pl.39. 5 1/2" *Mostly yellowish olive, brighter below; throat (broadly), belly, and
large eye-patch white; crown and ear-patch blackish brown.*

ORIOLES, BLACKBIRDS - ICTERIDAE - CALANDRIAS, TORDOS

Thirty-one residents; widespread Mexico; small to medium large; legs, neck, wings,
and tail medium-short to medium-long; bill medium-small to medium-large; ground to
tree-tops; grassland, semi-desert, to humid forest; new world, temperate, tropical.
Distinguish dark species by bill- and tail-shape and size, eye-color, wing-patch, voice;
orioles by pattern, back color, wing-bars, spots or streaks. **Plates 44, 45, and 47.**
Red-winged Blackbird. *Agelaius phoeniceus.* Z62a56.   Tordo Charretero
AK-CR. Resident up to 9000', nBC, nP, H (Chihuahua+Hidalgo to Chiapas), A, Y;
transient or winter visitor sBC, csP. Common; marshy areas, moist grassy fields,
summer; open fields, pastures, crop-land, marshes, winter, often in single-sex flocks.
Pl.44. 8" *M: Black; red wrist-patch, yellowish- or whitish-bordered. F: Dark gray
or blackish; heavily streaked below; may show trace of red on wrist-patch and
pinkish on throat. Im.M: Blackish, "scaled" or mottled; dull red wrist-patch.*
Tricolored Blackbird. *Agelaius tricolor.* Z62a57.   Tordo Capitán
US-M. Resident, near sea level, nBC. Abundant, local; breeds in colonies in marshy
areas; in winter often with Red-winged B. in pastures, other grassy or cultivated fields.
Pl.44. 8 1/2, 7 1/2" *Like* Red-winged B., *but (male) wrist-patch broadly bordered
white; (female) trace of red on wrist-patch (much less than on im. m. Red-w. B.).*
Eastern Meadowlark. *Sturnella magna.* Z62a68.   Triguero Común
Can-SAm. Resident up to 11,000', nP, H, A, Y (Yucatán). Rare+; grassy areas.
Pl.44. 9" *Streaked above; streaked head; black breast-patch, side streaks; mostly
yellow below; white outer tail-feathers; some races paler.* See Western M.
Western Meadowlark. *Sturnella neglecta.* Z62a69.   Triguero de Occidente
Can-M. Resident up to 8000', nBC, nP (Sonora), nH (Chihuahua+Nuevo León to
Zacatecas; winter visitor sBC, cH, nA. Rare+; open grassy areas. V: abrupt, mellow,
chortling, descending series (Eastern Meadowlark sings a slurred *chee-wee, chee-wee.*).
9" *Like* Eastern M., *but usually more yellow on malar area; slightly less white on tail.*

Yellow-headed Blackbird. *Xantho. xanthocephalus.* Z62a53. Tordo Cabeziamarilla
Can-M,CR,P. Resident, near sea level, nBC, nA; transient or winter visitor, sBC, ncP,
H. Common, irregular; usually cat-tail or bulrush marshes, fields, pastures, crop-lands.
Pl.44. 9, 8" *Ad.M: Black; yellow head and breast; white wing-patch. F.+Im: Dark
brown above; head brown and yellowish; breast dull yellow; belly white-streaked.*
Singing (Melodious) **Blackbird.** *Dives dives.* Z62a82.   Tordo Cantor
M-N. Resident, up to 4500', A, Y. Common; humid borders, open woodlots, lush
hedgerows, orchards, tree-dotted pastures; usually in pairs in small flocks. V: a loud,
whistled note, then one or two lower-pitched; often sung antiphonally and in rounds.
Pl.45. 11" *Black; male has green gloss; iris dark brown; tail medium, square.*

Brewer's Blackbird. *Euphagus cyanocephalus.* Z62a92. Tordo de Ojos Amarillos
Can-M,G. Resident up to 4000', nBC; winter visitor BC, ncP, ncH, nA. Common;
farmyards, corrals, crop-lands, pastures, parks, gardens, vacant lots, usually in flocks.
Pl.44. 9" M: Iridescent black; iris yellow; tail medium. F: Gray-brown; iris brown.

Great-tailed Grackle. *Quiscalus mexicanus.* Z62a84. Clarinero
US-SAm. Resident, up to 9000', nBC, P, H, A, Y. Abundant; seldom in dense forest.
*Pl.44. 17, 13" Yellow iris. M: Iridescent black; tail long, keel-shaped. F: Blackish
brown; paler on face, throat and breast; tail rather long, somewhat keel-shaped.*

Bronzed Cowbird. *Molothrus aeneus.* Z62a96. Tordo Ojirojo
US-Pan. Resident up to 9000', P, H, A, Y; casual nBC. Common; farms, tree-dotted
pastures, open woods, edges. Courting male hovers 3 or 4 feet above female on ground.
Pl.44. 8, 7" Glossy black; iris red; ruff may show on hind-neck. F: Not as glossy.

Brown-headed Cowbird. *Molothrus ater.* Z62a97. Tordo Negro
AK-M. Resident up to 8000', nBC, nP (Sonora to Sinaloa), ncH (Chihuahua+Coahuila
to Morelos+Puebla), ncA; winter visitor sBC, sA. Common; scrubby woods, borders.
*Pl.44. 7 1/2, 6 1/2" M: Glossy black; with dark brown head and upper breast; tail
short; bill black, short. F: Dull brownish gray, somewhat paler below.*

Giant Cowbird. *Scaphidura oryzivora.* Z62a98. Tordo Gigante
M-SAm,x.ES. Resident near sea level, csA (Puebla+Veracruz to Quintana Roo). Rare;
clearings or openings or emergent trees in humid forest, borders, tree-dotted pastures,
often on high, exposed branches, usually in loose flocks in or near oropendola colonies.
*Pl.45. 14, 12" M: Glossy black; prominent ruff; iris red. F: Similar but duller
black; ruff small or absent; iris red. Im: Iris whitish.*

Black-cowled Oriole. *Icterus dominicensis.* Z62a43. Calandria de Sureste
M-Pan. Resident near sea level, csA, Y. Rare; humid forest openings, clearings, edge.
*Pl.45. 7 1/2" Ad: Black; but bright yellow belly, untacs, rump, uptacs, wrist-patch.
Im: Like ad., or yellowish; but black face, throat, tail, and wing (except wrist-patch).*

Wagler's (Black-vented) **Oriole.** *Icterus wagleri.* Z62a42. Calandria Palmera
M-N,x.B. Resident up to 7000', nP (Sonora to Sinaloa), H; transient or winter visitor
sP. Rare+, local; scrubby woods, hedgerows, around palms in gardens, parks, fields.
*Pl.45. 8" Like Black-cowled O., but Ad: has a more orange tinge; rump-patch
smaller; uptacs, untacs black; and Im: more brownish; may have yellow face, throat.*

Bar-winged Oriole. *Icterus maculialatus.* Z62a48. Calandria Guatemalteca
M,G,ES. Resident 3000 to 4000', sP (Chiapas). Rare, local; scrub woods, forest edge.
*Pl.45. 8" One white wing-bar. M: Black; with yellow belly, untacs, rump, and
wrist-patch. F: Mostly yellowish green, yellower below; face and throat black.*

Orchard Oriole. *Icterus spurius.* Z62a40. Calandria Café
Can-SAm. Summer resident, 2500 to 8000', nP (Sonora), ncH (Chihuahua to Michoa-
cán+México); transient or winter visitor P, H, A, Y; accidental BC. Rare, summer;
common transient; tree-dotted fields, borders, hedgerows; also marshes, weedy fields.
*Pl.44. 6 1/2" Ad.M: Dark reddish brown below; also rump and wrist-patch; black
wings (one white bar), tail, back, and entire head. F: Grayish green above,
yellowish below; belly yellower than in "Bullock's" O., paler (and bill straighter)
than in Hooded O.; two white wing-bars. Im.M: Like f., but throat-to-eye black.*

Ochre Oriole. *Icterus fuertesi.* Z62a41. Calandria de Fuertes
M. Resident, near sea level, ncA (s.Tamaulipas and n.Veracruz). Rare, local; grassy,
brushy fields, hedgerows, tree-dotted wet meadows and marshes, open woods edge.
*Pl.45. 6 1/2" Like Orchard O., but Ad.M: pale orange-brown replaces dark reddish
brown; and F+Im: buffier yellow below.*

Hooded Oriole. *Icterus cucullatus.* Z62a36. Calandria Zapotera
US-M,B. Resident, up to 5000', sBC, nP (Sonora), A, Y; summer resident nBC;
winter visitor cP, nH. Common; semi-desert, farmyards, gardens, orchards, borders.

***Pl.44.** 7 1/2" Bill decurved. Ad.M: Bright orange, except black back, tail, wings (two white bars), and breast-to-eye. F+Im: Like* Orchard O., *but more orange tinge.*

Yellow-backed Oriole. *Icterus chrysater.* Z62a26.   Calandria Real
M-SAm,x.CR. Resident, up to 9000', sH (Chiapas), csA, Y. Rare+; humid forest borders, openings, partial clearings, or open mountain pine or pine-oak forest, or edge.
***Pl.45.** 8 1/2" No white on wing. Ad: Bright lemon-yellow rump, crown, and back. Im: Like adult but duller; breast-to-eye patch may be complete, partial, or absent.*

Yellow-tailed Oriole. *Icterus mesomelas.* Z62a30.   Calandria Acahualera
M-SAm,x.ES. Resident near sea level, csA, Y. Rare+; humid forest openings, borders.
***Pl.45.** 8" Ad: Mexico's only black-backed, orange-crowned oriole with no white in wing; tail mostly bright yellow below. Im: Mostly dull greenish above, yellow below; may have blackish lower-throat patch; tail mostly greenish yellow.*

Streaked-backed Oriole. *Icterus pustulatus.* Z62a35.   Calandria de Fuego
M-CR,x.B. Resident up to 5000', P. Common; scrubby woods, borders, tree-dotted brushy grassland, gardens, orchards, river-bank woods; may hang nest on utility wires.
***Pl.45.** 8" Ad.M: Orange; with black tail and breast-to-eye patch, black-and-white wings, and heavily streaked back (sP birds have wider streaks, may seem as black on back as* Hooded or Altamira O., *but tail-corners are pale gray, and wrist-patches, are orange-and-white, not plain orange, or black-and-white). Ad.F: Like m., but duller; back greener, has faint streaks. Im: Like ad.f. but some lack* throat-patch.

Orange Oriole. *Icterus auratus.* Z62a29.   Calandria Anaranjada
M. Resident near sea level, Y. Rare; scrubby woods, borders, tree-dotted clearings.
***Pl.45.** 7 1/2" M: Bright orange; black wings (one bar), tail, and breast-to-eye patch. F: Similar but duller, especially greener back; which may have faint streaks; brighter below than* similar immature orioles of other species (Hooded, Altamira, etc.).

Spotted (Spot-breasted) **Oriole.** *Icterus pectoralis.* Z62a33.   Calandria Pecho Pinto
US-CR,x.B. Resident, up to 3000', csP (Colima to Chiapas). Rare+; scrubby woods, borders, tree-dotted brushy fields, lush hedgerows, orchards, gardens, river borders.
***Pl.47.** 10" Ad: Orange, with black back, wings, tail, breast-to-eye patch, and breast-spots. Im: Similar, duller; may have breast-spots; back may be grayish green.*

Altamira Oriole. *Icterus gularis.* Z62a34.   Calandria Campera
US-N. Resident up to 4000', csP (Guerrero to Chiapas), A, Y. Common; tree-dotted clearings, open woods, hedgerows, borders, roadsides; may hang nests on utility wires.
***Pl.44.** 10" Ad.M: Orange, with black back, tail, and breast-to-eye patch, and black wings with white bar and orange wrist-patch.* (Hooded O. is smaller, has black-and-white wrist-patch, and slender, curved bill.) *F: Similar but duller. Im: Greenish back, rather dull yellow below; some may have black throat.*

Audubon's Oriole. *Icterus graduacauda.* Z62a47.   Calandria Hierbera
US-M. Resident up to 8000', nP (Nayarit), cH (Jalisco+San Luis Potosí to Oaxaca), ncA. Rare, local; tree-dotted pastures, gardens, parks, orchards, borders, open woods.
***Pl.44.** 9" Yellowish green above; lemon-yellow below; except entire head and upper breast, wings and tail, black; white wing-bar, yellow wrist-patch.* See Scott's Oriole.

Northern Oriole. *Icterus galbula.* Z62a38.   Calandria Norteña
Baltimore group. *I. g. galbula.*   Calandria Norteña
Can-SAm. Transient or winter visitor P, cH, A. Rare+; borders, gardens, parks.
***Pl.44.** 7 1/2" Ad.M: Bright orange, including much of tail, and wrist-patch; except entire head and upper breast, back, wings (one white bar), and center of tail, black. F.+Im: Grayish green above, with faint or dark mottling on crown and back; dull yellowish orange below; two whitish wing-bars.*

Bullock's group. *I. g. bullockii.*   Calandria Cañera
Can-M,G,CR. Resident up to 8000', nP (Sinaloa+Nayarit), nH (Chihuahua+ Coahuila to Durango); summer resident nBC, nP (Sonora); transient or winter visitor cP, csH, A. Rare+; river-border woods, open woods, borders, orchards.
***Pl.44.** 8" Ad.M: Like "Baltimore" O., but face broadly orange; large white*

wing-patch. F.+Im: Dull yellowish gray above; two wing-bars; belly and untacs whitish, not yellowish or pale dull orange of Orchard O. and Hooded O.

Abeille's Oriole. *Icterus abeillei.* Z62a39.   Calandria de Agua
M. Resident, 5000 to 9000', ncH (Durango+Nuevo León to Oaxaca). Rare; tree-dotted fields, small open woodlots, tall hedgerows or borders especially near water.
   Pl.45. 8" (Often "lumped" with Northern Oriole) *M: Entire upperparts, cheeks, throat, sides, flanks, center and tip of tail, and much of wing, black; large white wing-patch; tail-sides, untacs, belly, breast, and side of neck to bill, orange-yellow. F: Like "Bullock's" O., but more contrasty black and white wings and wing-bars.*

Scott's Oriole. *Icterus parisorum.* Z62a49.   Calandria Tunera
US-M. Resident up to 9000', BC, ncH; winter visitor ncP. Rare+; grassland with scattered large trees or hedgerows, semi-desert scrub, prickly-pear cactus, borders.
   Pl.44. 8" Ad.M: Lemon-yellow, but entire head, upper breast, back, much of tail, and wing (white bar, yellow wrist-patch) black. Im.M: Duller; head and upper breast scalloped with black; back streaked; two whitish wing-bars. F: Dull yellowish green; crown and back streaked; two whitish wing-bars; adult may have scalloped throat.

Yellow-billed Cacique. *Amblycercus holosericeus.* Z62a23.   Pico Blanco
M-SAm. Resident up to 5000', A, Y. Rare+, very secretive; undergrowth of dense humid forest, thickets along edge, dense hedgerows near forest, or river borders. V: a loud, mellow *whee-haw,* or *wa-wee-a* , somewhat like Bobwhite's, or a high-pitched *eek,* then a rasping trill, *br-r-r-r-r,* (which may be from a different individual).
   Pl.45. 9" Black; bill pale yellow (appears white); iris white. Im: Iris pale brown.

Mexican (Yellow-winged) **Cacique.** *Cacicus melanicterus.* Z62a22.   Zanate de Oro
M,G. Resident up to 3000', P. Common; open woods, river banks, orchards, borders.
   Pl.45. 12, 10" M: Black (including floppy, ragged crest); except yellow rump, wing-patch, outer tail-feathers, and untacs; bill pale yellow, pointed. F: Duller.

Wagler's (Chestn.-h.) **Oropendola.** *Psarocolius wagleri.* Z62a7.   Zacua Montañera
M-SAm,x.ES. Resident up to 3000', sA. Rare, local; tree-dotted pastures, clearings, openings in or near humid forest, tall trees above the forest canopy; nests in colonies.
   Pl.45. 14, 11" Black and dark reddish brown, tail yellow below; bill pale greenish, pointed, swollen base forms shield on top of head. See Montezuma Oropendola.

Montezuma Oropendola. *Psarocolius montezuma.* Z62a8.   Zacua Gigante
M-Pan,x.ES. Resident near sea level, A. Rare+, local; large trees in clearings, openings, or along borders, tall trees above forest canopy. V: many odd snapping, squeaking, popping, or gurgling sounds, and a distinctive rasping, resonant *chock* note.
   Pl.45. 20, 17" Much larger than Wagler's Oropendola, *and colors mostly reversed, head black, not reddish brown; breast, belly and wings reddish brown, not black; tail yellow below; blue skin and pink wattles around bill-base; bill black, orange-tipped.*

EMBERIZIDAE

   One hundred and one species in three sub-families; widespread Mexico; very small to medium-small; legs medium, neck short, wings rounded, tail medium; bill short, medium-stout to very stout; ground to tree-tops; grassland, desert, to marsh, humid forest; world-wide except Australasian. Distinguish by voice, colors, patterns, size and shape of bill and tail. **Plates 40, 41, 42, 43, 46, 47.**

GROSBEAKS, BUNTINGS - (CARDINALINAE) - CARDENALES

Gray Saltator. *Saltator coerulescens.* Z65b22.   Chucho Páez
M-CR,SAm. Resident up to 4000', P (Sinaloa to Chiapas), A, Y. Common; tree-dotted fields, hedgerows, gardens, orchards, borders. V: a loud *chew-chew-wheet.*
   Pl.41. 9" Gray above; pale line over eye; buff below; throat white, black-bordered.

Buff-throated Saltator. *Saltator maximus.* Z65b19.   Piquigordo Brincón
M-SAm,x.ES. Resident up to 4000', csA. Rare+; humid areas, forest edge, hedgerows.
Pl.41. 9" Like buff-throated race of Black-headed S., *but smaller; nape medium
gray, not mostly black; and V: gentler, more musical, mellow, warbling sounds.*

Black-headed Saltator. *Saltator atriceps.* Z65b18.   Chorcha
M-Pan. Resident up to 4500', csP (Guerrero to Chiapas), A, Y. Common; thickets at
forest borders, open woods, tree-dotted fields and hedgerows; very noisy, small flocks
or family groups. V: a shrill descending chatter *chut-chut-chut-chut-chut;* a shrill *chreet.*
*Pl.41. 10" Rich yellow-green above, crown and nape broadly black; sides of head
black or blackish gray; throat* white *with broad black border (a race in a small area of
c. Veracruz has a* buff *throat); breast and belly gray; untacs rufous* . See Buff-thr. S.

Black-faced Grosbeak. *Caryothraustes poliogaster.* Z65b11.   Pepitero Dorado
M-Pan,x.ES. Resident up to 3500', csA. Rare+; upper branches, dense humid forest;
very active, often in flocks. V: call is an unmusical note, then a loud doubled whistle.
*Pl.41. 7" Yellow-green wings, tail, back; pale gray rump; very pale gray or whitish
belly and untacs; broadly bright greenish-yellow all around black face and throat.*

Crimson-collared Grosbeak.*Rhodothraupis celaeno.* Z65b14.   Cardenal del Bosque
M. Resident up to 3500', ncA (Tamaulipas to Veracruz+Puebla). Rare; river-border
woods, humid forest and forest borders, tree-dotted overgrown fields, lush hedgerows.
*Pl.41. 8" M: Black; broad red collar, and most of underparts; black marks on red,
some red tinge on black. F: Dull yellow-olive, brighter below; black face and throat.*

Northern Cardinal. *Cardinalis cardinalis.* Z65b8.   Cardenal Común
Can-M,G,B. Resident up to 5000', BC, ncP (Sonora to Nayarit; Colima to Oaxaca), A,
Y. Common to very rare; scrubby woods, borders, brushy fields, hedgerows, thickets.
*Pl.40. 8" Crested (quite long in some races); heavy red bill in adult. M: Bright red;
black around base of bill. F: Grayish-brown and buffy-brown, with red tinge on
wings, tail, crest; dark gray around base of bill. Im: Dull dark brown, including bill.*

Pyrrhuloxia. *Cardinalis sinuata.* Z65b10.   Cardenal Torito
US-M. Resident up to 7000', BC, nP (Sonora to Nayarit), ncH (Chihuahua+Coahuila
to Michoacán+Querétaro), nA. Rare+, irregular; arid brushy areas, semi-desert, thickets.
*Pl.40. 8" Crested; bill heavy, pale dull yellow, with curved culmen. M: Grayish,
with face-throat-breast patch, tail, part of wings, tip of crest, red. F: Duller; yellower;
no red on throat or breast. Bill differs from* N.Cardinal's, *and no dark feathers at base.*

Yellow Grosbeak. *Pheucticus chrysopeplus.* Z65b2.   Guillo
M,G. Resident up to 7000', P, sH. Rare+; dense scrub woods, borders, hedgerows.
*Pl.41. 9" M: Bright orange or yellow, with black-and-white wings and tail, and
very heavy black bill* (any bright Mexican oriole has a much smaller bill, and some
black on head or throat). *F: Duller; heavily streaked above; two white wing-bars.*

Rose-breasted Grosbeak. *Pheucticus ludovicianus.* Z65b6.   Ahorcado
Can-SAm. Transient or winter visitor BC, P, csH, A, Y. Common; river-border
woods, borders, parks, gardens, orchards, open woodlots, scrub woods, hedgerows.
*Pl.43. 7 1/2" M(ad.): Red under-wing; black head and back; black-and-white wings
and tail; red breast-patch; mostly white below and on rump. M (im.+win.): Like ad.
m., but dark areas browner, pale areas duller, streaked or mottled. F: Yellow
under-wing; heavily streaked above (and on head) and below; white wing-bars.*

Black-headed Grosbeak. *Pheucticus melanocephalus.* Z65b7.   Tigrillo
Can-M. Resident, 5000 to 12,000', ncH; summer resident nBC; winter visitor sBC,
ncP. Common; in pine, pine-oak, or fir forest, or forest borders, tree-dotted gardens.
*Pl.40. 7 1/2" Yellow under-wing. Ad.M: Black head; orange brown breast and
partial collar, shading to yellowish buff to whitish untacs; heavily streaked back;
wings and tail black and white. F.+im.M: Like* female Rose-breasted G., *but rich
brownish buff (not* whitish) *below, with fewer, finer streaks.*

Blue-black Grosbeak. *Cyanocompsa cyanoides.* Z65b31. <u>Prusianito</u>
M-SAm,x.ES. <u>Resident up to 2500', csA</u>. Rare, secretive; undergrowth of dense humid forest, borders, weedy forest-openings, thickets. V: rasping, clinking call-notes. *Pl.41. 6 1/2" Very heavy dark bill. M: Appears black; blackish blue with slightly paler forehead, sides of crown, and wrist-patch. F: Dark, rich, chocolate brown.*

Blue Bunting. *Cyanocompsa parellina.* Z65b33. <u>Azulejito</u>
M-N. <u>Resident up to 5000', P (Sinaloa to Chiapas), A, Y</u>. Rare+; scrubby woods, undergrowth of open river-edge woods, weedy borders and thickets, overgrown fields. *Pl.41. 5 1/2" M: Dark blue, except powder-blue forehead, malar streak, rump, and wrist-patch. F: Brown; paler and buffier below.*

Blue Grosbeak. *Guiraca caerulea.* Z65b34. <u>Piquigordo Azul</u>
US-M. <u>Resident up to 10,000', P, H (Durango+Coahuila to Chiapas), ncA; summer resident nBC, additional nH; winter visitor sBC</u>. Common H; scattered thickets in open, dry and rocky, grassy fields, scrubby woods borders, weedy, grassy hedgerows. *Pl.40. 6" Heavy bill. Ad.M: Dark violet-blue; with black-streaked back, blackish wings (rufous wing-bars) and tail; black patch around bill-base. F: Brownish; streaked above; buffy below, faint streaks; buff wing-bars; rump may be tinged blue.*

Rosita (Rose-bellied) **Bunting.** *Passerina rositae.* Z65b39. <u>Gorrión Rosado</u>
M. <u>Resident up to 2000', sP</u>. Rare, local; dense scrub woods, thickets, on dry slopes. *Pl.41. 5 1/2" M: Medium blue, darker and richer on head; patchy red and blue breast; rose-pink belly and untacs. F: Brown; blue-tinged above; pink-tinged below.*

Lazuli Bunting. *Passerina amoena.* Z65b36. <u>Gorrión Cabeziazul</u>
Can-M. <u>Resident near sea level, nBC; transient or winter visitor sBC, nP, ncH</u>. Rare+; tree-dotted brushy fields, weedy hedgerows and thickets, open scrub-woods, borders. *Pl.40. 5" Whitish wing-bars; bluish rump. M: Blue head; streaked back; tawny breast; white belly and untacs. F: Plain brown head and back; buff and white below.*

Indigo Bunting. *Passerina cyanea.* Z65b35. <u>Azulito</u>
Can-SAm. <u>Transient or winter visitor P, csH, A, Y; casual BC</u>. Common; short-grass fields with scattered shrubs, grassy openings near hedgerows, thickets or scrub woods. *Pl.43. 5" Sum.M: Rich dark blue. Win.M: Dark brown above, whitish below; rump and breast tinged blue. F.+im.M: Brown above; paler below, faintly streaked.*

Varied Bunting. *Passerina versicolor.* Z65b37. <u>Gorrión Morado</u>
US-M,G. <u>Resident up to 5500', sBC, P, ncH, ncA</u>. Rare+; dense, scrubby woods, semi-desert scrub, hedgerows, thickets, overgrown fields in dry situations, or borders. *Pl.40. 5" M: Purple; with bluish rump, and red nape-patch; somewhat mottled or scaly in winter. May appear all-black. F: Brownish gray, paler below; unstreaked.*

Orange-breasted Bunting. *Passerina leclancherii.* Z65b40. <u>Amarillito</u>
M. <u>Resident up to 4500', csP (Jalisco+Puebla to Chiapas)</u>. Rare+; open, scrubby woods, woodland borders, or grassy openings, partial clearings, hedgerows. *Pl.41. 5" M: Bright blue above; rich bright yellow and orange below. F: Dull gray-green above; wings and tail tinged bluish; yellower below than other buntings.*

Painted Bunting. *Passerina ciris.* Z65b38. <u>Sietecolores</u>
US-Pan. <u>Summer resident around 4000', nH (Chihuahua+Coahuila); transient or winter visitor P, cH, A, Y; accidental BC</u>. Rare+; weedy fields, borders, openings, thickets. *Pl.40. 5" M: Red below and on rump; dark violet-blue head; bright yellow-green back. F.+Im: Distinctive bright lime-green above; dark wings; yellower below.*

Dickcissel. *Spiza americana.* Z65b1. <u>Gorrión Cuadrillero</u>
Can-SAm. <u>Transient or winter visitor P,H,A; accidental BC</u>. Rare+, irregular; in grassy fields with scattered thickets, or near hedgerows among farm-fields and pastures. *Pl.43. 6" Yellowish line over eye; dark sub-malar streak; rufous wrist-patch. M: Black or dark gray throat-patch; yellow breast; gray belly; streaked back and crown. F.+Im: Duller; underparts buffy or partly yellow, finely streaked or plain.*

EMBERIZINAE

White-naped (Brush-) **Finch.** *Atlapetes albinucha.* Z65c249.   Saltón Cerquero
M. Resident, 3000 to 7000', csH (Puebla to Chiapas), cA (Veracruz+Oaxaca). Rare;
overgrown fields, partial clearings, thickets at forest borders, brushy fields near forest.
*Pl.42. 7" Dark gray above; black head with broad white center-stripe on crown and
nape; yellow below including throat; olive-gray wash on flanks.*

Yellow-throated (Br.-) **Finch.** *Atlapetes gutturalis.* Z65c250.   Saltón Raya Blanca
M-SAm,x.B. Resident, 6000 to 8000', sH (Chiapas). Rare+; forest borders, thickets.
Pl.42. 7" Like White-naped F., *but only the throat yellow; breast pale gray; center
of belly white; flanks and untacs dark brownish gray.*

Rufous-capped (Br.-) **Finch.** *Atlapetes pileatus.* Z65c254.   Saltón Hierbero
M. Resident, 4000 to 10,000', ncH. Common; pine, pine-oak or other mountain forest
undergrowth, borders, weedy clearings; agitated chips if alarmed, abrupt tail-movement.
Pl.42. 5 1/2 " Gray-brown above; crown rufous; blackish eye-patch; yellow below.

Chestnut-capped Finch. *Atlapetes brunneinucha.* Z65c271.   Saltón Collarejo
M-SAm,x.B. Resident, 3000 to 10,000', sP, csH (Guerrero to Chiapas), csA (San
Luis Potosí to Chiapas). Rare+, secretive; undergrowth, humid forest or edge, thickets.
*Pl.42. 7" Bright olive-green above; crown and nape rich reddish brown; extended
black mask; white below except black breast-band, and dark sides, flanks, untacs.*

San Martín Finch. *Atlapetes apertus.* Z65c272.   Saltón de Tuxtla
M. Resident, 1000 to 5000', cA (c.Veracruz, Sierra deTuxtla). Common; humid forest.
Pl.42. 7" Like Chestnut-capped Finch, *but no black breast-band.*

Green-striped Finch. *Atlapetes virenticeps.* Z65a275.   Saltón Cabeza Verde
M. Resident, 4000 to 11,000', ncH (Durango+Sinaloa to Morelos+Puebla). Rare+,
secretive; on the ground in dense pine-oak or fir forest, or dense thickets in open woods.
*Pl.42. 7" Olive-green above; crown and nape striped black and yellow-green;
extended black mask; throat and belly white; breast, sides, and flanks dark gray.*

Orange-billed Sparrow. *Arremon aurantiirostris.* Z65c242.   Pico de Oro
M-SAm,x.ES. Resident up to 3000', csA (Veracruz to Chiapas). Rare+, secretive; on
or near the ground, in thickets and other dense undergrowth of dense humid forest.
*Pl.42. 6 1/2" White throat, belly, and line over eye, on black and gray head and
underparts; dark olive-green above, with blacker wings and tail; may show yellow
wrist-patch; bill bright orange.*

Olive Sparrow. *Arremonops rufivirgatus.* Z65c245.   Gorrión Oliváceo
US,M,G,B,CR. Resident up to 5500', P (Sinaloa to Chiapas), A, Y. Common; in
thickets and undergrowth at humid forest borders, open scrubby woods, hedgerows.
*Pl.46. 6" Dull olive above; head striped reddish brown and gray, including
center-crown stripe, and stripe through eye; whitish and pale olive-gray below.*

Green-backed Sparrow. *Arremonops chloronotus.* Z65c247.   Talero de Norte
M,G,B,H. Resident, up to 2000', sA. Rare+; tall grass, shrubs, trees; border thickets.
Pl.42. 6" Like Olive Sp., *but brighter olive-green above; crown- and eye-stripes
blackish brown and dull gray; throat and belly whiter, contrasts more with gray
breast, sides and flanks; and buffy olive untacs.*

Rusty-crowned (Ground-) **Sparrow.** *Melozone kieneri.* Z65c237.   Zorzal Llanero
M. Resident up to 7000', ncP, ncH (Guanajuato to Morelos+Puebla). Rare+; ground
level in dense shrubby dry woods, mixed trees, thickets, rocky grassy areas, openings.
*Pl.42. 6 1/2" Head-pattern blackish, white, and mostly rufous; large black
breast-spot on white below; grayish olive above, and on sides and flanks; bill black.*

Prevost's (Ground-) **Sparrow.** *Melozone biarcuatum.* Z65c238.   Zorzal Chiapaneco
M-CR,x.B,N. Resident up to 7000', sP (Chiapas), sH (Chiapas). Rare+; weedy,
shrubby overgrown fields, hedgerows and thickets bordering or near humid woodland.
Pl.42. 6 1/2" Like Rusty-crown. Sp., *but more white on face; no* black breast-spot.

White-eared (Ground-) **Sparrow.** *Melozone leucotis.* Z65c239. Zorzal Orejiblanca
M-CR,x.B,H. Resident, 2000 to 6000', sP (Chiapas). Rare+; thickets, brushy borders.
Pl.42. 6 1/2" Entire head black, except gray center-crown stripe, white spot before eye and on ear, and yellow line behind eye; mostly gray-brown above; white below, with black breast-spot, and rich brown flanks and untacs.
Green-tailed Towhee. *Pipilo chlorurus.* Z65c230. Toquí Cola Verde
US-M. Winter visitor BC, ncP, ncH, nA. Rare; overgrown fields, gardens, borders.
Pl.43. 7" Olive-green above; crown rufous; sides of head gray with white malar streak, black sub-malar streak; throat and belly white; breast and sides gray.
Collared Towhee. *Pipilo ocai.* Z65c231. Toquí Gargantilla
M. Resident, 5000 to 12,000', cH (Jalisco+Veracruz to Oaxaca). Common; thickets at borders of pine, pine-oak, and fir-forest, forest undergrowth or openings, hedgerows.
Pl. 42. 8 1/2" Head and broad collar black, with white throat-patch, malar streak, and line over eye, and rufous crown and nape; yellow-olive above; whitish below, with buffy-olive flanks, buffy-brown untacs; bill black; iris red. See (hybrids?) next.
(Collared Towhee. Z65c231. x[?] Rufous-sided Towhee. Z65c232.) A great variety of plumage patterns and colors, apparently intermediate between those of the Collared Towhee and the Mexican form of the Rufous-sided Towhee, occur mostly in western and central cH. Most authorities consider these to be hybrids between two species, the Collared Towhee and the Rufous-sided Towhee (we adopt this treatment here); other authorities, however, consider them to be intergrades between two groups (the Collared group and the Rufous-sided group) of a single species, the Rufous-sided Towhee; still others consider them to be distinct races of either the Collared Towhee species or the Rufous-sided Towhee species. Six representative plumage types are shown in small figures on Plate 42.

Rufous-sided Towhee. *Pipilo erythrophthalmus.* Z65c232. Chouís Común
Can-M,G. Resident up to 13,000', BC, H. Common; thickets, borders, undergrowth.
Pl.42. 8" Mexican representatives of this species are as follows: M: Upperparts, and entire head, throat, and upper breast black, with two white wing-bars, white spots on scapulars, and white tail-corners; breast and belly white; sides, flanks, and untacs rufous. F: Like male, but dark brown replaces black. See (hybrids?) above.
Socorro Towhee. *Pipilo socorroensis.* Z65c233. Chouís de Socorro
M. Resident near sea level, cP (Socorro I.). Rare+; undergrowth, borders, hedgerows.
8" M and F: Like male of Mexican form of Rufous-sided Towhee, but feet larger.
Brown Towhee. *Pipilo fuscus.* Z65c235. Ilama
US-M. Resident up to 10,000', BC, nP (Sonora+Sinaloa), ncH. Common to abundant; small-tree-dotted brushy open areas, dry rocky hillsides, gardens, hedgerows, borders.
Pl.46. 8" Gray-brown above; crown dull rufous; whitish or buffy below; untacs buffy brown; necklace of dark spots around buffy throat, may have large central spot.
Abert's Towhee. *Pipilo aberti.* Z65c234. Toquí de Abert
US-M. Resident near sea level, nBC, nP (Sonora). Common; brush, stream-valleys.
Pl.46. 8 1/2" Brown above, buff below; black area all around base of thick bill.
White-throated Towhee. *Pipilo albicollis.* Z65c236. Chorriento
M. Resident, 4000 to 10,000', cH (Guerrero, Puebla, Oaxaca). Common; thickets in shrubby grassy areas, hedgerows, dry rocky fields, scrub woods edge, gardens, parks.
Pl.42. 7 1/2" Like Brown T., but lower throat contrasty white; spotty breast-band.
Blue-black Grassquit. *Volatinia jacarina.* Z65c161. Marinerito
M-SAm. Resident up to 5500', P, A, Y. Common; overgrown fields, weedy or grassy hedgerows, cornfields, weedy shrubby vacant lots, borders. Courting male repeatedly flutters into the air two or three feet above an open perch, then back down, calling *si-ew*.
Pl.41. 4" Bill rather small. Sum.M: Glossy black; with small white patch on side under wing. Win.M., F.,+Im: Brown; paler, and has blurred streaks, below.

Slate-colored Seedeater. *Sporophila schistacea.* Z65c164.   Sirindango Gris
M,H,CR-SAm. Resident cA, near sea level, (Oaxaca). Very rare; humid forest borders.
4 1/2" M: Dark gray, with white belly, untacs, and wing-spot; may have small white wing-bar and neck-patch; bill yellow; legs greenish. F: Olive-brown above; pale olive-brown below to more buffy or whitish on belly and untacs; bill dark.

Variable Seedeater. *Sporophila aurita.* Z65c167.   Puntiblanco
M-SAm,x.ES. Resident near sea level, csA. Rare; tall grass, weeds, borders, openings.
Pl.41. 4 1/2" (Mexican form) M: Like Blue-black Grassquit, *but bill slightly heavier; white spot on base of primaries (may be hidden), and white wing-linings. F: Greenish brown above; paler and buffier below, unstreaked; wing-linings white.*

Collared Seedeater. *Sporophila torqueola.* Z65c169.   Sirindango Común
Cinnamon-rumped group. *S. t. torqueola.*   Sirindango Occidental
   M. Resident up to 7000', P (Sinaloa to Chiapas), cH (Guanajuato+Puebla to Oaxaca). Common; brushy fields, weedy grassy borders, gardens, hedgerows.
   Pl.40. 4" M: Back, wings (with white spot but no wing-bars), and tail, grayish brown; rump, belly, untacs rich orange-buff; head and breast-band black; throat buff; partial collar white. F: Brown above; yellowish buff below.
White-collared group. *S. t. morelleti.*   Sirindango Común
   M-Pan. Resident up to 5000', csA, Y. Common; brushy fields, weedy borders.
   Pl.40. 4" M: Black; but wing-bars, wing-spot, throat, partial collar, belly, untacs white; rump pale. F: Brown above; buff wing-bars, rump, underparts.
Sharpe's group. *S. t. sharpei.*   Sirindango de Sharpe
   US-M. Resident up to 5000', nA. Common; brushy fields, borders, grassy areas.
   Pl.40. 4" M: Black or dark brown head and back; pale gray or buffy rump; whitish partial collar and throat; whitish or buffy below, with blotchy breast-band or none; white wing-bars and wing-spot. F: Like White-collared group, *but browner, duller-rumped.*

Ruddy-breasted Seedeater. *Sporophila minuta.* Z65c185.   Canelillo
M-SAm,x.B. Resident near sea level, P (Nayarit to Chiapas). Rare+; long-grass fields, marshes with tall grasses or sedges, weedy grassy vacant lots, weedy orchards, edges.
Pl.41. 3 3/4" Sum.M: Blue-gray above; rufous below and on rump. F.+win.M: Greenish brown above, buff and brownish-buff below; two pale gray wing-bars.

Thick-billed Seed-Finch. *Oryzoborus funereus.* Z65c196.   Negrito Común
M-SAm,x.ES. Resident up to 3000', csA. Rare; wet grassy clearings, ditch-banks.
Pl.41. 4 1/2" Like (Mexican form of) Variable Seedeater, but bill much larger, very heavy at base; and F: much darker richer brown.

Blue Seedeater. *Amaurospiza concolor.* Z65c198.   Semillero Azul
M-SAm,x.G,B.   Resident, 2000 to 8000', cP (Guerrero, Morelos, Oaxaca), csH (Guerrero+Chiapas). Very rare, local; thickets, brush, in or near humid or scrub forest.
Pl.41. 5 1/2" M: Dull slaty blue or dark rich blue. F.+Im: Gray-brown; paler below.

Yellow-faced Grassquit. *Tiaris olivacea.* Z65c207.   Mascarita
M-SAm. Resident up to 5000', A, Y. Common; grassy fields, hedgerows, borders.
Pl.41. 4" M: Mostly grayish olive; head and breast (broadly) black; throat and line over eye bright yellow. F: Dull gray-green; chin and short line over eye dull yellow.

Slaty Finch. *Haplospiza rustica.* Z65c109.   Semillero Pizarra
M-SAm,x.G,B,N.   Resident 3500 to 5500', sP (Chiapas), csH (Veracruz+Chiapas).
Very rare; in dense humid mountain forest, or small openings in brushy scrubby woods.
Pl.42. 5" Tail short, notched; bill short, black, culmen straight, tip sharp. M: Dark slate-gray. F: Medium brown; streaked. V: a weak musical chew, chew, pee-toot.

Grassland Yellow-Finch. *Sicalis luteola.* Z65c153.   Semillero Amarillo
M-SAm,x.ES.   Resident up to 8000', cP (Morelos+Puebla), cH (D.F.), csA (Veracruz+Chiapas). Rare, local; often in flocks, humid grassy fields, pastures, cane or rice fields.
Pl.41. 5" M: Plain rich yellow below; streaked blackish gray on greenish yellow

above; yellow line over eye. F: Duller; browner above; grayer below.

Bridled Sparrow. *Aimophila mystacalis.* Z65c82.   Zacatonero Patilludo
M. Resident, 3500 to 6500', cP(Oaxaca), cH (México+Veracruz to Oaxaca). Common;
semi-desert, or other dry, rocky areas with mixed scrubby trees, thorny shrubs, cactus.
*Pl.47. 6" Black chin and upper throat with white-line border: rufous above and on
flanks, untacs; heavily streaked black on back; two white wing-bars.*

Black-chested Sparrow. *Aimophila humeralis.* Z65c83.   Zacatonero de Collar
M. Resident up to 5000', cP (Jalisco to Guerrero). Rare+; brushy semi-desert, borders.
*Pl.47. 6" White throat, with black border and broad breast-band; head mostly dark
gray-brown; white malar streak and spot before eye; streaked back; pale wing-bars.*

Striped-headed Sparrow. *Aimophila ruficauda.* Z65c84.   Charralero
M-CR,x.B. Resident up to 6000', P (Durango+Puebla to Chiapas). Common; thickets
in dry overgrown fields or pastures, hedgerows, scrubby woods, vacant lots, borders.
V: series of sharp, high-pitched notes in chorus or duet, *pich-ee-pich-ee-pich-ee-pich-ee.*
*Pl.47. 6 1/2" Black-and-white crown and superciliary stripes; black ear-patch;
streaked back; whitish and pale gray below, may have broad gray breast-band.*
Resembles ad. White-crowned Sparrow, *but has black ear-patch; blackish bill.*

Sumichrast's Sparrow. *Aimophila sumichrasti.* Z65c85. Zacatonero de Sumichrast
M. Resident up to 3500', cP (Oaxaca). Common; borders, hedgerows, scrub woods.
*Pl.47. 6 1/2" Crown striped dark brown, with whitish center stripe and superciliary
line; front of face whitish with narrow black line below and above white malar streak;
lower mandible pale yellowish, tail cinnamon-rufous.* See Rusty and Rufous-w. Sp.

Botteri's Sparrow. *Aimophila botterii.* Z65c89.   Zacaterillo
US-CR,x.ES.   Summer resident up to 9000', ncP, ncH (Durango+San Luis Potosí to
Oaxaca), A, Y (Yucatán). Rare+; pastures, weedy fields, grassy plains (few shrubs).
*Pl.46. 5 1/2" Grayish above with dark rufous stripes on back; fine streaks on rufous
crown; sides of head and underparts grayish buff; with slightly darker line through
eye; tail rounded, grayish brown.* See Cassin's Sp.

Cassin's Sparrow. *Aimophila cassinii.* Z65c90.   Zacatonero de Cassin
US-M.   Resident up to 6000', nH (Chihuahua+Coahuila to San Luis Potosí), nA
(Tamaulipas); winter visitor nP. Rare, local; open grassy plains, short-grass pastures.
Pl.46. 5 1/2" Like Botteri's S., *but tail darker, grayer; narrow pale tail-feather tips.*

Rufous-winged Sparrow. *Aimophila carpalis.* Z65c91.   Zacatonero Alirrojo
US-M. Resident up to 4000', nP (Sonora+Sinaloa). Common; dry grassy plains with
mixed shrubs and small trees, grassy openings or borders, scrubby overgrown fields.
Pl.46. 5 1/2" Like Sumichrast's Sparrow, *but tail dark gray , not rufous; has more
fine   streaks in broad crown stripes; and supra-malar line not so obvious.*

Rufous-crowned Sparrow. *Aimophila ruficeps.* Z65c92. Zacatonero Corona Rojiza
US-M. Resident up to 8000', BC, ncH; winter visitor ncA. Rare+; short-grass areas.
*Pl.46. 6" Grayish brown above; dull rufous streaks on back ; crown and line
through eye plain rufous; line over eye, sides of face, and underparts pale brownish
gray, with slightly darker breast; black sub-malar streak.*

Oaxaca Sparrow. *Aimophila notosticta.* Z65c93.   Zacatonero de Oaxaca
M. Resident, 5000 to 6000', cH (Oaxaca). Rare, local; dry brushy hillsides or ravines.
*Pl.47. 6 1/2" Back brownish with blackish brown streaks; crown rufous, may be
finely streaked; sides of head gray; blackish sub-malar streak and line through eye;
pale gray below, dark flanks, untacs; bill black; tail rather long, gray.* See Rusty Sp.

Rusty Sparrow. *Aimophila rufescens.* Z65c94.   Zacatonero Rojizo
M-CR.   Resident up to 8000', P (Sinaloa to Chiapas), H, csA (Veracruz, Puebla,
Chiapas). Common; thickets, weedy undergrowth in open woods, borders, hedgerows.
*Pl.47. 7" Races vary. Typically brownish above, with heavily black-streaked back;
crown rufous, may be finely streaked, mottled, have grayish partial center-stripe;*

blackish line through eye; black sub-malar streak; tail rufous; lower mandible pale grayish. See Sumichrast's and Oaxaca Sparrows.

Striped Sparrow. *Orirurus superciliosus.* Z65c96.   <u>Zorzal Rayado</u>
M. <u>Resident, 5000 to 14,000', w.nH+cH (Sonora+Chihuahua to Oaxaca)</u>. Common; high-mountain bunch-grass fields, grassy areas with scattered pines, grassy borders. *Pl.42. 6 1/2" Heavily striped above; pale gray below; crown rufous, with finely black-streaked gray center-stripe; whitish line over eye; black ear-patch and bill.*

Chipping Sparrow. *Spizella passerina.* Z65c71.   <u>Chimbito Común</u>
AK-N. <u>Resident, 3500 to 10,000', nBC, H; winter visitor BC, nP, ncA</u>. Common; in open pine woods, grassy woods borders, clearings; in flocks in dry grassland (winter). *Pl.43. 5" Sum.Ad: Back heavily streaked; crown rufous, sharply bordered by white line over eye; black line through eye; black bill ; pale gray nape, cheeks, <u>rump</u>, and underparts. Im.+win.ad: Similar, but crown fine-streaked; superciliary line and ear-patch brownish gray; bill yellowish.*

Clay-colored Sparrow. *Spizella pallida.* Z65c75.   <u>Chimbito Pálido</u>
Can-M,G. <u>Winter visitor BC, nP, H, ncA</u>. Common; dry grassy fields, borders, parks. *Pl.46. 5" Heavily streaked black on buffy brown back; crown finely black-streaked, with <u>gray center-stripe</u>; nape grayish; ear-patch buff-brown; rump grayish-tan like back-color; whitish below.* See Chipping and Brewer's Sp.

Brewer's Sparrow. *Spizella breweri.* Z65c76.   <u>Chimbito de Brewer</u>
Can-M. <u>Winter visitor BC, ncP, ncH</u>. Common; dry short-grass fields, semi-desert. *Pl.46. 5" Like* Clay-colored Sp., *but has white eye-ring; no* center-crown stripe.

Field Sparrow. *Spizella pusilla.* Z65c72.   <u>Chimbito Llanero</u>
Can-M. <u>Winter visitor nH, nA</u>. Rare; grassy plains, grassy openings, edges, pastures. *Pl.43. 5" Heavily streaked black and rufous on buff back and scapulars; crown, nape and line behind eye rich dark rufous; white eye-ring and wing-bars; breast pale gray; rufous wash on sides and flanks; bill pinkish.*

Worthen's Sparrow. *Spizella wortheni.* Z65c73.   <u>Chimbito de Worthen</u>
M. <u>Resident, 4000 to 7500', ncH (Zacatecas+Coahuila to Veracruz)</u>. Very rare; dry grassy weedy fields with thickets, hedgerows, grassy openings in dense brushy areas. *Pl.47. 5" Like* Field Sparrow, *but somewhat paler over all; no* dark rufous line behind eye*; more prominent eye-ring.*

Black-chinned Sparrow. *Spizella atrogularis.* Z65c74.   <u>Chimbito Carbonero</u>
US-M. <u>Resident, 3500 to 8000', BC, ncH</u>. Rare+; grassy scrubby slopes, semi-desert. *Pl.46. 5" M: Dark gray; <u>streaked</u> brown and blackish <u>back</u>; black upper throat and eye-patch; whitish belly, untacs, and wing-bars; pinkish bill. F.+Im: Similar, but little or no black or blackish gray on throat and around eye.*

Vesper Sparrow. *Pooecetes gramineus.* Z65c77.   <u>Gorrión Torito</u>
Can-M,G. <u>Winter visitor BC, nP, H, ncA</u>. Rare+; tree-dotted grassland, grassy edges. *Pl.43. 6" Streaked above and below with blackish brown; tail notched, with white outer feathers; brownish ear-patch against whitish background; white eye-ring.*

Lark Sparrow. *Chondestes grammacus.* Z65c78.   <u>Chindiquito</u>
Can-ES+H. <u>Resident up to 8000', nBC, nH; transient or winter visitor all sub-regions</u>. Common; pastures, grassy fields, farmyards, hedgerows, overgrown fields, borders. *Pl.46. 6" Striking head-pattern: center-crown, line over eye, malar stripe, and throat white; side-crown and ear-patch chestnut; sub-malar streak and line through eye black. Whitish below, black spot on breast; streaked black and brownish above; tail rounded, broadly white-cornered. Juv: Head much duller; streaked breast.*

Black-throated Sparrow. *Amphispiza bilineata.* Z65c79.   <u>Chiero Barbanegra</u>
US-M. <u>Resident up to 7500', BC, nP (Sonora to Sinaloa), ncH (Chihuahua+Coahuila to Guanajuato+Hidalgo), nA</u>. Common; brushy, thorny semi-desert, dry scrubby fields. *Pl.46. 5 1/2" Crown, nape, and ear-patch black and gray; and throat to upper breast black; white line over eye and below ear-patch; mostly white below, brownish gray*

above; white tail sides. Juv: Similar, but streaked above and below; throat not black.

Sage Sparrow. *Amphispiza belli.* Z65c80.   Chiero de Lunar
US-M. Resident up to 4000', BC; winter visitor nP, nH. Rare+; dry scrub, semi-desert.
Pl.46. 5 1/2" Blackish or gray crown, nape, and sides of head, with white malar streak, black sub-malar streak, and black breast-spot; fine streaks on dark gray above, and on white (especially sides and flanks) below.

Five-striped Sparrow. *Amphispiza quinquestriata.* Z65c81. Zacatonero Cinco Rayas
US-M. Resident, 1500 to 5500', nP. Rare+; densely shrubby areas, dry brushy slopes.
Pl.47. 5 1/2" Dark grayish brown above; dark brown head, with white line over eye and malar streak; broad black (sub-malar) streak each side of white throat; medium gray breast, sides, and flanks; white belly; black spot on breast.

Lark Bunting. *Calamospiza melanocorys.* Z65c47.   Gorrión Cañero
Can-M. Winter visitor BC, nP, nH, nA. Rare+; grassy plains, roadsides, dry brush.
Pl.43. 7" Sum.M: Black; large white wing-patch; white tail-tip spots; bill dark, rather heavy. F: Finely streaked black on dark brown above, brown on whitish below; ear-patch outlined buffy; wing-patch buffy or whitish. Win.M: Like female, but much more contrasty; spotty or blotchy black throat.

Savannah Sparrow. *Passerculus sandwichensis.* Z65c61.   Gorrión Zanjero
AK-ES+H. Resident up to 9000', BC, nP (Sonora to Sinaloa), ncH; transient or winter visitor A, Y. Common; grassy fields, marshes, grassy borders of marshes; hedgerows.
Pl. 46. 5" Races vary, but mostly streaked above and below (usually white belly and untacs); may have central breast-spot; tail notched; may have yellow above eye.

Baird's Sparrow. *Ammodramus bairdii.* Z65c65.   Gorrión de Baird
Can-M. Winter visitor nP, nH. Rare; tree-dotted grassy plains, dry grassy rocky slopes.
5" Crown and nape finely black-streaked, with tawny buff center stripe; narrowly black-bordered ear-patch, and line over eye, buffy; black sub-malar streaks; upperparts streaked; underparts whitish, with streaky necklace, sides, and flanks; short, notched tail. Much like Grasshopper Sp., except sub-malar and breast streaks.

Grasshopper Sparrow. *Ammodramus savannarum.* Z65c67.   Gorrión Chapulín
Can-SAm. Resident, up to 5500', nBC, nP (Sonora), ncH (Zacatecas+México), csA; transient or winter visitor all sub-regions. Rare and local, summer; common, winter; grassy meadows, grassy borders of farm fields, mixed grass, weeds, and low shrubs.
Pl.46. 5" Rich buff throat, breast, sides, untacs, may have faint streaks; crown striped black on buff; back striped black, rufous, buff; tail short, feather-tips pointed.

Sierra Madre Sparrow. *Xenospiza baileyi.* Z65c48.   Gorrión Serrano
M. Resident, 8000 to 10,000', ncH (Durango to Morelos). Very rare, local; lush grass on open slopes, often bunch-grass, or borders of grassy thickets in mountain meadows.
Pl.42. 5" Heavily streaked black on rufous above; gray line over eye; sides of head gray with fine black streaks; heavy black streaks on whitish below. Somewhat like a dark-streaked Song Sp., but more slender, and no large central breast-spot.

Fox Sparrow. *Passerella iliaca.* Z65c49.   Gorrión Vulpino
AK-M. Winter visitor nBC. Common; thickets, forest borders, hedgerows, gardens.
Pl.43. 6 1/2" Races visiting Mexico may have unstreaked blackish-brown, brown, or gray crown, side of head, and back; rufous or brownish rump and tail; malar streak pale gray; throat speckled; breast, sides and flanks heavily streaked.

Song Sparrow. *Melospiza melodia.* Z65c50.   Zanjero Cantor
AK-M. Resident up to 9000', BC, nP (Sonora), ncH (Durango to México). Common, irregular; gardens, parks, borders, thickets, marshes with dense growth, marshy ponds.
Pl.46. 6" BC and nP races mostly pale rufous and gray, lightly streaked, to dark brownish, heavily streaked, above and below; ncH races mostly very dark, heavily streaked. All have a slightly rounded tail, moved up and down in flight; and most have a rather large central breast-spot.

Lincoln's Sparrow. *Melospiza lincolnii.* Z65c51.   Zorzal de Lincoln
AK-Pan. Transient or winter visitor all sub-regions.   Common, except Y; in thickets,
undergrowth in pine, pine-oak, fir forests, shrubby borders, hedgerows, scrub woods.
*Pl.43. 5" Fine blackish streaks on rich buff breast and sides; lower breast, belly and
untacs white; center-crown stripe gray, lateral crown-stripes black and reddish
brown; pale line over eye; black sub-malar streak; black-streaked back and scapulars.*

Swamp Swarrow. *Melospiza georgiana.* Z65c52.   Zorzal Pantanero
Can-M. Winter visitor nP, ncH, nA. Rare; in marshes, swamps, flooded woods, bogs.
*Pl.43. 5 1/2" Sum.Ad: Streaked brown and black back; wings and rump mostly
rufous; crown rufous; throat and underparts whitish, with grayer breast; ear-patch
and line over eye gray, with black sub-malar and supra-malar streak and line through
eye. Win.Ad: Crown finely streaked black, brown, and gray. Im: Ear-patch buffy.*

Andean (Ruf.-coll.) **Sparrow.** *Zonotrichia capensis.* Z65c53.   Cerquerito
M-SAm,x.B,N. Resident, 5000 to 10,000', sH (Chiapas). Common; parks, gardens,
orchards, patios, hedgerows, borders. V: two or three loud and musical extended notes.
*Pl.47. 5 1/2" Back heavily streaked brownish and black; crown and nape black,
with gray center; line over eye gray; ear-patch dark; throat broadly white; blotchy
black breast-band; rufous partial collar; belly and untacs dull brownish; tail notched.*

White-throated Sparrow. *Zonotrichia albicollis.* Z65c56.   Zacatero Garganta Blanca
Can-M. Winter visitor nP, nA; accidental BC. Very rare; thickets, hedgerows, borders.
*Pl.43. 6" Ad: Streaked above; head-stripes black, white, gray (ear-patch), or
blackish-brown, dull buff, and dull gray, with contrasty white throat, and bright or
dull yellow spot in front of eye; white wing-bars; pearly gray, or faintly to lightly
streaked dull gray, breast; pale gray to whitish belly and untacs. Juv: Like duller
adult, but still duller crown, and heavily streaked below.*

Golden-crowned Sparrow. *Zonotrichia atricapilla.* Z65c57. Zacatero Corona Dorada
AK-M. Winter visitor BC. Rare+; thickets, hedgerows, gardens, borders, vacant lots.
*Pl.43. 6 1/2" Streaked above; crown-patch dull yellow, with broad black borders;
wing-bars white; throat, sides of head, breast and sides pale gray and brownish gray.
Im: Crown fine-streaked, with trace of yellow and black pattern or not; browner face.*

White-crowned Sparrow. *Zonotrichia leucophrys.* Z65c55.   Zacatero Mixto
AK-M. Winter visitor BC, ncP, ncH, nA. Abundant (nw.) to rare; thickets, hedgerows.
*Pl.43. 6" Ad: Contrasty black-and-white crown-pattern and line through eye; breast
and sides of head pearly gray; throat, belly, and untacs whitish; bill pinkish or
yellowish; back streaked black, brown and whitish; two white wing-bars. Im:
Stripes on crown brown, buff, and whitish.*

Dark-eyed Junco. *Junco hyemalis.* Z65c59.   *Pl.46.*   Carbonero Apizarrado
Slate-colored group. *J. h. hyemalis.*   Carbonero Apizarrado
AK-M. Winter visitor nBC, nP, nH. Very rare; openings, hedgerows, borders.
      6" Dark gray; white belly, untacs, outer tail-feathers; pale bill. F: Duller.
"White-winged" sub-group: *Paler gray; two white wing-bars.*
Oregon group. *J. h. oreganus.*   Carbonero Oregonense
AK-M. Resident, 4000 to 6000', nBC; winter visitor BC, nP, nH.Rare+; borders.
      *6" Entire head and upper breast black; back rusty-brown; belly, outer tail-
      feathers white; sides rufous; bill pale. F: Duller.*
"Pink-sided" sub-group: *Head pale gray; back dull brown; sides, flanks pinkish.*
Gray-headed group. *J. h. caniceps.*   Carbonero Viejo
US-M. Winter visitor nBC, nP, nH. Rare+; thickets, hedgerows, woods borders.
      *6" Rump, and top and sides of head pale to medium gray; back bright rufous;
      very pale gray below; bill typically pale.*
"Red-backed" sub-group: *Bill larger, blackish above, pale grayish below.*
Guadalupe group. *J. h. insularis.*   Carbonero de Guadalupe
   M. Resident up to 4500', nBC (Guadalupe I.). Common; open woods, borders.
      6" Like "Pink-sided" sub-group of "Oregon" group, but darker; bill grayish.

Yellow-eyed Junco. *Junco phaeonotus.* Z65c60.   *Pl.46.*   Ojilumbre Mexicano
Mexican group. *J. p. phaeonotus.*   Ojilumbre Mexicano
US-M. Resident, 3500 to 14,000', ncH. Common; forest undergrowth, borders.
 *6" Head (and rump) mostly medium gray; lores black; throat, breast, and sides
 pale gray; back rich reddish brown; outer tail-feathers white; iris yellow; bill
 blackish above, yellowish below.*
Baird's group. *J. p. bairdi.*   Ojilumbre del Cabo
M.Resident, 3500 to 6000', sBC. Common; forest undergrowth, openings, edge.
 *5 1/2" Like Mexican group, but paler head; less contrast between paler, duller
 back, and browner rump; pale rufous sides and flanks; paler breast.*
Chiapas group. *J. p. fulvescens.*   Ojilumbre de Chiapas
M. Resident, 5000 to 9000', sH (Chiapas). Common; partial clearings, borders.
 6" Like Mexican group, but darker below; back duller; rump less contrasty.
Guatemala group. *J. p. alticola.*   Ojilumbre de Guatemala
M,G. Resident, 7500 to 11,000', sH (se. Chiapas). Common; borders, openings.
 6 1/2" Like Chiapas group, but larger and much duller and darker above.
McCown's Longspur. *Calcarius mccownii.* Z65c41.   Arnoldo de McCown
Can-M. Winter visitor nP, nH. Rare+; treeless grassy plains, dry open fields, pastures.
 *Pl.43. 5 1/2" Tail white with central black "T".   Sum.M: Streaked above; head
 whitish, with black crown and malar streak; whitish below with black breast-patch;
 rufous wrist-patch. F.+win.M: Wrist-patch (often concealed) as in summer male;
 crown finely streaked; buff malar streak and line over eye; scaly breast-patch
 prominent, faint, or absent.*
Chestnut-collared Longspur. *Calcarius ornatus.* Z65c44.   Arnoldo Collar Castaño
AK-M. Winter visitor nP, ncH; accidental BC. Rare+; grassy plains, large open areas.
 *Pl.43. 5 1/2" Tail white with broad black "V".   Sum.M: Black-and-white head, with
 pale yellow throat; chestnut hind-neck to side of neck; heavily streaked above; mostly
 black below; black-and-white wrist-patch. Sum.F: Like McCown's L., but see tail
 pattern; no trace of rufous wrist-patch; and more heavily streaked below. Win.M:
 Head and throat mostly buff, with scaled blackish and buff crown and underparts.*

FINCHES, SISKINS - (CARDUELINAE) - DOMINIQUITOS
Purple Finch. *Carpodacus purpureus.* Z65a84.   Gorrión Purpúreo
Can-M. Resident, about 4000 to 5000', nBC. Rare+; pine or pine-oak woods, borders.
 *Pl.40. 5 1/2" M: Raspberry red or tinged red, except unstreaked whitish belly and
 untacs; back streaked, about same color as crown. F: Heavily streaked whitish and
 dark gray; malar streak and line behind eye, whitish.* See House and Cassin's Finch.
Cassin's Finch. *Carpodacus cassinii.* Z65a85.   Gorrión de Cassin
Can-M. Resident, 5000 to 7000', nBC; winter visitor nP, ncH. Rare+; upper branches
in mountain pine, or pine-oak forest, or borders, or tree-dotted openings, or clearings.
 *Pl.40. 6" Like Purple Finch, but untacs streaked, not plain; and M: crown brighter
 red, more contrasty with grayish brown nape and back; more extensively whitish
 below; and F: more sharply streaked, face pattern less contrasty.* See House Finch.
House Finch. *Carpodacus mexicanus.* Z65a86.   Gorrión Común
Can-M. Resident up to 10,000', BC, nP, ncH. Abundant; all areas except deep forest.
 *Pl.40. 5 1/2" Culmen of bill slightly curved. M: Rump and most of head and
 breast rosy-red, nape and back more brownish gray, streaked; streaked below,behind
 rosy breast-patch. F: Streaked; but no contrasty face streaks.* See Purple Finch.
Red Crossbill. *Loxia curvirostra.* Z65a108.   Picocruzado
AK-N. Resident, 3000 to 13,000', nBC, H. Rare+, irregular; pine or pine-oak forest,
borders, scattered pines on rocky, grassy slopes. V: call in flight a *dip-dip* or *clip-clip*.
 *Pl.46. 6" Bill crossed; wings and forked tail black. M: Brick red (im. m. is
 mottled red and yellowish green). F: Dull yellow-green; back and crown streaked.*

Pine Siskin. *Carduelis pinus.* Z65a45.   Piñonero Rayado
AK-M. Resident, 5500 to 13,000', nBC, H; winter visitor nP. Common; pine,
pine-oak or fir forests, openings, tree-dotted clearings, borders. V: buzzy *zree-ee-ee.*
*Pl.40. 4 1/2" Streaked blackish brown on pale gray; wings and forked tail blackish
with yellow patch, and pale wing-bars (sP birds may have plain blackish crown,
fewer streaks below). Im: May be yellow between dark streaks.* See Blk-capped S.

Black-capped Siskin. *Carduelis atriceps.* Z65a46.   Piñonero Encapuchado
M,G. Resident, 8000 to 10,000', sH (Chiapas). Rare; open pine or pine-oak forests.
*Pl.41. 4 1/2" M: Wings and forked tail black with yellow patch; crown black;
grayish olive-green above; grayish green below. F: Crown dark gray. Im: Streaked,
like Pine S., but darker above, duller below; has only one (buffy) wing-bar.*

Black-headed Siskin. *Carduelis notatus.* Z65a55.   Piñonero Cabezinegro
M-N. Resident, 3000 to 10,000', mainly H, and slopes of P and A. Rare+; in pine or
pine-oak mountain forest, or deciduous slope-forest, or tree-dotted gardens, or borders.
*Pl.41. 4 1/2" M: Wings and tail (with yellow patch), and most of head to upper
breast black; bright yellow below; back dull yellow-green. F: Duller. Im: Head dull
yellow-green, not black; two dull yellow wing-bars.*

Lesser Goldfinch. *Carduelis psaltria.* Z65a61.   Dominiquito Dorado
US-SAm. Resident up to 9000', BC, P, H, ncA, Y. Common; open pine or pine-oak
woods, tree-dotted clearings, borders, weedy fields, vacant lots, gardens, and orchards.
*Pl.46. 4" M: Black above, bright yellow below (but nw. birds - "Green-backed"
G. - have streaked olive-green back and rump); tail black above, white below; wings
black with white patch and wing-bar. F: Dull olive-green above, faintly streaked;
yellow below; wings blackish with two white bars. Im: Like adult female, but duller.*

Lawrence's Goldfinch. *Carduelis lawrencei.* Z65a62.   Dominiquito de Lawrence
US-M. Resident up to 5000', nBC; winter visitor BC, nP. Rare; tree-dotted brushy
fields, overgrown fields, open pine or pine-oak woods, borders, hedgerows, gardens.
*Pl.46. 4" Sum.M: Pale gray above, yellow below (whitish sides and untacs); with
black throat, face, and fore-crown; tail black above, white below; wings black with
broad yellow wing-bars and patches. Win.M: Browner above; duller below. F: Like
winter male but no black on head.*

American Goldfinch. *Carduelis tristis.* Z65a60.   Dominiquito Viajero
Can-M. Resident near sea level, nBC; winter visitor BC, nP, nH, ncA. Rare;
tree-dotted brushy fields, open woods, borders, hedgerows, weedy overgrown fields.
*Pl.43. 4 1/2" Sum.M: Bright yellow, but black crown-patch, wings, tail; white
untacs and uptacs; yellowish wrist-patch, white wing-bar. F.+win.M: olive-green or
buffy olive; whitish belly and untacs; wing-bar and wrist patch, or two bars.*

Hooded Grosbeak. *Hesperiphona abeillei.* Z65a124.   Bellotero
M,G. Resident, 4000 to 11,000', H (Chihuahua+México to Chiapas), ncA. Rare,
local; cloud forest, pine, pine-oak or fir forest, lush gardens, partial clearings, borders.
*Pl.41. 6 1/2" Bill heavy, pale greenish. M: Greenish yellow; but head, tail, and
wings (with whitish patch) black. F: Yellow-olive, with black crown; white
tail-corners. V: a loud, mellow, tyew-tyew or clew, clew.*

Evening Grosbeak. *Hesperiphona vespertina.* Z65a123.   Pepitero Vespertino
Can-M. Resident, 5000 to 11,000', ncH (Chihuahua+Hidalgo to Oaxaca). Very rare;
upper branches of mountain pine, pine-oak, or fir forest. V: a rolling, musical *chir-r-rp.*
*Pl.40. 7" Like Hooded Grosbeak, but head blackish brown with broadly yellow
forehead. F: Much duller; and has gray top of head; no yellow on head.*

HOUSE SPARROWS - PASSERIDAE - GORRIONES
House Sparrow. *Passer domesticus.* Z66a11.   Gorrión Inglés
AK-SAm. Resident up to 10,000', BC, P, H, A. Common; cities, villages, farmyards.
*Pl.33. 6" M: Crown gray; chestnut and white face; throat gray to black; gray breast,
belly; streaked back; wing-bar. F: Brownish; back streaked black; buff line over eye.*

Birds which have been reported as accidental or casual in Mexico; or which have been introduced and possibly established; or which may have very recently been found to be regular. Some of these records are well documented, others are somewhat hypothetical. (Species which approach Mexico only in the Clipperton Island area are not included.)

Yellow-billed Loon. *Gavia adamsii.* B1a4. Casual nBC.
Red-necked Grebe. *Podiceps grisegena.* C1b3. Reported from northern Mexico.
Southern Fulmar. *Fulmarus glacialoides.* D2a3. Accidental nP.
Kermadec Petrel. *Pterodroma neglecta.* D2a16. Reported from offshore waters.
Pale- (Flesh-) footed Shearwater. *Puffinus carneipes.* D2c9. Casual nBC.
Buller's Shearwater. *Puffinus bulleri.* D2c8. Reported accidental nBC.
Fork-tailed Storm-Petrel. *Oceanodroma furcata.* D4b14. Reported nw. offshore.
White-tailed Tropicbird. *Phaethon lepturus.* E1a3. Accidental sP.
Red-tailed Tropicbird. *Phaethon rubricauda.* E1a2. Casual nBC, cP.
Lineated Heron. *Tigrisoma lineatum.* I1c4. Accidental sA.
Glossy Ibis. *Plegadis falcinellus.* I5a4. Pl.3. May be regular now A; casual Y.
- **Eurasian Wigeon.** *Anas penelope.* L2e17. Casual nBC; accidental nP.
Harlequin Duck. *Histrionicus histrionicus.* Casual nP.
Barrow's Goldeneye. *Bucephala islandica.* L2f12. Accidental nH.
Chukar. *Alectoris chukar.* M5b12. Introduced nBC, may not be established.
Ring-necked Pheasant. *Phasianus colchicus.* M5b141. Probably breeds nBC.
Whooping Crane. *Grus americana.* N4a6. Pl.10. Casual nH.
Eskimo Curlew. *Numenius borealis.* P17a6. Was regular nH; not reported recently.
American Woodcock. *Scolopax minor.* P17c6. Casual Y.
Little Gull. *Larus minutus.* P5a41. Accidental (sight report) cA.
Common Black-headed Gull. *Larus ridibundus.* P5a35. Accidental cA.
Lesser Black-backed Gull. *Larus fuscus.* P5a26. Casual (sight reports) nA, Y.
Roseate Tern. *Sterna dougallii.* P5b15. Casual or very rare transient.
Bridled Tern. *Sterna anaethetus.* P5b29. Now reported regular residents cP, Y.
White-capped (Black) Noddy. *Anous minutus.* P5b43. Accidental or casual Y.
White Tern. *Gygis alba.* P5b44. Accidental cP.
Pigeon Guillemot. *Cepphus columba.* P1a6. Casual nBC.
Ancient Murrelet. *Synthliboramphus antiquus.* P1a12. Casual nBC.
Crested Auklet. *Aethia cristatella.* P1a16. Accidental nBC.
Horned Puffin. *Fratercula corniculata.* P1a22. Accidental nBC.
N. (Yellow-shafted) Flicker. *Colaptes a. auratus.* Pl. 23. Reported ne.Mexico.
Gray Kingbird. *Tyrannus dominicensis.* Z10d71. Casual Y.
Giant Kingbird. *Tyrannus cubensis.* Z10d73. Accidental Y.
Blue-and-white Swallow. *Notiochelidon cyanoleuca.* Z15b18. Casual Chiapas.
Northern Wheatear. *Oenanthe oenanthe.* Z21a163. Accidental Y.
White Wagtail. *Motacilla alba.* Z17a7. Accidental sBC, nH.
Red-throated Pipit. *Anthus cervinus.* Z17a42. Accidental sBC.
Kirtland's Warbler. *Dendroica kirtlandii.* Z57a40. Accidental (sight report) cA.
Bobolink. *Dolichonyx oryzivorus.* Z62b1. Accidental sBC; casual Y.
Rusty Blackbird. *Euphagus carolinus.* Z62a91. Casual nBC.
Leconte's Sparrow. *Ammodramus leconteii.* Z65c64. Casual nH.
Sharp-tailed Sparrow. *Ammodramus caudacutus.* Z65c63. Casual nBC, Y.
Seaside Sparrow. *Ammodramus maritimus.* Z65c62. Casual nA.
Lapland Longspur. *Calcarius lapponicus.* Z45c42. Accidental or casual BC, Y.

BIBLIOGRAPHY

Alvarez del Toro, Miguel. 1964. *Lista de las Aves de Chiapas*. Instituto de Ciencias y Artes de Chiapas. Tuxtla Gutiérrez, Chiapas, México.

American Ornithologists' Union. 1983. *Check-list of North American birds,* 6th edition.

Blake, Emmet R. 1953. *Birds of Mexico*. University of Chicago Press. Chicago, IL.

Davis, L. Irby. *A Field Guide to the Birds of Mexico and Central America*. University of Texas Press. Austin, TX.

Edwards, Ernest P. 1968. *Finding Birds in Mexico*. Second Edition. Ernest P. Edwards. Sweet Briar, VA.
   1985. *1985 Supplement to Finding Birds in Mexico*. Ernest P. Edwards. Sweet Briar, VA.

National Geographic Society. 1983. *Field Guide to Birds of North America*. National Geographic Society. Washington, DC.

Peterson, Roger Tory. 1973. *A Field Guide to Mexican Birds*. Houghton Mifflin Co. Boston, MA.

Phillips, Allan R. 1986. *The Known Birds of North and Middle America. Part 1*. Allan R. Phillips. Denver, CO.

Ridgely, Robert S. 1976, 1981. *A Guide to the Birds of Panama*. Princeton University Press. Princeton, NJ.

Ridgway, Robert. (also Herbert Friedmann, author of parts 9-11) 1901-1950. *Birds of North and Middle America*. U.S.National Museum Bulletin 50, pts. 1-11. Washington, DC.

Robbins, Chandler S., Bertel Bruun, and Herbert S. Zim. Illustrated by Arthur Singer. 1966. *Birds of North America*. 1983. Golden Press. New York, NY.

Wilson, Richard G., and Hector Ceballos-Lascurain. 1986. *The Birds of Mexico City*. BBC Printing and Graphics Ltd. Burlington, Ont., Canada.

Also various articles in the *Auk, Condor,* and *Wilson Bulletin*; and the *Mexican Birds Newsletter,* and *Aves Mexicanas* (formerly *MBA "Bulletin Board"*).

INDEX OF ENGLISH NAMES AND LATIN GENERIC NAMES

INDEX OF SELECTED SPANISH GROUP NAMES